## DATE DUE

| NV 30 '98 | | | |
|---|---|---|---|
| | | | |
| OC 26 '98 | | | |
| AP 16 01 | | | |
| MY 14 01 | | | |
| JE 11 01 | | | |
| | | | |
| | | | |
| | | | |
| | | | |
| | | | |
| | | | |
| | | | |
| | | | |
| | | | |

DEMCO 38-296

# State Police
# in the
# United States

R

# State Police in the United States

## A Socio-Historical Analysis

*H. Kenneth Bechtel*

CONTRIBUTIONS IN CRIMINOLOGY AND PENOLOGY, NUMBER 47

GREENWOOD PRESS
Westport, Connecticut • London

**Library of Congress Cataloging-in-Publication Data**

Bechtel, H. Kenneth.
  State police in the United States : a socio-historical analysis /
H. Kenneth Bechtel.
    p.    cm.—(Contributions in criminology and penology, ISSN
0732–4464 ; no. 47))
  Includes bibliographical references (p.   ) and index.
  ISBN 0–313–26380–9 (alk. paper)
  1. Police, State—United States—History. I. Title. II. Series.
HV7965.B43  1995
363.2'0973—dc20        94–30929

British Library Cataloguing in Publication Data is available.

Library of Congress Catalog Card Number: 94–30929
ISBN: 0–313–26380–9
ISSN: 0732–4464

First published in 1995

Greenwood Press, 88 Post Road West, Westport, CT 06881
An imprint of Greenwood Publishing Group, Inc.

Printed in the United States of America

The paper used in this book complies with the
Permanent Paper Standard issued by the National
Information Standards Organization (Z39.48–1984).

10 9 8 7 6 5 4 3 2 1

To Deb

# Contents

# Tables

# Acknowledgments

Completion of a scholarly work represents the singular work of the author. Nevertheless, without the assistance from numerous individuals, a study of this scope would be impossible to complete. I therefore take this opportunity to express my most sincere appreciation for their support.

A very special note of appreciation is extended to my mentor, Chuck Snyder, who provided invaluable assistance and encouragement. His insight and intellectual contributions, as well as personal example and friendship, have contributed greatly to my intellectual growth and development. I am also greatly indebted to Ernest K. Alix, Howard Allen, Tom Burger, and Jerry Gaston for their support and thoughtful contributions and criticisms. I would also like to thank Phil Perricone, my department chairman, and Tom Mullen, Dean of the College at Wake Forest University, for providing the encouragement and assistance which made completion of this book possible.

Many libraries and historical societies helped along the way. I would like to pay special thanks to Carline B. Stottlar and Doug Carlson of the Illinois Historical Survey at the University of Illinois Library in Champaign-Urbana, Peggy R. Turner of the Colorado Division of State Archives and Public Records and Jennifer Bosley of the Colorado History Museum, who offered much needed assistance and put up with numerous requests and beleaguering questions. I am also grateful for the cooperation given by the staffs at the Chicago Historical Society, the Colorado Historical Society, the University of Illinois Archives, the

Illinois State Archives, the Chicago Public Library, the Denver Public Library, and the law libraries of the University of California at Los Angeles, the University of Minnesota, the University of Colorado, and the University of Illinois at Champaign-Urbana.

Last, but most important, this book would never have been completed had it not been for the presence and assistance of my wife Debra. Without her strong support and encouragement, patient friendship and love, this book would have been an empty exercise in abstract science, devoid of human spirit and warmth. It is to her that this book is dedicated.

*Chapter 1*

---

# Introduction

The increasing complexity of modern social life has placed greater demands on the various agencies of social control and order maintenance. This is especially true for those agencies intending to deal with problems of crime control. Dunham and Alpert have noted that "as problems of social control have grown and become more complex, so have the actions and reactions of the police."[1] Because the police are viewed by most people as the first line of defense against crime and disorder, the public expectations of what the police should and can do about crime and disorder have risen accordingly. There has also been a call for increased study of the police. And, as Dunham and Alpert indicate, beginning in the mid-1970s, increased federal funding for police research and a corresponding improvement in methodological sophistication have improved significantly our level of knowledge about the police.[2]

Despite the increase of research on the police, the United States police in general have been the subject of limited scientific study. Bayley has noted that this "discrepancy between the importance of the police in social life and the amount of attention given them by scholars is so striking as to require explanation."[3] Bayley suggests the lack of police research is a function of their pervasive presence, relatively routine occupational activities, and their absence as pivotal characters in major historical incidents.[4] The recent research interest in the police stems from their greater involvement in major social and political events.

Current studies of the United States police tend to explore topics with immediate policy implications such as encounters and interactions between police and the public, the occupational role of the police, or the critical analysis of the organizational and administrative dimensions of police work.[5] Continued research on these and related issues is of major importance for understanding the impact of police on society and to inform policy recommendations for changes in police structure or operation. But, in our haste to understand the current and future dimensions of the United States police system, we have overlooked the past.

The extent of our knowledge and understanding of the historical development and transformation of the United States police remains paltry. Palmer claims that historians tend to ignore institutions like the police, which "once established, exist[s] in perpetuity and grows by its own momentum."[6] With rare exceptions, such as the pioneering work of Seldon Bacon or the recent work of Monkkonen, questions of historical development, operation, and change have been given minimal attention at best.[7] There is a lack of quality data on the most basic questions of United States police history: How and why were the police created? Why and how did they take a particular form? What social, economic, and political forces over time gave us the present police structure in our society? Conley, writing in 1977, noted that we have lost sight of the connection of current problems with past developments and that historical research can bring a balance to our understanding of the police.[8] Conley's call for more historical study of the police has gone unanswered. Palmer, writing in 1988, is surprised that so few scholars have given any attention to police history; such research, he believes, can "educate us about a society's structure, dynamics and needs."[9]

This critical appraisal of police scholarship is not meant to imply that no historical study of the United States police has ever been undertaken. Beginning in the late 1960s research on the development of police began to appear in the literature. The pioneering efforts of Lane and Richardson, along with the studies of Silver, Parks, Carte and Carte, Harring and McMullin, and the previously mentioned Monkkonen, are of considerable importance.[10] Nevertheless, the United States effort at researching its police heritage remains embarrassingly deficient when compared to the work of police historians in Great Britain.[11] The fact that the United States has not produced a Leon Radzinowicz, a Charles Reith, or a T. A. Critchley reflects an apparent lack of interest on the part of United States scholars for conducting or encouraging research into their own police history.[12] This has begun to change, but most of the works on United States police history are descriptive studies of individual big-city police departments. The limited scope of these case studies makes it difficult to develop explanations that reach beyond individual departments and address the broader relationship between the police and society.

The major weaknesses of most historical studies of the United States police are their failure to identify the specific interests that were involved in developing, promoting, or opposing police development and reform, and their lack of a detailed description of the conflict that may have existed with regard to alternative ideas about police organization and operation. Without a comprehensive picture of police development, the scattered studies of municipal departments remain isolated pieces of the total puzzle of United States police history. This book is an effort to expand our knowledge of police history by analyzing the development of a previously ignored segment of law enforcement in the United States: the state police.

## THE STATE POLICE

Known as the highway patrol, state troopers, department of public safety, or state police, these law enforcement agencies of the state governments are an integral part of the United States police system. Yet, unlike the municipal police, state police forces have received no attention from police researchers or historians. Other than a mention of their existence and a brief description of their duties and jurisdiction, state police agencies are rarely given more than a cursory discussion in the criminal justice and law enforcement literature.[13] In fairness to criminal justice writers, the problem lies in the lack of credible literature about state police agencies. Most of the available data are outdated, nonscholarly, or both. (Chapter 2 will discuss the state police literature in more detail.)

Another reason for the limited information and lack of research attention given the state police may be their perceived role in the overall police system. When people think of the police, they have in mind the city police in their town or the large urban forces in New York, Chicago, or Los Angeles. It is the city police that are seen as the first line of defense in the battle against crime and social disorder. Therefore, municipal police departments receive most of the research attention in society's effort to contend with the problems of urban order maintenance. In sharp contrast is the common perception of state police activities as more mundane and service oriented. Unlike the crime-fighting image of city police, the state police bring to mind speed enforcement, traffic accidents, and helping stranded motorists.[14] Such an image, although accurate in a superficial sense, overlooks the important role state police have played in United States police history. The goal of this book is to describe the trends in state police development and to offer an explanation for the emergence of the state police as a significant part of police reform in the United States.

## WHY POLICE?—THE DEBATE

Recent discussion among police scholars, concerning the origins and reasons for creation of police forces, was a stimulus for the study of state police. Because of limited empirical evidence on this subject, differences of opinion exist concerning the etiology of the police. Currently three competing interpretations of police development can be identified in the literature: a social disorganization perspective, a conflict-oriented political process model, and a radical Marxist perspective.[15]

The social disorganization perspective is exemplified by the writings of urban historians Roger Lane and James Richardson in their respective studies of the nineteenth-century municipal police departments in Boston and New York.[16] According to social disorganization theory, the police emerged and developed in direct response to growing social problems generated by industrialization, urban growth, immigration, and the political transformation that took place during the second half of the nineteenth century. The old sheriff-constable system was inefficient and prone to corruption. Fear of rising crime and threats of riots produced the need for a more professional, rationally administered form of public protection.[17] The police were created and expanded in attempts to maintain "order" in a rapidly changing society.

The political process view of police development is illustrated in the works of Allen Levett and Samuel Walker. This perspective stresses the goals of centralization and professionalization as indicators of attempts by various groups to exert political influence over the police and thereby gain control of the urban political environment.[18] The forms of policing that developed were the outcome of this competition between contending factions of the urban scene, for example, elites versus immigrants, to organize the formal means of social control in support of their political and social interests.[19]

Both of these interpretations of police development have been challenged by a Marxist perspective that charges that "liberal analysis" of police development is mystifying and misleading. Exemplified by the works of Sidney Harring and Joel Summerhays, this perspective argues that capitalism dramatically altered older class relations, necessitating tighter control and discipline of the working classes.[20] Crime and disorder were symptoms of a fundamental threat to established order, and the traditional methods of order maintenance were not so much ineffective as they were "unsuitable" or "counterproductive" to the needs of the ruling class.[21] From this point of view, the police are neither a neutral by-product of the social disorganization produced by industrialization and urban growth, nor the outcome of some vague pluralistic competition among various factions of the urban political environment. Rather, the police constitute an integral component of the coercive apparatus of the state that directly serves the interests of the dominant capitalist class. Thus, the police in the United States have served to enforce the class, social, and cultural oppression inherent in the growth of capitalism and were "deradicalized" in response to the rioting and disorder of the working classes during the late nineteenth century.[22]

The central element in this debate is the relationship between the structure of vested interests and the formation of the police. But none of the three perspectives provides an adequate analysis of the specific interests involved in developing the United States police system. Social disorganization proponents focus on changing social conditions as contributing factors in the drive for police reform but fail to identify the groups involved or their relationship to the changing conditions and the police forces being created. Political process advocates address the question of political influence on the police but fail to deal adequately with the question of interest group involvement. Lacking in their explanation is a detailed analysis of the groups competing for control of the police and the changes taking place in the larger social environment. Marxist analysis asserts a direct relationship between the development of police forces and the desires of industrialists to protect their interests with respect to the lower class, immigrants, and organized labor. Nevertheless, the Marxist perspective fails to document the specifics of interest group involvement, reporting instead police actions as post-hoc indicators of the groups working for police reform.[23]

These three paradigms offer plausible explanations of the development of the police in the United States. But given the limited scope of historical research on police development, the relative validity of these perspectives for understanding the growth of the police remains open to debate. A deeper understanding of the relationship between the police and the changes affecting modern societies requires more historically oriented studies into the development, structure, and operation of the police at all levels of operation: local, county, state, and federal. This book brings additional knowledge to bear on the central questions of police development and provides opportunities for building upon, and moving beyond, existing literature on United States police history.

## RATIONALES FOR STATE POLICE RESEARCH

State police research affords the opportunity to study the law enforcement agencies that were specifically intended to operate in a rural, as opposed to an urban, setting. Most of the existing works on police history have been studies of large urban departments such as Boston, New York, or Buffalo. These studies have contributed important knowledge about the response of particular urban communities to the problems of social control. Similar studies of other cities are needed if we are to build a sound historical understanding of policing in the United States. Case studies, however, limit our knowledge to the particular city being studied.[24] The goal of social-historical scholarship on the police should be the building of a comprehensive and integrated picture of police development that includes local, county, state, federal, and private police. Research into the historical development and operation of the state police broadens the scope of police history by addressing the societal response to the problems of crime and social control in rural areas.

There is little information about police development during the twentieth century.[25] Since most urban police departments came into existence during the middle of the nineteenth century, the available data limit our knowledge of police development to pre- and post–Civil War periods. State police are primarily a twentieth-century phenomenon, with peak periods of emergence in the early 1920s and again in the 1930s. Given the historical significance of these two junctures of United States history (post–World War I, the Prohibition era, and the Great Depression), state police development offers an excellent opportunity to study the relationship between changing social conditions and the emergence and transformation of the mechanisms of social control.

Criticism of historical studies of the police have noted their failure to examine evidence about the identities, motives, and activities of the specific vested interests engaged in creating the police.[26] Historical study of the creation of state police forces addresses this weakness found in earlier studies of municipal police development. The creation of the state police was a legislative act that required the introduction and passage of specific pieces of legislation. This public legislative process makes it possible to identify the various individuals, groups, political factions, and other vested interests working for and against the passage of state police laws. An added feature of the legislative nature of the state police is the ability to locate development of the state police within a broader political climate as evidenced through legislative policymaking and debate.

Emergence of the state police in the United States coincides with what historians refer to as the Progressive Era. Covering the period from the late 1880s to the early 1920s, progressivism is characterized as a way of thinking about and responding to the nation's problems at the turn of the century.[27] Link and McCormick argue that progressives were the first to undertake solutions to the changes brought about by an increasingly urban and industrializing society. They point out that knowledge about "their [the progressives'] achievements and failures has considerable relevance for our own time."[28] Efforts at police reform are excellent examples of society's interest in, and willingness to use, various types of repression to bring about desired changes. The state police offer an excellent opportunity to study this process as it was a new form and type of police, created especially for the changes taking place. Analysis of state police development sheds additional light on the intentions behind progressive reform in general and repressive reform in particular.

Currently a great deal of attention is paid to the broad issues of control and operation of major law enforcement institutions in the United States. Yet there is little information available that can provide a glimpse into the political and social relationships that were involved in the creation and development of these institutions. This book explores the social, economic, and political forces instrumental in the creation of state police agencies and uncovers the interest structure that best explains how the state police were created. Although the state police are only a single component of the larger United States police system, the arguments and empirical evidence concerning the creation of the state police will move us a step closer toward understanding the evolution of the United States police system.

**PLAN OF THE BOOK**

Chapter 2 critically reviews the literature available on the state police. I do not attempt to evaluate every piece of literature on the state police, but rather focus on types of literature and the more significant items and authors. What is known about the state police and what criminal justice writers have had to rely on for their discussions of the state police is of poor quality. A review of the state police literature revealed several inadequacies. The most significant weakness was the lack of any current writings on the emergence and operation of the state police. Most of the materials were published before 1935 and were written with a pro–state police bias. Although much of the state police literature is flawed due to its proselytizing nature, this material, especially the early works, provides a look at the values, beliefs, and fears of those who were active in promoting the state police as an important police reform.

Chapter 3 offers a description of state police development beginning with a brief discussion of the early efforts at centralizing the police in Ireland and Canada. The state police concept was neither a United States invention nor a new idea in police organization. Searching for improved methods of social control to deal with anticipated social unrest, leaders in Ireland during the late 1780s and in Canada during the 1870s created highly centralized, paramilitary forces combining the structure and skills of the army with the civil, order-maintaining aspects of the city police. These two centralized police forces, especially the Irish Constabulary, served as models for those promoting the state police concept in the United States. The remainder of Chapter 3 presents a chronological analysis of the development of the United States state police. Using secondary literature, newspaper accounts, and state documents, I detail the legislative enactments pertaining to state police, highway patrols, and other centralized law enforcement agencies of the various states. The main purpose is to offer a historically and legislatively accurate description of the pattern of state police development. The first section will present a discussion of the experimental phase of state police development that took place during the nineteenth century. The remaining sections focus on the twentieth century, the primary period of state police activity.

The emergence of the state police in the United States cannot be understood in isolation. Therefore, the purpose of Chapter 4 is to connect the pattern of state police development to larger events and provide a social-historical explanation for why the state police were developed in the United States during the early twentieth century. Emerging as they did during the Progressive Era, the state police were an ideal reflection of the ideals, values, and beliefs of the progressive spirit, incorporating many of the features reformers were attempting to promote in the municipal police. I argue that the most influential factors in stimulating the movement to create the state police were the reemergence of nativism as a response to the increasing numbers of immigrants and the appearance of a politically active and aggressive labor movement. Responding to these factors, reformers sought to "modernize" all aspects of United States society by using the bureaucratic and rational dimensions of the business world to address society's problems.

These arguments are examined in more detail in Chapters 5, 6, and 7, where I present the findings of detailed historical analysis of the process creating the state police in Illinois and Colorado. These chapters are a response to the failure of many police histories to set forth the various interests, for and against, involved in creating a particular police agency. Chapters 5 and 6 contain data relevant to the unsuccessful attempts to create a Pennsylvania-style state police force in Illinois, while Chapter 7 describes the events pertaining to the creation and eventual disbanding of the state police in Colorado.

Chapter 8 presents a summary discussion of state police development by comparing the different outcomes of the state police movements in Colorado and Illinois. Using a law creation approach, the elements of social conflict involved in creating the state police are located. Based on this analysis, I argue that the emergence of the state police was a product of the progressive reform movement, with the primary motivating factors being the increase in immigration from eastern and southern Europe and the desire to curb the growing labor movement. Support for this argument is found in materials relating to the state police movement in other states. Chapter 8 also addresses the question of state police development within the context of the current debate over why, how, and for whom the police were created. Recent interest in police history has produced a number of studies concerning the emergence of the United States police. As discussed above, three perspectives on police development can be found in the literature: a social disorganization approach that focuses on the impact of industrialization and urban growth; a political process explanation that stresses the impact of competing political factions; and a Marxist approach that advocates a class analysis of police development. In applying these different perspectives to the data on the state police I found that a modified political process perspective offers the best explanation for the state police movement.

Finally, I have included an appendix. Much remains to be done in police history, and the state police offer a wealth of research topics. The appendix incudes a discussion of potential areas in need of further research and a research bibliography intended as a reference tool for police scholars that includes all known published and unpublished books, articles, and manuscripts pertaining to the state police.

## NOTES

1. Roger G. Dunham and Geoffrey P. Alpert, *Critical Issues in Policing: Contemporary Readings* (Prospect Heights, IL: Waveland Press, 1989), p. 1.

2. Ibid.

3. David H. Bayley, *Patterns of Policing: A Comparative International Analysis* (New Brunswick, NJ: Rutgers University Press, 1985), p. 5.

4. Ibid.

5. See, for example, Michael Banton, *The Policeman in the Community* (London: Tavistock, 1964); Jerome H. Skolnick, *Justice Without Trial: Law Enforcement in Democratic Society* (New York: John Wiley and Sons, 1966); David J. Bordua, *The Police: Six Sociological Essays* (New York: John Wiley and Sons, 1967); Arthur Niederhoffer, *Behind the Shield: The Police in Urban America* (Garden City, NJ: Doubleday, 1967); James Q. Wilson, *Varieties of Police Behavior* (Cambridge, MA: Harvard University Press, 1969); Egon Bittner, *The Functions of the Police in Modern Society* (Chevy Chase, MD: National Institute of Mental Health, 1970); Albert J. Reiss, *The Police and the Public* (New Haven, CT: Yale University Press, 1971); Robert Fogelson, *Big-City Police* (Cambridge, MA: Harvard University Press, 1977); Peter K. Manning, *Police Work: The Social Organization of Police* (Cambridge, MA: MIT Press, 1977); Jerome H. Skolnick and David H. Bayley, *The New Blue Line: Police Innovation in Six American Cities* (New York: Free Press, 1986);

Geoffrey P. Alpert and Roger G. Dunham, *Policing Urban America* (Prospect Heights, IL: Waveland Press, 1988); Herman Goldstein, *Problem-Oriented Policing* (New York: McGraw-Hill, 1990).

6. Stanley H. Palmer, *Police and Protest in England and Ireland, 1780–1850* (Cambridge: Cambridge University Press, 1988), p. 6.

7. Seldon Bacon, "The Early Development of the American Municipal Police: A Study of the Evolution of Formal Controls in a Changing Society" (Ph.D. diss., Yale University, 1939); Eric H. Monkkonen, *Police in Urban America, 1860–1920* (Cambridge: Cambridge University Press, 1981).

8. John Conley, "Criminal Justice History as a Field of Research: A Review of the Literature, 1960–1975," *Journal of Criminal Justice* 5 (Spring 1977): 15.

9. Palmer, *Police and Protest*, p. xix.

10. Roger Lane, *Policing the City: Boston, 1822–1885* (Cambridge, MA: Harvard University Press, 1967); Allen Silver, "The Demand for Order in Civil Society," in *The Police*, ed. David Bordua (New York: Basic Books, 1968); James F. Richardson, *The New York Police: Colonial Times to 1901* (New York: Oxford University Press, 1970); Evelyn Parks, "From Constabulary to Police Society," *Catalyst* 5 (Summer 1970): 76–97; Gene E. Carte and Elaine H. Carte, *Police Reform in the United States: The Era of August Vollmer, 1905–1932* (Berkeley: University of California Press, 1975); Sidney L. Harring and Lorraine M. McMullin, "The Buffalo Police, 1872–1900: Labor Unrest, Political Power and the Creation of the Police Institution," *Crime and Social Justice* 4 (Fall–Winter 1975): 5–14; Monkkonen, *Police in Urban America*.

11. Conley, "Criminal Justice History," p. 16.

12. Leon Radzinowicz, *A History of English Criminal Law and Its Administration from 1750*, vol. 3 (New York: Macmillan, 1968); Charles Reith, *The Police Idea: Its History and Evolution in England in the Eighteenth Century and After* (London: Oxford University Press, 1938), *A Short History of the British Police* (London: Oxford University Press, 1948), *A New Study of Police History* (London: Oliver and Boyd, 1956); T. A. Critchley, *A History of Police in England and Wales, 1900–1966* (London: Constable and Co., 1967).

13. Documentation of the indifference by scholars toward the state police can be found in the criminal justice and criminological literature. A survey by the author of fifty-one texts and readers on criminology, police, and criminal justice published during the past two decades revealed an almost total disregard for the state police. Only seven of these books discuss historical issues of origin, growth, and operation, with only one devoting more than two pages to a discussion of the state police.

14. A similar criticism has been raised concerning the lack of research attention given to small-town and rural police forces. See Victor H. Sims, *Small Town and Rural Police* (Springfield, IL: Charles C. Thomas, 1988).

15. An elaboration of these perspectives can be found in Robert Liebman and Michael Polen, "Perspectives on Policing in Nineteenth-Century America," *Social Science History* 2 (Spring 1978): 346–360; and Monkkonen, *Police in Urban America*. A detailed analysis of these perspectives as found in British police literature is contained in Robert Reiner, *The Politics of the Police* (New York: St. Martin's Press, 1985).

16. Lane, *Policing the City*; Richardson, *The New York Police*.

17. Reiner, *The Politics of the Police*, pp. 11–14.

18. Allen E. Levett, "Centralization of City Police in the Nineteenth Century United States" (Ph.D. diss., University of Michigan, 1975); Samuel Walker, *A Critical History of Police Reform* (Lexington, MA: D. C. Heath, 1977).

19. Monkkonen, *Police in Urban America*, p. 51.

20. Sidney L. Harring, "The Development of the Police Institution in the United States," *Crime and Social Justice* 5 (Spring-Summer 1976): 54–59; Center for Research on Criminal Justice, *The Iron Fist and the Velvet Glove: An Analysis of the United States Police* (Berkeley, CA: Center for Research on Criminal Justice, 1977); Joel Summerhays, "American Police Reform: An Alternative Perspective" (Ph.D. diss., University of California at Berkeley, 1979).

21. Reiner, *The Politics of the Police*, pp. 21–23.

22. Cyril D. Robinson, "The Deradicalization of the Policeman: A Historical Analysis," *Crime and Delinquency* 24 (April 1978): 132.

23. *Liebman and Polen, "Perspectives on Policing,"* pp. 347–348.

24. A few comparative studies of the municipal police have been done, but they remain largely unpublished. The classic study by Seldon Bacon is a case in point. Recent comparative studies by George A. Ketcham, "Municipal Police Reform: A Comparative Study of Law Enforcement in Cincinnati, Chicago, New Orleans, New York, and St. Louis, 1844–1877" (Ph.D. diss., University of Missouri, 1976) and David R. Johnson, "The Search for an Urban Discipline: Police Reform as a Response to Crime in American Cities, 1800–1875" (Ph.D. diss., University of Chicago, 1972) also remain unpublished.

25. Samuel Walker, "The Urban Police in American History: A Review of the Literature," *Journal of Police Science and Administration* 4 (September 1976): 252–260.

26. Liebman and Polen, "Perspectives on Policing," pp. 347–348.

27. Arthur S. Link and Richard L. McCormick, *Progressivism* (Arlington Heights, IL: Harlan Davidson, 1983), p. 2.

28. Ibid, p. 3.

# Chapter 2

# What Do We Know
# About the State Police?

Every state except Hawaii has some form of state police agency. In 1990, there were a total of 77,330 full-time state police employees, of which 52,372 were sworn officers.[1] The total operating expenditure in fiscal 1990 for all state police agencies was $3.7 billion, or approximately 9 percent of all operating expenditures for police protection at the state and local level including county sheriffs.[2] Yet, with few exceptions, the state police receive little if any commentary in current criminal justice or police science literature. Many authors do not even mention the state police, while others simply indicate that they exist. Authors that do discuss the state police rarely provide more than a few brief paragraphs of limited information.[3] The publication of the *Handbook of State Police, Highway Patrols, and Investigative Agencies* by Donald Torres is a welcome and needed resource. Primarily a reference text, Torres's book provides a wealth of information, previously unavailable in one volume, on the organizational structure, duties, jurisdiction, and training qualifications of sworn personnel for all state law enforcement agencies.[4] Nevertheless, neither Torres, nor any of the other criminal justice writers, provide anything but sketchy comments about the history of the state police. Questions concerning the dynamics of state police creation and development or the role of the state police in the historical process of police reform are either not discussed or covered in a superficial fashion.

Limited as it is, what does the current criminal justice literature tell us about the history of the state police? For the most part, the discussions are remarkably similar in format and content. After a perfunctory presentation about the development of the Texas Rangers as the first attempt at state policing in the United States, discussions usually turn to the early twentieth century and to the creation of the Pennsylvania state police in 1905. Other than to credit the Pennsylvania force as the first modern state police and the subsequent model for other states, very little is said about the historical evolution and developmental process of the state police in other parts of the country except to mention that a few states (Massachusetts, Arizona, New Mexico) also had experimented with the state police idea.

As to the reasons why the state police were developed, the standard presentation focuses on the apparent inability of the traditional sheriff-constable system to deal with a modern, mobile criminal element. This, combined with the reluctance of the urban political machines to reform the metropolitan police departments, forced law-abiding citizens to find an alternative that was efficient, had fewer jurisdictional restrictions, and was beyond political corruption.[5] A few authors offer some alternatives to this standard "change causes reform" argument. Some writers note that the Pennsylvania state police were created in direct response to disputes between labor and management and were intended to serve as a force to protect and defend mine owner interests. This allegedly led to opposition by organized labor, which attempted to have the state police disbanded.[6] A variant of this argument has the Pennsylvania state police emerging either in response to the coal strike of 1902 or to the early activity of the Molly Maguires, after which the state police were established to prevent the outbreak of similar activity in the future.[7] None of the writers have anything to say about the reasons for the creation of state police forces in other states, nor do they provide a description of the process and patterns of state police development across the country. At best, a few writers comment that other states simply copied the Pennsylvania model or link the emergence of the state police to the increased use of the automobile and the resulting problems of traffic control and auto thefts.[8] One author mentions the possibility that the state police may have been created to ensure enforcement of laws if local police officials refused to do so.[9]

Relying on such accounts, the reader is left with a superficial, questionable interpretation of the historical development and growth of the state police. Moreover, the similarity of the discussions is the result of a reliance on the same references. Some writers do not provide references for their comments on the state police, but those that do, cite the same two or three sources. Invariably, the most frequently cited works are Bruce Smith's book *The State Police*, published in 1925, and Katherine Mayo's story of the Pennsylvania state police, *Justice to All*, published in 1917.[10] The dependence on such outdated references invariably calls into question the accuracy of the state police discussions that are based on these sources. A critical review of the nature, quality, and usefulness of the material available about the state police is the primary focus of this chapter.

## THE STATE POLICE LITERATURE

Given the narrow discussion of the state police in the current criminal justice literature and the reliance on the same outdated sources, it would appear that there is very little material available to scholars interested in the state police. This is not the case. In conducting the research for this book, I was able to assemble a bibliography of over 250 specific references about the state police (see the research bibliography in the appendix). The problem is not the existence of written material on the topic, but rather the quality and accuracy of this material for research purposes.

The bulk of the existing material on the state police suffers from two weaknesses. First, much of the material is "police science" oriented, consisting primarily of descriptions of the administrative and organizational characteristics of state police departments. Second, and more important, is the lack of recent, up-to-date studies of the state police.[11] The bulk of the material written about the state police was published prior to 1935. This is not surprising, however, given that the period between 1917 and 1935 was the time when state police development was at its peak. A controversial innovation such as centralized policing by the state government was bound to generate considerable public debate and discussion. Because of the controversy surrounding this new form of police activity, however, most of this early literature is often little more than propaganda, extolling the virtues of state police as a needed reform for bringing about more efficient crime control.

The most obvious characteristic of the early literature on the state police is its proselytizing nature. Emphatic in their favor of state police, journalists, editors, reformers, and educators attempted to promote the advantages of centralized law enforcement. Therefore, most of the early publications about the state police were intended to convince the general public that the time had come for state-controlled police. The effort to generate favorable public opinion toward the idea of state police took two basic forms: sensationalism, which played upon the fears, prejudices, and nativistic attitudes of the general public; and a "scientific" approach, which sought to justify the need for state police on the premise that modern society had outgrown traditional methods of law enforcement, especially in the rural districts. Excellent examples of the sensationalist approach can be found in the writings of Katherine Mayo and Frederick Van de Water.

Mayo, a freelance writer on American history for popular magazines, wrote three books and published over a dozen articles about the Pennsylvania and New York state police. Convinced that some form of police protection other than the local sheriff was needed in the rural areas of New York, Mayo investigated the state constabulary system that was then operating in Pennsylvania. The result was her book *Justice to All: The Story of the Pennsylvania State Police*. Relying on selective newspaper accounts and interviews with state police officers, and playing on the public's fears of foreigners through the use of racial and ethnic stereotypes, Mayo produced a biased and distorted portrayal of early state police activity. Her numerous magazine articles repeat the sensationalist pattern and style of the stories in *Justice to All*.[12] Her two other books on the state police are nothing more than compilations of previously published articles.[13]

Although lacking scientific credibility with regard to the validity of their content, Mayo's writings are important for understanding the development of the state police in the United States. The introduction to *Justice to All* was written by Theodore Roosevelt. In it he strongly advocated the idea of state police and argues for expanding the concept to other states. Roosevelt's introduction, combined with the sensational and exaggerated descriptions of state police activity, made the book a potent and widely used propaganda tool in the movement to establish state police in New York and other states.

Similar to Mayo's book, both in content and style, is Frederick Van de Water's book on the New York state police.[14] As with Mayo, romanticized tales of state troopers rescuing rural New Yorkers from all types of danger, criminal and otherwise, are presented in a highly biased and sensational fashion. Gaining most of his information while traveling with the troopers, he explicitly took the side of the state police (Van de Water was an honorary New York state trooper) and wrote more to legitimate their existence than to provide an accurate description of their operations.

Playing on the fears and prejudices of the white old-stock American, Mayo and Van de Water attempted to generate popular support for the state police by presenting the trooper as a superhuman hero capable of protecting and bringing order to the isolated areas of the country. Although uninformative about state police development and "actual" operation of the state police, the writings of Mayo and Van de Water provide examples of the values, beliefs, and fears of those who were attempting to reform the police by promoting "more efficient" measures of social control.

No doubt the sensationalist accounts of state police officers combatting the evils of crime, vice, and immigrant disorder served to capture the interest of the general public and build support for the idea of a centralized rural police. Yet a more "scientific" approach toward promoting the state police also exists in the early literature. Written mostly by political and police scientists, public administrators, and legal scholars, this material argued in favor of state police on the basis of "facts" that supposedly proved the need for a more modern and efficient approach to rural law enforcement.

The academic writings on the state police during this early period consist of chapters in books on government or police administration, and published reports and articles by various committees, organizations, and individuals promoting the state police idea.[15] As a whole, this material takes a pro–state police stance, providing chronologies of state police development, arguments for why state police are needed, and organizational descriptions of law enforcement operations of various state police departments. None of these works attempt to fit the pattern of state police development into a broader historical context. This failure to relate the emergence of the various state police forces to larger events taking place in American history is the major weakness of these presentations.

Given the promotional nature of this literature, the prominent feature is a section outlining the rationale for creating state police forces. The arguments usually include the following points: lack of rural police protection due to the breakdown in the sheriff-constable system; change in the nature of rural crime brought about by the development of the automobile and expansion of good roads that offered convenient access to rural areas and effective means of escape; the realization that the state militia and National Guard were too expensive and inappropriate for use in general police work; the lack of uniformity of law enforcement created by a decentralized system of policing; and the problem of rising death and injury rates due to increased traffic on rural roads. Although representing the formal recommendations of individuals and groups explicitly promoting the state police concept, the arguments given in support of such a system provide valuable insight into the ideology used to convince the public and lawmakers about the merits of, and need for, state police.

Rarely do any of these early works mention opposition to the state police. In an American Institute of Criminal Law and Criminology report published in 1919, four arguments against the state police were given: (1) the state police would be militaristic; (2) state police would be a financial burden on the state budget; (3) the possibility of political corruption would exist; and (4) state police would be used against labor.[16] Similar arguments were reported by Conover, with the additions that state police would be an infringement on local government and possibly prejudicial to personal liberty.[17] The authors of these papers rejected such opposition arguments to the state police as both unwarranted and unfounded, and suggested they could easily be overcome through an educational campaign extolling the virtues of state police.

Of foremost importance among the academic scholarship on the state police are the works of Bruce Smith. A Columbia-educated specialist in police administration, Smith was a recognized expert on police methods and operation. Throughout his career, he was involved with many state and local governments, committees, and crime commissions as a consultant on police administration and organization. His writing on the state police was the logical outcome of his interest in police reform at all levels. Smith believed that state police were a necessary and welcome improvement in United States police practices.

Smith's primary work on the state police was published in 1925. This work was concerned with the organization, administration, and statutory powers of state police forces in existence at the time.[18] Information about the state police was derived from secondary sources, consisting primarily of studies by local and state government committees, and Smith's personal experience with a number of the departments. Based on these data, he argued that state police emerged as a result of changes in the character of rural crime, as the expansion of the railroads and development of the automobile brought the urban criminal element into contact with the rural areas. While the nature of rural crime had changed, law enforcement had not kept pace and was, he argued, inadequate to handle the new problems of social control. Smith claimed that the sheriff and constable were unwilling and incapable of dealing with these new problems, and that various alternatives such as the state militia and private police contained inherent disadvantages that made them unsuitable for general police work. Smith then promoted the idea of state police as the logical solution. This was consistent with the general movement on the part of state governments to assume more of the administrative functions of the local communities.[19]

Although a valuable source of information, Smith's work lacked a critical awareness regarding the role of police in society. From his romantic portrayal of early rural life to simple solutions for the "rural crime problem," Smith espoused the ideals of the status quo; in his view the police were a necessary feature of modern society. Smith made no effort to discuss any controversies surrounding social policy and the operation of the state police. Nevertheless, Smith's writings were significant contributions toward gaining acceptance of the state police idea as his work served as a model and reference for other commentators on the subject.

Beginning in 1935 the available literature on the state police declined substantially.[20] Works that were written after 1935 were similar in content and style to the earlier writings that were either administrative in approach or strictly descriptive accounts of trends in state police development.[21] They lack any attempt to explain the rise and growth of state police in terms other than a general need for more efficient rural law enforcement. These writings are characterized by two types of studies not generally found in the early period: (1) articles describing individual state police departments[22] and (2) in-house histories, usually written by a member or former member of the force, in which the story of the department's growth is told in generally favorable terms.[23]

Two of the better case studies on the state police are by Kaloupek on the Iowa highway patrol and Coakley on the New Jersey state police.[24] In addition to the standard administrative discussion of structure and operation, these works present both a discussion of the social setting precipitating the development of state police and the legislative process leading to the enactment of the specific statutes.

The main thesis of Kaloupek's paper is that changes in the social structure generated new needs for government services. Specifically, the increase in population in urban areas, industrialization of rural areas, and improved means of transportation generated government recognition that more effective control agencies were required. The result was the establishment of state police and highway patrols.[25] Following a discussion of why state police were necessary, which essentially restates the arguments of Bruce Smith, Kaloupek presents a lengthy discussion of the process that culminated in the establishment of the Iowa highway patrol. He traces the various bills through the legislature from 1915 until 1935, when the act creating the patrol was finally passed. Although he provides an informative analysis, the reliance on legislative journals produces a superficial investigation lacking any in-depth study of specific interests involved in the issue. However, Kaloupek, for the first time in the state police literature, attempts an examination of the process surrounding the creation of a state law enforcement agency.

Coakley was a sergeant in the New Jersey state police and makes no claims to objectivity. Nevertheless, he provides a good description of the social and political forces involved in the movement to establish a state police in New Jersey. According to Coakley, state police were created to supply an enforcement apparatus for the governors to deal with labor disputes and to increase the effectiveness of rural law enforcement. As did earlier commentators on state police, Coakley views the inability of the sheriff-constable system to cope with rising crime as the key issue around which the debate over state police for New Jersey revolved. Rural proponents of state police pointed to the increase in crime brought about by the popularity of the automobile, while urban supporters brought up the issues of labor disputes and the "foreign" element. Opponents of state police claimed such a force would be used against labor. All three views were well represented in the legislature, but it was the labor issue that brought about the first bill on state police. Immediately following a period of violent strikes during 1914–1915, a measure providing for a state police was introduced and passed in the Senate, but died in a House committee. State police bills were introduced in succeeding sessions, with each bill moving a little closer toward enactment. But opposition forces, claiming that a state police would be an antilabor force as well as a hindrance to the war effort, were too powerful to overcome. It was not until 1921 that the General Assembly, under pressure to do something about "increased criminal activity," passed a state police bill over the governor's veto.[26]

The remainder of Coakley's book is of little value for understanding the creation of the state police, as it consists of colorful stories about the important and sensational cases, such as the Lindbergh kidnapping, that engaged the New Jersey state police over the fifty-year period covered by the book. While a step in the right direction, and an improvement over Kaloupek, Coakley falls short of producing a systematic treatment of the relationship between society and the state police, and the historical characteristics of that relationship as shaped by the larger social context.

Conti's work, a more recent study of the Pennsylvania state police, is disappointing.[27] A former officer in the force, Conti tells the story of this department from the executive level. Thus, twenty out of the twenty-four chapters are devoted to descriptive biographical presentations of the various superintendents and commissioners who had headed the department over the years. While providing much information on the personal lives of these men, the book lacks any critical or objective analysis of the development of the state police in Pennsylvania. Introductory sections describing the establishment of the force are cursory and less informative than similar discussions provided by Kaloupek and Coakley. Overall the book is eulogistic in tone and, in many ways, is a modern version of Mayo's *Justice to All*. This is unfortunate because the Pennsylvania state police, created in 1905, was the first department of its type to be permanently established in the United States. Militaristic in structure, the Pennsylvania state police served as the ideal on which other states attempted to model their forces. Many of the bills introduced in other states (Colorado, New Jersey, New York) were identical to the Pennsylvania law. Because of the benchmark status of the Pennsylvania state police, research into the social, political, and economic factors related to its creation, growth, and operation would provide crucial elements necessary for grounding explanations for the rise of the state police. To date, no such study has been undertaken.

## SUMMARY

The preceding discussion indicates that much of the available literature relating to the state police is inadequate for fully understanding the emergence and development of state-level police forces. Most of the studies were written during the 1920s when the state police movement was reaching its peak. Much of this material on the state police takes the need for such a force for granted and deals with how these agencies operated, or on how to educate the public about the advantages of the state police in order to promote their adoption in other states, or simply to tell the state police story, thereby documenting their value to society. The rest of the literature is either police science, with a focus on organizational structure and administration, or in-house histories, detailing the heroic exploits of the men who made up the various forces. The major weakness of the existing state police literature is the lack of a social scientific perspective.

The failure to address the sociopolitical context of state police development is most apparent in the rudimentary attempts to deal with the issues of why the state police emerged when they did. According to the literature, rising rural crime rates and a decentralized and ineffective police system were the primary causes for establishing the state police. As Monkkonen has noted, the weakness of this argument is the assumption that creation of police forces is a "natural occurrence" in response to increased crime and the failure of existing agencies to control it.[28] This may or may not be correct, but due to the lack of empirical documentation or analysis, the issue remains open to question.

Furthermore, simply to state that the state police were created to replace an outdated and inefficient sheriff-constable system, or as a response to increased rural crime, raises more questions than it answers. Inefficient according to whom? The local residents and farmers, city politicians, reformers, businessmen? What aspect was deemed inefficient—training, financing, or operation? Or was the complaint of inefficiency a reaction by vested interests to the influence of local sentiment on the sheriffs' selective enforcement of the law? Was the rise in rural crime real or manufactured to serve vested interests? Who was complaining about the increase, farmers or city businessmen? These and other questions need to be addressed in order to penetrate the official ideology and rhetoric of those who were calling for the establishment of the state police.

Except for Coakley, none of the works attempt to identify the vested interests involved in the creation of state police forces. With only passing remarks in the literature such as "it was a partisan issue," or "politics were involved," or "citizens pressured the lawmakers," the question of who was behind state police legislation has long been a mystery. On the other hand, most of the works that discuss opposition to the creation of state police agree that the major, if not the only, obstacle was organized labor. However, this claim is simply stated and no effort is made to investigate the components, activities, and ideology of labor opposition. Was labor unified in its opposition to state police or were there factions within the labor movement with different ideas and approaches to the issue? Was labor the only opposition or were there other interest groups (e.g., farmers, immigrants, or African Americans) that may have been opposed to the state police? These and other questions concerning vested interests need to be critically examined if an accurate account of state police development is to be produced. The following chapters are intended to provide some answers to these important questions.

## NOTES

1. U.S. Department of Justice, Bureau of Justice Statistics, *Sourcebook of Criminal Justice Statistics, 1992*, edited by Kathleen Maguire, Ann L. Pastore, and Timothy J. Flanagan (Washington, DC: Government Printing Office, 1993), p. 40.

2. Ibid.

3. See Clemens Bartollas, *American Criminal Justice: An Introduction* (New York: Macmillan, 1988); John E. Conklin, *Criminology*, 2nd ed. (New York: Macmillan, 1986); Don C. Gibbons, *Society, Crime, and Criminal Behavior*, 5th ed. (Englewood Cliffs, NJ: Prentice-Hall, 1987); Henry W. Mannle and J. David Hirschel, *Fundamentals of Criminology* (Englewood Cliffs, NJ: Prentice-Hall, 1988); Robert D. Pursley, *Introduction to Criminal Justice* (New York: Macmillan, 1987); Lawrence F. Travis, *Introduction to Criminal Justice* (Cincinnati, OH: Anderson Publishing, 1990); Lewis Yablonski, *Criminology: Crime &Criminality*, 4th ed. (New York: Harper and Row, 1990).

4. Donald A. Torres, *Handbook of State Police, Highway Patrols, and Investigative Agencies* (Westport, CT: Greenwood Press, 1987).

5. George T. Felkenes, *The Criminal Justice System: Its Functions and Personnel* (Englewood Cliffs, NJ: Prentice-Hall, 1973); James A. Inciardi, *Criminal Justice* (Orlando, FL: Academic Press, 1984); Larry J. Siegel, *Criminology*, 3rd ed. (St. Paul, MN: West Publishing, 1989); Ronald J. Waldron, *The Criminal Justice System: An Introduction*, 4th ed. (New York: Harper and Row, 1989); Paul B. Weston and Kenneth M. Wells, *Law Enforcement and Criminal Justice: An Introduction* (Pacific Palisades, CA: Goodyear, 1972).

6. Felkenes, *The Criminal Justice System*; N. Gary Holten and Melvin E. Jones, *The System of Criminal Justice*, 2nd ed. (Boston: Little, Brown, 1982); Peter C. Kratcoski and Donald B. Walker, *Criminal Justice in America: Process and Issues*, 2nd ed. (New York: Random House, 1984); Weston and Wells, *Law Enforcement and Criminal Justice*.

7. Sue T. Reid, *Criminal Justice*, 2nd ed. (New York: Macmillan, 1990); Samuel Walker, *A Critical History of Police Reform* (Lexington, MA: D. C. Heath, 1977).

8. Neil C. Chamelin, Vernon B. Fox, and Paul M. Whisenand, *Introduction to Criminal Justice* (Englewood Cliffs, NJ: Prentice-Hall, 1975); Inciardi, *Criminal Justice*.

9. George F. Cole, *The American System of Criminal Justice*, 5th ed. (Pacific Grove, CA: Brooks-Cole, 1989).

10. Bruce Smith, *The State Police* (New York: Macmillan, 1925); Katherine Mayo, *Justice to All: The Story of the Pennsylvania State Police* (New York: G. P. Putnam's Sons, 1917).

11. The few exceptions are Leo J. Coakley, *Jersey Troopers: A Fifty Year History of the New Jersey State Police* (New Brunswick, NJ: Rutgers University Press, 1971); Stanley L. Swart, "The Development of State-Level Police Activity in Ohio, 1802–1928" (Ph.D. diss., Northwestern University, 1974); Philip Conti, *The Pennsylvania State Police: A History of Service to the Commonwealth, 1905 to the Present* (Harrisburg, PA: Stackpole Books, 1977).

12. See "Cherry Valley," *Atlantic Monthly* 121 (February 1918): 175–181; "New York State Troopers," *Outlook* 118 (April 1918): 622–623; "Guardians of the Countryside," *Country Life in America* 35 (December 1918): 61–63; "Demobilization and State Police," *North American Review* 209 (June 1919): 786–794; "State Troopers, Operator," *Outlook* 133 (February 1923): 398–400.

13. *The Standard-Bearers: True Stories of Heroes of Law and Order* (Boston: Houghton Mifflin, 1918); *Mounted Justice: True Stories of the Pennsylvania State Police* (Boston: Houghton Mifflin, 1922).

14. Frederick F. Van de Water, *Grey Riders: The Story of the New York State Troopers* (New York: G. P. Putnam's Sons, 1922).

15. See Leonard F. Fuld, *Police Administration* (New York: Putnam, 1909); P. S. Reinsch, "The Pennsylvania Constabulary," in *Readings on American Government*, ed. P. S. Reinsch (Boston: Ginn, 1911); Edgar Dawson, "New York State Police," *American Political Science Review* 11 (August 1917): 539–541; F. P. Stockbridge, "New York State Troopers," *World's Work* 35 (1918): 264–272; P. O. Ray, "Metropolitan and State Police," *Journal of Criminal Law and Criminology* 10 (November 1919): 351–355; Milton Conover, "State Police," *American Political Science Review* 15 (February 1921): 82–93; C. Burke, "Experiences of the State Police," *American Magazine* 98 (1924): 26–28.

16. Ray, "Metropolitan and State Police," p. 353.

17. Milton Conover, "State Police Developments, 1921–1924," *American Political Science Review* 18 (November 1924): 773–784.

18. Smith, *The State Police*.

19. Ibid, pp. 1–46 passim.

20. Excluding editorials and newspaper articles, an analysis of the author's references (N = 250) on the state police revealed that approximately 80 percent were published prior to 1935; 13 percent between 1935 and 1959; and only 7 percent from 1960 to the present.

21. See August Vollmer and Alfred Parker, *Crime and the State Police* (Berkeley: University of California Press, 1935); E. W. Puttkammer, "The Organization of the State Police," *Journal of Criminal Law and Criminology* 26 (January–February 1936): 727–740; Edward J. Hickey, "Trends in Rural Police Protection," *Annals of the American Academy of Political and Social Science* 291 (January 1954): 22–30; Virgil W. Peterson, "Local and State Law Enforcement Today," *Current History* 53 (1967): 8–14, 49–50.

22. Paul E. Fidler, "The Texas Highway Patrol," *Texas Municipalities* 22 (April 1935): 91–95; Victor A. Rapport, "The Growth and Changing Functions of the Connecticut Department of State Police," *Journal of Criminal Law and Criminology* 30 (September–October 1939): 359–369; Robert M. Graves, "A History of the Utah State Bureau of Criminal Identification and Investigation," *Utah Historical Quarterly* 24 (April, 1956): 171–179.

23. Oscar G. Olander, *Michigan State Police: A Twenty Year History* (Lansing: Michigan Police Journal Press, 1942); Basil L. Sherril, "Twenty-Five Years of Service," *Popular Government* 20 (May 1954): 3–6; E. Wilson Purdy, *Pennsylvania State Police* (Harrisburg: Pennsylvania State Police, 1963); William F. Powers, *The One-Hundred Year Vigil: The Story of the Nation's First Statewide Enforcement Agency* (Boston, MA: Department of Public Safety, 1965); William E. Kirwan, *The New York State Police: History and Development of Collective Negotiations* (New York: New York State Police, 1969); William F. Powers, *In the Service of the State: The Rhode Island State Police, 1925–1975* (Providence: Rhode Island Bicentennial Commission Foundation, 1975).

24. Walter E. Kaloupek, "The History and Administration of the Iowa Highway Safety Patrol," *Iowa Journal of History and Politics* 36 (October 1938): 339–386; Coakley, *Jersey Troopers*.

25. Kaloupek, "History and Administration," p. 339.

26. Coakley, *Jersey Troopers*, pp. 4–26 passim.

27. Conti, *The Pennsylvania State Police*.

28. Eric H. Monkkonen, *Police in Urban America, 1860–1920* (Cambridge: Cambridge University Press, 1981), p. 7.

# Chapter 3

# State Police Development, 1835–1941

The United States saw little in the way of police reform in the direction of state-controlled police in the nineteenth century. The emphasis was on building and expanding the municipal police that had begun to appear in the larger cities around the 1840s. The movement to establish state police is primarily a product of the first three decades of the twentieth century. Although a few states experimented with different forms of state-controlled law enforcement in the nineteenth century, the majority of the state police agencies were created between 1917 and 1935.

The establishment of state police was one of the major police reforms to occur in the historical development of the United States police system. However the state police, like the municipal police, were not a United States invention, but had forerunners in various forms of centralized police systems that previously had been established in other countries. Centralized police systems were established as early as 1544 when France's rural police, the Maréchausseé, were established. By 1750 this force numbered three thousand men, who were uniformed and heavily armed and controlled by the central government.[1] In Italy a state police force called the Carabinieri was established in 1814, and Prussian leaders established the Schutzmannshaft in Berlin, a 1,400-man royal state police.[2] However, it is the state-controlled police, established in Ireland during the late 1700s and in Canada during the middle of the nineteenth century, that demand our attention.

Political leaders in Ireland and Canada desired new methods of control that could effectively maintain stability and the established order. Officials in both countries were anxious about the possibility of disorder arising from conflict between antagonistic groups—whether anticipated revolution from Irish nationalists or a bloody range war between settlers and Indians. The solution in both instances was the creation of highly centralized, paramilitary forces combining the structure and skills of the army with the civil, order-maintaining aspects of the city police. It was these characteristics, along with their reputed success, that led proponents of the first state police forces in the United States to use the Royal Canadian Mounted Police and the Royal Irish Constabulary as models.

## THE ROYAL IRISH CONSTABULARY

Known mostly for its activity against Irish nationalists during the political disturbances of the early 1900s, the Royal Irish Constabulary (R.I.C.) traces its history to 1786, when the first centralized police force was created in Ireland. The impetus for police reform in Ireland, however, did not come from increased public disorders or from increasing crime. Instead, its origins were political and resulted from a surge of Irish nationalism.[3] In 1786, fears of growing political unrest in Ireland prompted Chief Secretary Thomas Orde to propose to Parliament a bill to reform the police of Dublin. After looking at various existing police forces as models, including the highly centralized Paris police, Orde finally presented a plan for a centralized force which

> would consist of one high constable, four constables, forty petty constables, and four hundred night watchmen. The men were to be young, Protestant and in good health; they would be salaried and prohibited from other employment. The force would be recognizable by its uniform and arms, to consist of bayonets and muskets.[4]

Upon introduction in the Parliament, Orde's proposal generated considerable debate and faced hostile opposition from those who saw the measure as a further indication of England's domination of Ireland. Nonetheless, Parliament was effectively controlled by the government, and the bill passed on April 5, 1786.[5]

Having succeeded in centralizing the Dublin police, Orde turned his attention toward the rural sections of the country. Palmer notes that two different plans were suggested. One plan consisted of "120 constables for every medium-sized county, or overall, some 3,500 armed and Castle-controlled constables throughout Ireland." The second plan was to model the rural police after the French Maréchausseé, a national rural police of three thousand men scattered over thirty districts.[6]

Orde favored the French model but was well aware of the uproar that would result from trying to impose anything French on the people of Ireland. In an effort to assure the passage and acceptance of his rural police plan, Orde made a number of modifications designed to deflate possible opposition. Besides being confined to Catholic areas, the new force was "temporary," only to be renewed after three years. The concessions notwithstanding, the new force was highly centralized, with almost complete control of operations placed in the hands of the lord lieutenant and the only remaining local input being maintenance of the forces in their respective areas.[7]

By 1787, Ireland was the center of British experimentation in centralizing and reforming the police. Further efforts to reform the Irish police—to make it more efficient as well as acceptable to the people—fell to later administrators, most notably Sir Robert Peel. Eventually known as the architect of the first modern police of London, Peel developed and tested many of his ideas on policing in Ireland during his tenure as under secretary from 1812 to 1818.

Although the Dublin Police Act of 1786 and the Rural Police Act of 1787 had radically transformed the police in Ireland into a more centralized organization, many features of these forces continued the ideas of the old constabulary and watch systems of the past—characteristics Peel felt contributed to inefficiency and incompetent leadership. The outcome of Peel's search for a better approach to policing Ireland resulted in the creation of the Peace Preservation Force in 1814.[8]

Since the basic fear of the Crown with regard to Ireland was political disturbance, particularly agrarian and patriotic revolution, the Peace Preservation Force appeared to be the most appropriate solution. The force was "a body of trained policemen in mobile units, led by a stipendiary magistrate, and under the authority of the central government."[9] In addition, the lord lieutenant could "proclaim any county or city or portion of any county to be in a 'state of disturbance,' in which case he could appoint a chief magistrate, a chief constable, and fifty sub-constables to such an area or district of disturbance."[10] The emphasis placed on dealing with large-scale political disturbances, as opposed to criminal matters, is also evident in the military-like organization of the Peace Preservation Force. The members of the force, especially constables and subconstables, "were to be drawn from discharged soldiers . . . accustomed to discipline and capable of acting in formation—both absolutely essential in handling banditti groups of superior strength."[11]

Police reform continued in Ireland with the Irish Constables Act of 1822. This act created a constabulary for each county to be under the jurisdiction of the county magistrate. Local control was limited. Four provincial inspectors "were appointed by and answerable to the central government, as were the chief constables who commanded the separate detachments. . . . the Castle was given the right to discharge any member of the constabulary."[12] As with previous Irish police reforms, more control was located with the central government, while local officials gradually lost influence over police activity. This process of centralization culminated in the creation of the Irish Constabulary in 1836, which became the Royal Irish Constabulary (R.I.C.) in 1867.

The Irish Constabulary contained many of the ideas and proposals of previous administrators such as Orde and Peel. While the county organization of the 1822 Constables Act continued, control of local magistrates was eliminated altogether and the power to appoint all members of the force was given to the central government, with the entire constabulary system placed under the authority of one official—the inspector general.[13] In addition, the military character of previous forces was further developed as "most of the senior officers were men of military experience," while the men lived in barracks and were "armed with carbines and . . . instructed in military drill."[14] Thus, with a total of over seven thousand officers and men in 1836, the Irish Constabulary more closely resembled an army than a civilian police force. This paramilitary nature of police reform in Ireland can be found in ever increasing degrees, beginning with the early acts of 1786 and 1787, and becoming more apparent in the later forces, particularly the Peace Preservation Force of 1814 and the Constabulary Act of 1836.[15]

Over a period of fifty years, Irish police reforms gradually worked their way through various plans to centralize and make the forces more efficient. Ireland thus served, as W. L. Burns has stated, as "a social laboratory" where "Englishmen were willing to experiment . . . on lines which they were not prepared to contemplate or tolerate at home."[16] In these early police experiments in Ireland, we find some of the first attempts at developing agencies of social control that were not restricted by local influences or jurisdictions, but instead were controlled by a central government administration and were able to operate anywhere in the country. The relationship between changing social conditions and the desire for new forms of social control can also be found in Canada with the formation of the Northwest Mounted Police.

## THE ROYAL CANADIAN MOUNTED POLICE

Commentators have consistently credited the London police created by Robert Peel in 1825 with being the model the British used in creating law enforcement agencies in other regions of their empire. In reality, the

R.I.C. played a more important, if overlooked, role in the historical development of the police. Palmer notes that British development of colonial police forces "took one of two paths, either the outright adoption of the Irish model or a resort to it after the civilian British model failed."[17] Such was the situation in the Canadian west as the government sought to reduce potential conflict among Indians and settlers by creating the Northwest Mounted Police (NWMP), a force modeled directly on the R.I.C.[18]

Although the "Mounties" have long been idealized through romantic tales, alternative descriptions have dispelled many of the popular beliefs about them."[19] The primary myth maintains that the NWMP was created by a "benevolent government" to protect the Indians from whiskey traders and provide "a system of law impartially enforced and guaranteeing equal rights for all."[20]

Despite this popularly held belief, the actual reason for the development of the NWMP is to be found in the changing economic and social conditions in Canada's western provinces. Ideas for a mounted police were discussed within the government in 1869 as part of the plans for taking control of the lands chartered to the Hudson's Bay Company. Prime Minister Sir John MacDonald "was anxious that Canadian expansion into the Northwest should not be accompanied by violent conflict between the Indian population and settlers," a situation which, it was feared, would "retard development of the Northwest."[21] To ensure that this development was successful, bankers, politicians, and other interested parties believed it was necessary to wrest control of the Northwest from the Indians. Thus, the idea was to have the NWMP serve as an "advance guard" to control the conflict between the settlers and Indians.[22] Established as a semimilitary force, the NWMP was "designed to keep order on the prairies and to facilitate the transfer of most of the territory of the region from the Indian tribes to the federal government with a minimum of expense and bloodshed."[23]

To maximize the chances of success in this effort, Prime Minister MacDonald devised a plan that would combine military and civil qualities. The structure of the Royal Irish Constabulary seemed to be the ideal model on which to base the proposed mounted police force. The military nature of the Irish constabulary appealed to the prime minister and in 1870 he wrote to London requesting information on the Irish police.[24] As stated by MacDonald:

It was the intention of the government . . . to ask the house for a moderate grant of money to organize a mounted police force, somewhat similar to the Irish mounted constabulary. They would have the advantage of military discipline, would be a civil force, each member of which would be a police constable, and therefore a preventive officer.[25]

The NWMP was officially established by an act of Parliament in the spring of 1873. The semimilitary force was directly controlled from Ottawa with no control given to the local government officials in the Northwest territories. The passage of the act was unopposed in Parliament and received minimal attention in the press.[26]

Although the NWMP, between 1873 and 1885, was less brutal than the United States Army in dealing with similar circumstances, it was still "a crucial part of the conscious scheme by which powerful economic and political interests destroyed the . . . way of life of entire peoples and wrested vast territory from its inhabitants for a pittance."[27] Besides asserting government control over the Indians, the NWMP gradually took on the function of protecting corporate interests as these moved into the frontier. Most notable was the close relationship that developed between the NWMP and the Canadian Pacific Railway. Of all corporate interests in the Northwest, "the railway . . . supposedly represented advancing civilization" and "in any dispute between the Canadian Pacific Railway and the Indians or . . . its own employees, the police automatically sided with the corporation and often made no attempt to hide the fact."[28]

As settlement of the Northwest areas continued into the 1890s and early 1900s, the NWMP also grew in size and importance. When in 1905 Saskatchewan and Alberta become provinces and retained the mounted police instead of establishing police forces of their own, it appeared that the NWMP was to be a permanent feature of the Canadian Northwest. In 1904 the name was changed to the Royal Northwest Mounted Police (RNWMP) in recognition of its service to that area of the country.[29]

During the early part of World War I, the RNWMP worked with other police forces in Canada to preserve order, investigate "enemy aliens" in the western provinces, patrol the border with the United States, and enforce special wartime regulations. Also, during the war the commissioner of the RNWMP instituted a "network of plainclothes detectives and undercover men" to form a security and intelligence branch that eventually became "notorious in later years as Canada's secret police."[30]

By 1917, with westward settlement all but complete and the new provinces establishing police forces of their own, the number of men on active duty with the RNWMP began to decline. In fact, government authorities proposed to disband the force at the end of the war. However, postwar events presented a situation in which the government found the RNWMP an indispensable agency for maintaining order. As did the United States, Canada suffered from postwar disturbances such as labor disputes, strikes, and other "red scare" activities that generated anxiety among businessmen and government leaders. Because of the military structure of the RNWMP, its loyalty to the government, and a tradition of antilabor activity, the force proved to be more effective in dealing with civilian strikes and disturbances than did the army, which was often sympathetic to the civilian cause.[31] Toward the end of 1919 "the government had already built the force up to a strength of 1,600 men, and in November the act was passed to absorb the Dominion police into the RNWMP and change the name to the Royal Canadian Mounted Police."[32]

Modeled after the Irish constabulary, the mounted police of Canada were created to facilitate westward expansion and minimize conflict between settlers and Indians. Serious conflict could have delayed western development for years, thus destroying the plans of government officials and their corporate allies, especially the railroad.[33] The answer was thought to be a federal force of "soldier-policemen, trained for warfare on the plains but with wide judicial powers and responsibilities, giving the federal government a firm grasp over the maintenance of order."[34]

First in Ireland, and later in Canada, dominant political and economic interests created new forms of social control designed not only to protect their material interests, but also to ensure their continued control of the social order. The subversion of local control over the police, along with the centralizing of police control in the hands of the government, was a response to major changes taking place in the political economy of each country. The emergence of the state police in the United States follows a similar pattern as business and political leaders strove to reform police agencies to deal with new problems of order maintenance—problems stimulated by the social and economic changes affecting the United States as the country moved into the twentieth century.

The following sections describe the state-controlled law enforcement agencies established by various states. The first section presents a discussion of the experimental phase of state police development which took place during the nineteenth century. The remaining sections focus on the twentieth century, the primary period of state police activity in the United States. Table 3.1 contains a list of the states indicating the type of law enforcement agency created and the year in which they were established.

## THE FIRST STATE POLICE FORCES, 1835–1900

Texas has the distinction of being the first state to establish a statewide law enforcement agency, the Texas Rangers. Romantic tales, told in story,

**Table 3.1**
**State Police Departments: Agency Type and Date Established**

| State | Type of Agency | Date | Session Law |
|-------|----------------|------|-------------|
| Alabama | Special Force | 1919 | no. 551 |
| | Special Force | 1920 | no. 12 |
| | State Highway Patrol* | 1935 | no. 331 |
| Alaska | Highway Patrol* | 1941 | chap. 65 |
| | Territorial Police | 1953 | chap. 144 |
| Arizona | Rangers | 1901 | chap. 2, no. 46 |
| | Rangers | 1903 | no. 64 |
| | Highway Patrol* | 1931 | chap. 104 |
| Arkansas | State Road Patrol* | 1929 | no. 299 |
| | State Police | 1935 | no. 120 |
| California | Highway Patrol* | 1929 | chap. 308 |
| Colorado | Department of Safety | 1917 | chap. 12 |
| | Highway Courtesy Patrol | 1935 | chap. 125 |
| Connecticut | State Police | 1903 | chap. 141 |
| Delaware | County Detectives | 1891 | chap. 47 |
| | State Detectives | 1898 | chap. 64 |
| | Traffic Officers | 1921 | chaps. 195, 196 |
| Florida | Dept. of Public Safety* | 1939 | chap. 19551, no. 556 |
| Georgia | Home Guard | 1917 | no. 224 |
| | Dept. of Public Safety* | 1937 | no. 220 |
| Hawaii | No state police; each island has its own police force. | | |
| Idaho | State Constabulary | 1919 | chap. 103 |
| | State Police | 1939 | chap. 60 |
| Illinois | Highway Patrol Officers* | 1921 | — |
| | Highway Maintenance Police | 1923 | — |
| Indiana | Deputies* | 1921 | chap. 265 |
| | State Police | 1933 | chap. 71 |
| Iowa | Special Agents | 1915 | chap. 203 |
| | Highway Safety Patrol | 1935 | chap. 48 |
| Kansas | Inspectors* | 1933 | chap. 109 |
| | Highway Patrol | 1937 | chap. 330 |
| Kentucky | Highway Patrol* | 1932 | chap. 106, sec. 18 |
| | State Police | 1948 | chap. 80 |
| Louisiana | Highway Police* | 1928 | no. 296 |
| | Highway Patrol | 1932 | no. 21, sec. 11 |
| | State Police | 1936 | no. 94 |
| Maine | Special Constables | 1917 | chap. 284 |
| | State Highway Police* | 1921 | chap. 211 |
| Maryland | Motorcycle Deputies* | 1916 | chap. 687 |
| | State Police | 1935 | chap. 303 |
| Massachusetts | State Police | 1865 | chap. 249 |
| | State Detective Force | 1875 | chap. 15 |
| | District Police | 1879 | chap. 305 |
| | Dept. of Public Safety | 1919 | chap. 350 |
| Michigan | State Troops | 1917 | no. 53 |
| | State Police | 1919 | no. 26 |
| Minnesota | Highway Patrol* | 1929 | chap. 355 |

**Table 3.1**
(continued)

| State | Type of Agency | Date | Session Law |
|-------|----------------|------|-------------|
| Mississippi | Highway Patrol* | 1938 | chap. 143 |
| Missouri | Highway Patrol | 1931 | pp. 230–231 |
| Montana | Highway Patrol* | 1935 | chap. 185 |
| Nebraska | Special Assistants | 1919 | chap. 173 |
| | Law Enforcement Dept. | 1927 | chap. 157 |
| | Highway Safety Patrol* | 1937 | chap. 141 |
| Nevada | State Police | 1908 | chap. 4 |
| New Hampshire | State Police | 1937 | chap. 34 |
| New Jersey | State Police | 1921 | chap. 102 |
| New Mexico | Mounted Police | 1905 | chap. 9 |
| | Motor Patrol | 1933 | chap. 79 |
| | State Police | 1935 | chap. 119 |
| New York | State Police | 1917 | chap. 161 |
| North Carolina | Highway Patrol* | 1929 | chap. 218 |
| North Dakota | Highway Patrol* | 1935 | chap. 148 |
| Ohio | Highway Patrol* | 1933 | pp. 93–96 |
| Oklahoma | Highway Patrol | 1937 | chap. 50 |
| Oregon | Field Deputies* | 1921 | chap. 371, sec. 53 |
| | State Police | 1931 | chap. 139 |
| Pennsylvania | State Police | 1905 | no. 227 |
| Rhode Island | Constabulary | 1917 | chap. 1469 |
| | State Police | 1925 | chap. 588 |
| South Carolina | State Police | 1868 | no. 11 |
| | Highway Patrol* | 1930 | no. 603 |
| South Dakota | State Constabulary | 1917 | chap. 355 |
| | Dept. of Justice | 1935 | chap. 97 |
| Tennessee | State Constabulary | 1915 | no. 74 |
| | State Police | 1919 | chap. 96 |
| | Highway Patrol* | 1929 | chap. 25 |
| Texas | Texas Rangers | 1835 | Laws, p. 20 |
| | State Police | 1870 | chap. 13 |
| | Ranger Force | 1901 | chap. 34 |
| | Highway Patrol* | 1929 | chap. 42 |
| | Dept. of Public Safety | 1935 | chap. 181 |
| Utah | Patrols* | 1923 | chap. 65 |
| | Highway Patrol* | 1941 | chap. 14 |
| Vermont | Enforcement Officers* | 1925 | no. 70 |
| Virginia | Motor Vehicle Inspectors* | 1924 | chap. 99 |
| | Patrol Officers | 1932 | chap. 342 |
| Washington | Highway Patrol | 1921 | chap. 108 |
| West Virginia | Dept. of Public Safety | 1919 | chap. 12 |
| Wisconsin | Traffic Inspectors* | 1939 | chap. 10 |
| Wyoming | Dept. of Law Enforcement | 1921 | chap. 18 |
| | Highway Patrol | 1935 | chap. 51 |

* Indicates those agencies restricted to the enforcement of traffic and motor vehicle laws.

song, and motion pictures, have made the "Texas Ranger" synonymous with law and order.[35] Although they operated as a police force, they were not created as such. The rangers were formed as a paramilitary unit which was intended as a "frontier pacification force" to secure the expanding frontiers of the republic and eventually the borders of the state of Texas.[36]

The first appearance of the term "rangers" occurs in 1823 when continued Indian problems prompted Stephen F. Austin to call a meeting of district representatives to discuss the problem of defense. It was decided to keep a permanent force of rangers in service at all times. Little is known about this force and it is not certain if they were ever placed on active duty.[37] Most writers date the Texas Rangers from 1835 at the outbreak of the Texas revolution. On November 24, 1835, the revolutionary government of Texas passed an ordinance which created three companies of "rangers," each company consisting of fifty-six men. Distinct from both the army and the militia, the rangers were an irregular mounted force, furnishing their own horses and arms, and devoid of the usual trappings of the regular army.[38] The Republic of Texas was established in 1836 and over the next ten years various laws were passed for protecting the frontier. Although these forces were not specifically called "rangers," but rather "mounted riflemen," "mounted gunmen," or "mounted volunteers," they are all accepted as part of the tradition that has come to be known as the Texas Rangers.[39]

When Texas became a state in 1845, the United States government took over the job of protecting the frontier, and the rangers eventually became insignificant as a force for fighting Indians. During the next fifteen years ranger service was sporadic, with periods of activity usually only from three to six months at a time. During the Civil War there was virtually no ranger force as almost everyone capable of military service was thrown into the war effort. From 1865 to 1874 there were no Texas Rangers at all since the federal government did not allow any of the southern states to maintain organized armed forces.[40]

The Texas Rangers were reestablished in 1874 by a newly elected Democratic governor and the state legislature. Two distinct forces were created: a "frontier battalion" comprising six companies of seventy-five men each for controlling the Indians on the western frontier, and a "special force" of rangers sent to the southwest sections in order to suppress bandit activity along the Mexican border.[41] By 1880 the threat of Indian attack had been removed and the frontier virtually closed. With the main reason for their existence eliminated, the rangers turned inward, becoming a quasi-state police, pursuing outlaws and acting as "trouble-shooters . . . handling situations beyond the control of local peace officers."[42] For the next twenty years, the rangers, and especially the frontier battalion, became an institutional anachronism. And with their turn to interior activities, they became subject to criticism, opposition, and legal attack. Finally, in 1900, a ruling by the Texas attorney general effectively destroyed the rangers by declaring that all noncommissioned officers and privates had no legal authority to execute criminal process or make arrests.[43]

A temporary force was permitted to operate on a limited basis until 1901 when the law of 1874 was amended and a new ranger force created. The new force consisted of four companies of not more than twenty men each. The purpose was to protect the frontier against marauding thieves and to suppress lawlessness and crime throughout the state. In 1919 the ranger force was reorganized and reduced in size. Finally, in 1935, the rangers were merged with the highway patrol to form a new department of public safety.[44]

Although most commentators on the subject attribute the first state police force to Pennsylvania in 1905, Texas is entitled to that distinction because of its creating a statewide police force in 1870. Following the Civil War, Texas was in a state of political turmoil. Several studies conducted during 1868 and 1869 documented the problems of rising crime and homicide rates, and the inability of local law officers to cope with them. These findings provided justification for intervention by the government and a state constabulary was recommended as a solution to the problem.[45]

In 1869, strict military control of the Reconstruction period gave way to "radical rule" with the election of a Republican governor, E. J. Davis.[46] Davis was convinced that Texas needed a strong militia and a state police and upon taking office recommended the creation of two forces: a state guard and militia to deal with "extreme emergencies," and a state police to deal with individual criminals and general disorder in those counties where local officials were unable or unwilling to enforce the law. Both acts were opposed on constitutional grounds by conservatives who believed law enforcement should remain in the hands of local officials. In addition, it was feared that these forces would place an inordinate amount of power in the governor's office. Both bills survived heated debate and finally passed.[47]

The newly created state police numbered 258 officers and men. The chief was appointed by the governor with the advice and consent of the Senate. The specific duties were to enforce all state laws and to repress and prevent crime of any kind throughout the state. In addition, the governor was given the authority to bring the men together to act as a combined unit anywhere in the state. The law was amended in 1871 to increase the size of the force by adding more officers and sergeants, as well as to permit the force to act independently of local law officers.[48]

However, the most interesting feature of the state police was the racial composition of the force. It was approximately 60 percent white and 40 percent black. This was enough to give the force a "Negro militia" connotation which generated much hostility among the conservative elements in the state.[49]

The state police received both praise and condemnation. According to Walter Webb in his history of the Texas Rangers, the force was nothing but a mechanism which allowed the carpetbag government to build up its political machine, while its history is a story of "official murder and legalized oppression."[50] Baenziger argues differently, indicating that evidence suggests most of the opposition to the state police was due to its racial composition and association with Republican rule. The state police became the focus of political backlash, resulting in "hostility towards the force . . . an expression of conservative resentment of Negro and radical domination."[51] Democrats regained control of the legislature in 1873 and quickly eliminated the state police. Introduced only days after the legislature convened, a bill for repeal passed both houses without opposition. But Governor Davis questioned the wisdom of disbanding the force at a time when lawlessness was still prevalent in sections of the state and vetoed the bill. Nonetheless, on April 22, 1873, the repeal act was passed over the veto by a 58 to 7 margin.[52]

Texas was not the only state experimenting with statewide law enforcement agencies during the nineteenth century. In 1865, Massachusetts began a series of state police developments that continued into the 1900s. The Massachusetts legislature passed a law in 1865 that created a "state police" force of approximately twenty men.[53] In reality, the act authorized the governor to appoint a chief constable who would be in charge of a force made up of all the state constables and their deputies. The force was charged with preserving the peace and preventing crime through the suppression of liquor shops, gambling houses, and brothels, and was given police powers anywhere in the state.

During the ensuing years, the Massachusetts legislature made numerous modifications in the state police. A law passed in 1871 replaced the chief constable with three police commissioners appointed by the governor and increased the size of the force from twenty to seventy men, although no changes were made in the duties or powers of the force. However, this law was abolished in 1874 and the chief constable was reinstated. In 1875 Massachusetts enacted a law that repealed all previous laws pertaining to state police and established a "state detective force." The force was limited to thirty men and led by a chief detective appointed by the governor. The detective force was specifically charged with aiding the attorney general of Massachusetts and all the district attorneys and magistrates in procuring evidence on criminal activities and in suppressing riots. The state detectives were abolished in 1879 and replaced by the "district police," who were appointed by the governor. This force was limited to two men per district and was headed by a chief who was selected by the governor. However, no changes were made in the powers or duties, which remained similar to the previous state detective force.[54]

In 1891, Delaware created a county detective force consisting of two men appointed by the governor who were under the direction of the attorney general. Although specifically established for the county of New Castle, the detectives were authorized to make arrests and act without restriction anywhere in the state, upon all requests made by the governor. A law passed in 1898 changed the name to "state detectives" and removed the county requirement of the earlier law, but the powers, duties, and size of the agency remained the same.[55]

The only other state to experiment with a state-controlled law enforcement agency during the nineteenth century was South Carolina. In 1868 an act establishing a "state police" was passed which authorized the governor to appoint an officer designated as the "chief constable" of the state. The chief constable was to appoint, in each county, a chief deputy constable and as many deputy constables as requested by the governor. The primary duties of this organization were to enforce all state laws, repress disorder, prevent crime, and execute orders of the governor with regard to preserving the public peace. The office of chief constable was made provisional in 1878, to be activated only when the governor determined that a public emergency warranted extra control. This act also restricted the number of deputy constables that could be appointed to a maximum of two in each county. Beginning in 1892, and continuing into the early 1900s, the constabulary was placed under the control of the Dispensary Commission and was restricted to regulating the manufacture and sale of liquor within the state. In 1935, the constabulary was placed under the absolute control of the governor and given the authority to enforce all state laws.[56]

## THE FIRST MODERN STATE POLICE FORCES, 1900–1909

In 1901 Arizona organized a ranger force similar to the Texas Rangers. Intended to protect the frontier and patrol the border with Mexico, the force was known as the Arizona Rangers and consisted of one captain, one sergeant, and twelve privates. The bill authorized the governor to select the members of the force from the best cattlemen and law officers on the border and specified that "skill in roping, shooting, riding, trailing, and general knowledge of the country" should determine the applicants' fitness for service.[57] The ranger law was revised in 1903, increasing the force to one captain, one lieutenant, four sergeants, and not more than twenty privates. But due to political differences and negative public opinion, the ranger law was repealed in 1909 over the governor's veto.[58] Arizona did not have another state law enforcement agency until 1931 when a highway patrol was established.

Development of the small, specialized forces originating in Delaware and Massachusetts was continued by Connecticut in 1903 when the legislature created a "state police department." The force numbered no more than ten men who were under the direction of a supervisor appointed by a board of five commissioners. While the Delaware and Massachusetts forces were responsible for liquor and vice laws, the Connecticut police were to investigate and detect all criminal matters and assist any sheriff or chief of police in preventing crime and preserving order. For this purpose the force was granted powers equal to those of sheriffs, police officers, and constables anywhere in the state.[59]

With the exception of the short-lived Texas state police of 1870, the first major development in the creation of state police came in 1905 when Pennsylvania established its constabulary force. Modeled after the Royal Irish Constabulary, the Pennsylvania state police were a paramilitary type of enforcement agency, mounted on horses and heavily armed.[60] A number of "new" features were incorporated into the Pennsylvania force. The size (numbering 228 men) was quite large in comparison to earlier forces. The troops were selected by a superintendent who, although appointed by the governor, was completely autonomous in running the department. The men were housed in barracks and were to constantly patrol the rural sections of the state. They were given total police power to serve all warrants, arrest without warrant all witnessed law violators, and preserve law and order throughout the state.[61] This type of state police, however, did not have an immediate impact, as over the next ten years only two other states created law enforcement agencies—New Mexico and Nevada.

In 1905 the governor of New Mexico, responding to pressure from stockmen and the railroad, recommended to the Territorial Assembly the creation of a force to "patrol the ranges, to prevent the theft of stock and aid in the apprehension of criminals."[62] Shortly thereafter, Senator W. A. Greer, a wealthy cattleman, introduced a bill to organize a company of mounted police. The measure establishing the "New Mexico Mounted Police" passed the assembly and was signed by the governor on February 15, 1905.[63] The force was small, numbering only eleven men, who were under direct control of the governor. Given authority to make arrests anywhere in the state, the mounted police were expected to follow and capture lawbreakers and marauding Indians and carry out any measure necessary to secure the frontier.[64]

The New Mexico mounted police performed a wide range of duties. They informed the governor of local conditions and attitudes, enforced federal liquor laws pertaining to Indians, coordinated the law enforcement activities of other state agencies, and performed investigations involving state officials and other prominent citizens.[65] The force withstood the transition to statehood in 1912 but became inactive in 1915 when the legislature failed to provide appropriations for its operation. However, the mounted police were revived by the special wartime session of the legislature in 1917, which passed a bill authorizing appropriate operating funds. Although the force was increased in size to twenty-two men during 1919, the 1921 legislature, reacting to changing social conditions and political pressures, abolished the force by repealing all acts relating to the mounted police.[66]

Nevada created a state police force in 1908 ostensibly to protect the mining regions of the state. Small in size, consisting of thirty regular officers and 250 reserves, the Nevada force was organized in a similar fashion to the Pennsylvania state police. Under the direction of a superintendent appointed by the governor, the Nevada state police were charged with the arrest of all persons violating any state law and with the suppression of all riots or disturbances of any kind. In order to carry out these duties, the force was given the power to arrest without warrant and detain all suspected persons.[67]

## STATE POLICE RESURGENCE, 1915–1921

Beginning in 1915, the movement to establish state police forces gained momentum. From 1915 to 1921, twenty-three states organized some type of statewide law enforcement agency. Initial activity took the form of small, specialized forces, usually attached to the adjutant general or governor's office. In 1915, Tennessee and Iowa established such forces. The "special force" model was continued by Alabama and Nebraska in 1919 and by Wyoming in 1921. Although these forces were directed to enforce all state laws and maintain public order, their small size precluded patrolling the rural areas and limited their activities to investigations and other specific assignments.[68]

Entrance of the United States into World War I prompted a number of states to create police forces in order to make up for the loss of their National Guard troops. Colorado, Georgia, Maine, Michigan, New York, and Rhode Island formed "war emergency" enforcement units. Most of these forces were large, mounted on horses, and stationed throughout the state to patrol the countryside and small towns. Given complete police powers anywhere in the state, they could arrest with or without warrant anyone violating state or federal law. The Michigan and Georgia forces were essentially duplicates of the National Guard, being established according to the authority and guidelines of the state's military laws. Intended as war measures, a number of these forces, for example, Colorado, Georgia, and Rhode Island, were legislatively required to be disbanded after the war. However, Michigan and Colorado made their forces permanent.[69]

The New York state police represented the first continuation of the modern state police begun with the Pennsylvania constabulary in 1905. Efforts to set up a constabulary in New York began before 1915 when a number of influential citizens, impressed with the effectiveness of the Pennsylvania state police and alarmed by the lack of rural police protection, sought to establish a state police in New York. While their initial efforts failed on account of political opposition, the entrance of the United States into the war provided the spark its proponents needed to press for passage of the state police law in 1917.[70]

Modeled after the Pennsylvania system, the New York state police force was large, consisting of 232 men and officers, under the direction of a superintendent who was appointed by the governor. Intended to detect and prevent crime in the rural districts, the state police were given the power to arrest without warrant anyone violating the law or peace in their presence as well as the authority to execute all search and arrest warrants. The only restriction placed on the force was that they could not be used to suppress riots in cities without approval of the governor.[71]

Following the war, the constabulary type of state police became the ideal, as five states—Michigan, Massachusetts, Tennessee, New Jersey, and West Virginia—established this type of state law enforcement agency. Following the models of Pennsylvania and New York, these forces were large (usually numbering over one hundred men), military in structure, and mounted on horses or equipped with motorcycles. Given the power to arrest without warrant anyone violating any state or federal law throughout the state, they were to patrol the rural areas, maintain order, and generally perform any law enforcement duty requested by the governor. However, because of pressures from organized labor, restrictions were placed on these forces with regard to policing labor disputes and acting as a unit in cities and towns.[72]

Owing to the growing presence of the automobile, a number of states began to develop enforcement agencies designed to deal with traffic problems. The first such force was created by Maryland in 1916 when the commissioner of motor vehicles was authorized to appoint "motorcycle deputies" to enforce the provisions of the motor vehicle act throughout the entire state. In 1921, six other states—Delaware, Illinois, Indiana, Maine, Oregon, and Washington—created forces to enforce the traffic laws. These "highway patrols" were generally small, unarmed, and restricted to arresting only those who violated laws pertaining to the operation of motor vehicles on state roads and highways.[73]

Finally, two somewhat unique state law enforcement agencies were introduced during this period. In 1917, South Dakota established the office of "state sheriff." Appointed by the governor, the state sheriff was in command of the state constabulary, which consisted of all sheriffs, deputy sheriffs, and three additional members appointed by the state sheriff. Individual members were given authority to operate anywhere in the state but were expected to confine law enforcement to their respective counties. However, on orders of the state sheriff, the members of the constabulary could be mobilized to act as a unit in any part of the state.[74]

In 1919 Idaho created a Department of Law Enforcement to execute state regulatory, motor vehicle, and penal laws. Adjunct to this department was the "state constabulary" created the same year. This force was directed by the commissioner of the Department of Law Enforcement and consisted of all of the department's officers and all state and local peace officers. Given jurisdiction anywhere in the state, the constabulary was to enforce the criminal laws of the state, assist in detecting and investigating all criminal matters, and maintain all state laws relating to temperance and morality. In 1921 control of the constabulary was taken out of the Department of Law Enforcement and given to a chief who was appointed by the governor. The force was also restructured, made up of the chief, two regular deputies, and as many special deputies as deemed necessary. Powers and duties, however, did not differ from those outlined in the 1919 legislation. The constabulary was abolished in 1923 and the Department of Law Enforcement was reinstituted as the primary state law enforcement body.[75]

## PERIOD OF ADJUSTMENT, 1923–1928

After 1921, further development of state police agencies declined, with only seven states creating law enforcement agencies during the period from 1923 to 1928.[76] Four of the states—Louisiana, Utah, Vermont, and Virginia—were creating police forces for the first time, while Illinois, Nebraska, and Rhode Island were making second attempts.

Continuing the trend begun in 1921, most of the forces established during this period were "highway patrols" which were restricted to enforcing only motor vehicle laws. The forces created in Illinois and Utah in 1923, Virginia in 1924, Vermont in 1925, and Louisiana in 1928 were this type of agency. The Illinois force, called the "highway maintenance police," was an expansion of the small group of highway patrol officers which had been assigned to the Department of Public Works and Buildings in 1921. The significant change was an increase in size to 100 men and the power to arrest violators of all state laws, although primary responsibility remained regulation of traffic.[77]

In 1925, Rhode Island created a small police force. Although numbering only twenty-four men, they were given full police powers to enforce all criminal laws and to investigate any criminal matter throughout the state. Unless ordered by the governor, however, they could not perform riot duty in any city of the state. This was Rhode Island's second effort at state policing, after it had created a constabulary in 1917 as a war preparedness measure. That force had been disbanded in early 1918.[78]

The only other state to establish a state-controlled police force during this period was Nebraska, in 1927. The act authorized the governor to appoint as many "law enforcement officers" as deemed necessary to enforce the state's criminal laws. The chief of the enforcement officers was designated the "state sheriff," while his assistants were called "deputy state sheriffs." This group of law officers was essentially an expansion of the "special assistants" appointed by the governor in 1919.[79]

## DEPRESSION ERA EXPANSION—THE HIGHWAY PATROL, 1929–1941

Fifteen states organized state law enforcement agencies for the first time during this period: Arkansas, California, Minnesota, and North Carolina in 1929, Missouri in 1931, Kentucky in 1932, Kansas and Ohio in 1933, Montana and North Dakota in 1935, Oklahoma and New Hampshire in 1937, Mississippi in 1938, and Florida and Wisconsin in 1939. Except for Missouri, Oklahoma, and New Hampshire, which had total police powers, all of the others were highway patrols, usually small in number and restricted to arresting those who had violated the provisions of the respective state motor vehicle laws.[80]

Nineteen other states made second or third attempts at establishing state law enforcement agencies during this period. The general trend of these reforms was to create larger forces with more extensive police powers. Seven of these states—Oregon in 1931, Indiana in 1933, Alabama, Iowa, Maryland, and Wyoming in 1935, and Utah in 1941—formed highway patrols or state police forces to replace small, specialized agencies. Virginia in 1932 and Kansas in 1937 simply increased the size of their highway patrols and removed the restrictions so that the forces were now allowed to arrest violators of all state laws. On the other hand, Tennessee in 1929, South Carolina in 1930, and South Dakota in 1935 created highway patrol departments to augment existing agencies. Also, Louisiana removed the restrictions on its highway patrol in 1932, created a separate state police in 1936, and finally merged both in 1942 to form the Department of Public Safety. Similarly, Nebraska established a highway patrol in 1937 to complement the state sheriff system and then in 1941 merged both into a single law enforcement department.[81]

Finally, five states established new forces after having abolished previously created state police agencies. Georgia created a state police force in 1937 after having formed a home guard in 1917 which was designed to protect the state for the duration of the war. Idaho formed a state police in 1939 after having abolished a state constabulary in 1923. After having abolished state police forces under pressure from politicians and hostile public opinion, Arizona in 1931, New Mexico in 1933, and Colorado in 1935, established highway patrols. In all three states, the new agencies were smaller in size and more limited in terms of police power than their earlier counterparts—a reaction to lingering opinion concerning the experiences of the past. Colorado went the furthest in its efforts to discourage negative public opinion by calling its force a "courtesy patrol."[82]

## SUMMARY

Development of the state police can be divided into four distinct periods of activity. The first period begins in the 1830s and extends up to 1900. Only four states (Texas, Massachusetts, Delaware, and South Carolina) created state-controlled law enforcement agencies during this period. These forces were small, usually attached to the adjutant general or governor's office, and intended for specific purposes, such as frontier and border patrol or the enforcement of liquor and vice laws. Although Texas formed a constabulary force in 1870, it was short-lived and did not stimulate much public interest in the idea of state police. Popular beliefs about policing were similar to those of the British, as most people in the United States at this time were suspicious of state-controlled agencies, preferring instead local control of law enforcement.

The second period covers the first decade of the twentieth century. Only a few states created state police forces during this time, and most were similar in structure and purpose to the specialized forces established earlier. Most significant is the constabulary form of state police that made its appearance with the creation of the Pennsylvania state police in 1905. Modeled after the Royal Irish Constabulary and the Royal Canadian Mounted Police, the Pennsylvania police were mounted on horses, heavily armed, on constant patrol in the rural areas, and under the direction of an autonomous superintendent. Combined with its military organization, these features made the Pennsylvania state police a model of the ultimate form of police. Nevertheless, during the next ten years only two other states created constabulary forces, and these were on a smaller scale than that of the Pennsylvania force. The constabulary form of state police was considered a challenge and a threat to those who maintained a belief in the local control of policing. Many states, therefore, took a "wait and see" attitude, content to let Pennsylvania experiment with this new form of law enforcement.

The third period begins during the years 1915 to 1919 and continues throughout the twenties. Stimulated by the perceived success of the Pennsylvania state police, the war, and growing social unrest, many states began to embrace the concept of state-controlled police forces. Beginning in 1915 and continuing through 1923, twenty-seven states created some type of state police force. The model that many states looked to was the Pennsylvania constabulary system. Yet, after ten years of operation, certain negative aspects of this type of state police had appeared, particularly with regard to their use in policing labor disputes and strikes. For these reasons, many states placed restrictions on their forces to eliminate these problems. Also, the emergence and growing popularity of the automobile created a need for motor vehicle regulation. In response, some states began to create highway patrols during this period. Reaching a peak in 1921, state police development dropped off dramatically as only a few states created new forces during the remainder of the 1920s.

Beginning in 1929, the final stage of state police development covers the entire period of the Great Depression. The creation of new forces and the modification of older ones began to escalate, reaching a peak in 1935 when eleven states organized police forces. The basic feature of this period was the emphasis on highway patrols rather than the military-like state constabularies characteristic of the early twenties. Over 80 percent of the forces created during this period were of the highway patrol type, and these generally were restricted to enforcing only traffic laws. By the end of 1941, every state had established some type of state police or highway patrol.[83]

The process of state police development in the United States began with a long period of slow and gradual emergence via individual experimentation by a few states, continued with a period of quickened activity which focused on the constabulary model of policing, and ended with a period of redirection during the thirties, with the focus on traffic control.

## NOTES

1. Stanley H. Palmer, *Police and Protest in England and Ireland, 1780–1850* (Cambridge: Cambridge University Press, 1988), pp. 11–12.

2. Ibid., p. 15.

3. Stanley H. Palmer, "The Irish Police Experiment: The Beginnings of Modern Police in the British Isles 1785–1795," *Social Science Quartely* 56 (December 1975): 413.

4. Ibid., p. 415.

5. Ibid., pp. 416–418.

6. Ibid., p. 419.

7. Ibid.

8. Galen Broeker, *Rural Disorder and Police Reform in Ireland, 1812–36* (London: Routledge and Kegan Paul, 1970), p. 230.

9. Ibid., p. 232.

10. Seamus Breathnach, *The Irish Police: From Earliest Times to Present Day* (Dublin: Anvil Books, 1974).

11. Broeker, *Rural Disorder*, p. 70.

12. Ibid., p. 234.

13. Ibid., p. 238.

14. Ibid., p. 225.

15. Ibid., p. 223.

16. Quoted in Palmer, "The Irish Police Experiment," p. 411.

17. Palmer, *Police and Protest*, p. 543.

18. Ibid., p. 544.

19. S. W. Horrall, "Sir John MacDonald and the Mounted Police Force for the Northwest Territories," *Canadian Historical Review* 53 (June 1972): 179–200; Lorne Brown and Caroline Brown, *An Unauthorized History of the Royal Canadian Mounted Police* (Toronto: James Lewis & Samuel, 1973).

20. Brown and Brown, *An Unauthorized History*, p. 7.

21. Horrall, "Sir John MacDonald," pp. 180–181.

22. Ibid., p. 181.

23. Brown and Brown, *An Unauthorized History*, p. 10.

24. Horrall, "Sir John MacDonald," p. 182.

25. Quoted in ibid., p. 190.

26. Ibid., p. 191; Brown and Brown, *An Unauthorized History*, p. 13.

27. Brown and Brown, *An Unauthorized History*, p. 23.

28. Ibid., p. 24.

29. Ibid., p. 33.

30. Ibid., pp. 33–35.

31. Ibid., p. 41.

32. Ibid., p. 45.

33. Ibid., p. 14.

34. Horrall, "Sir John MacDonald," p. 199.

35. Julian Samora, Joe Bernal, and Albert Pena, *Gunpowder Justice: A Reassessment of the Texas Rangers* (South Bend, IN: University of Notre Dame Press, 1979), p. 1.

36. Ibid., p. 15.

37. Walter P. Webb, *The Texas Rangers: A Century of Frontier Defense* (Boston: Houghton Mifflin, 1935), pp. 20–21.

38. Ibid., p. 24.

39. Samora, *Gunpowder Justice*, p. 23.

40. Ibid., pp. 31–38.

41. Webb, *The Texas Rangers*, pp. 307–308.

42. Ibid., pp. 425–426.

43. Ibid., p. 453.

44. Texas State Legislature, *Session Laws*, 1901, chap. 34; 1919, chap. 144; 1935, chap. 181.

45. Ann P. Baenziger, "The Texas State Police During Reconstruction: A Reexamination," *Southwestern Historical Quarterly* 72 (1967): 471–473.

46. Webb, *The Texas Rangers*, p. 219.

47. Baenziger, "The Texas State Police," pp. 473–474.

48. Texas State Legislature, *Session Laws*, 1870, chap. 13; 1871, chap. 67.

49. Baenziger, "The Texas State Police," p. 475.

50. Webb, *The Texas Rangers*, p. 486.

51. Baenziger, "The Texas State Police," p. 486.

52. Webb, *The Texas Rangers*, pp. 228–229; Baenziger, "The Texas State Police," pp. 487–488; Texas State Legislature, *Session Laws*, 1873, chap. 31.

53. Massachusetts State Legislature, *Session Laws*, 1865, chap. 249.

54. Massachusetts State Legislature, *Session Laws*, 1871, chap. 394; 1874, chap. 405; 1875, chap. 15; 1879, chap. 305.

55. Delaware State Legislature, *Session Laws*, 1891, chap. 47; 1898, chap. 64.

56. South Carolina State Legislature, *Session Laws*, 1868, no. 11; 1878, no. 601; 1892, no. 28; 1894, no. 518; 1896, no. 61; 1903, no. 12; 1907, no. 226; 1935, no. 232.

57. Joseph Miller, *The Arizona Rangers* (New York: Hastings House, 1972), p. 2.

58. Arizona State Legislature, *Session Laws*, 1903, no. 64; 1909, chap. 4.

59. Connecticut State Legislature, *Session Laws*, 1903, chap. 141.

60. Although a good analysis of the Pennsylvania state police is not available, there are a number of sources that provide useful but generally biased information about the structure and operation of the Pennsylvania constabulary. See, for example, P. S. Reinsch, "Pennsylvania Constabulary," in *Readings on American State Government*, ed. P. S. Reinsch (Boston: Ginn, 1911); Blair Jaekel, "Pennsylvania's Mounted Police," *World's Work* 23 (1912): 641–652; Pennsylvania State Federation of Labor, *The American Cossack* (Harrisburg: Pennsylvania State Federation of Labor, 1915); John P. Guyer, *Pennsylvania's Cossacks and the State's Police* (Reading, PA: John P. Guyer, 1924); Lawrence G. Holmes, "An Analysis of State Police," *Trade Winds* (May 1925): 16–20; C. E. Perry, "Origin of the Pennsylvania State Police," *The Police Journal* (New York) 14 (October 1926): 6; E. Wilson Purdy, *Pennsylvania State Police* (Harrisburg: Pennsylvania State Police, 1963); Philip Conti, *The Pennsylvania State Police: A History of Service to the Commonwealth, 1905 to the Present* (Harrisburg, PA: Stackpole Books, 1977).

61. Pennsylvania State Legislature, *Session Laws*, 1905, no. 227.

62. From Governor Otero's message to the Territorial Assembly, January 16, 1905, quoted in Chuck Hornung, *The Thin Gray Line: The New Mexico Mounted Police* (Fort Worth, TX: Western Heritage Press, 1971), p. 14.

63. Hornung, *The Thin Gray Line*, p. 14.

64. New Mexico State Legislature, *Session Laws*, 1905, chap. 9.

65. Frank R. Prassel, *The Western Peace Officer: A Legacy of Law and Order* (Norman: University of Oklahoma Press, 1972), p. 165.

66. Hornung, *The Thin Gray Line*, p. 178; Prassel, *The Western Peace Officer*, p. 167; New Mexico State Legislature, *Session Laws*, 1919, chap. 94; 1921, chap. 12.

67. Nevada State Legislature, *Session Laws*, 1908, chap.4.

68. Tennessee State Legislature, *Session Laws*, 1915, no. 74; Iowa State Legislature, *Session Laws*, 1915, chap. 203; Alabama State Legislature, *Session Laws*, 1919, no. 551; Nebraska State Legislature, *Session Laws*, 1919, chap. 173; Wyoming State Legislature, *Session Laws*, 1921, chap. 18.

69. Colorado State Legislature, *Session Laws*, 1917, chap. 12; Georgia State Legislature, *Session Laws*, 1917, no. 224; Maine State Legislature, *Session Laws*, 1917, chap. 284; Michigan State Legislature, *Session Laws*, 1917, no. 53; New York State Legislature, *Session Laws*, 1917, chap. 161; Rhode Island State Legislature, *Session Laws*, 1917, chap. 1469.

70. Those favoring a state police for New York formed the Committee for a State Police under the leadership of Seth Low, Oswald Garrison Villard, and Katherine Mayo. The committee engaged in an active campaign to promote public support for the state police as well as lobbying congressmen and testifying before hearings on the state police bills. Examples of their activities along with lists of members can be found in their published annual reports for the years 1917, 1918, 1919, and 1920. An excellent historical study of the development of the New York state police can be found in the recent doctoral dissertation by Gerda Ray, "Contested Legitimacy: Creating the State Police in New York, 1890–1930," (Ph.D. diss., University of California at Berkeley, 1990). Useful but biased information on the operation of the New York State Police can be found in Edgar Dawson, "New York State Police," *American Political Science Review* 11 (August 1917): 539–541; New York. Division of State Police, *The New York State Police: The First Fifty Years, 1917–1967* (Albany, 1967); and William E. Kirwan, *The New York State Police: History and Development of Collective Negotiations* (New York: New York State Police, 1969).

71. New York State Legislature, *Session Laws*, 1917, chap. 161.

72. Michigan State Legislature, *Session Laws*, 1919, no. 26; Massachusetts State Legislature, *Session Laws*, 1919, chap. 350; New Jersey State Legislature, *Session Laws*, 1919, chap. 102; Tennessee State Legislature, *Session Laws*, 1919, chap. 96; West Virginia State Legislature, *Session Laws*, 1919, chap. 12.

73. Maryland State Legislature, *Session Laws*, 1916, chap. 687; Delaware State Legislature, *Session Laws*, 1921, chaps. 195–196; Illinois State Legislature, *Session Laws*, 1921, p. 571; Indiana State Legislature, *Session Laws*, 1921, chap. 265; Maine State Legislature, *Session Laws*, 1921, chap. 211; Oregon State Legislature, *Session Laws*, 1921, chap. 371; Washington State Legislature, *Session Laws*, 1921, chap. 108.

74. South Dakota State Legislature, *Session Laws*, 1917, chap. 355.

75. Idaho State Legislature, *Session Laws*, 1919, chap. 103; 1921, chap. 67; 1923, chaps. 12 and 152.

76. By comparison, during the previous six-year period from 1915 to 1921, twenty-three states created state police forces.

77. Illinois State Legislature, *Session Laws*, 1923, p. 562; Utah State Legislature, *Session Laws*, 1923, chap. 65; Virginia State Legislature, *Session Laws*, 1924, chap. 99; Vermont State Legislature, *Session Laws*, 1925, no. 70; Louisiana State Legislature, *Session Laws*, 1928, no. 296.

78. Rhode Island State Legislature, *Session Laws*, 1925, chap. 588.

79. Nebraska State Legislature, *Session Laws*, 1927, chap. 157.

80. Arkansas State Legislature, *Session Laws*, 1929, no. 299; California State Legislature, *Session Laws*, 1929, chap. 308; Minnesota State Legislature, *Session Laws*, 1929, chap. 355; North Carolina State Legislature, *Session Laws*, 1929, chap. 218; Missouri State Legislature, *Session Laws*, 1931, pp. 230–236; Kentucky State Legislature, *Session Laws*, 1932, chap. 106, sec. 18; Kansas State Legislature, *Session Laws*, 1933, chap. 109; Ohio State Legislature, *Session Laws*, 1933, pp. 93–96; Montana State Legislature, *Session Laws*, 1935, chap. 185; North Dakota State Legislature, *Session Laws*, 1935, chap. 148; Oklahoma State Legislature, *Session Laws*, 1937, chap. 50; New Hampshire State Legislature, *Session Laws*, 1937, chap. 134; Mississippi State Legislature, *Session Laws*,

1938, chap. 143; Florida State Legislature, *Session Laws*, 1939, chap. 19551, no. 556; Wisconsin State Legislature, *Session Laws*, 1939, chap. 10.

81. Oregon State Legislature, *Session Laws*, 1931, chap. 139; Indiana State Legislature, *Session Laws*, 1933, chap. 71; Alabama State Legislature, *Session Laws*, 1935, no. 331; Iowa State Legislature, *Session Laws*, 1935, chap. 48; Maryland State Legislature, *Session Laws*, 1935, chap. 303; Wyoming State Legislature, *Session Laws*, 1935, chap. 51; Utah State Legislature, *Session Laws*, 1941, chap. 14; Virginia State Legislature, *Session Laws*, 1932, chap. 342; Kansas State Legislature, *Session Laws*, 1937, chap. 330; Tennessee State Legislature, *Session Laws*, 1929, chap. 25; South Carolina State Legislature, *Session Laws*, 1930, no. 603; South Dakota State Legislature, *Session Laws*, 1935, chap. 97; Louisiana State Legislature, *Session Laws*, 1932, no. 21, sec. 11; 1936, no. 94; 1942, chap. 110; Nebraska State Legislature, *Session Laws*, 1937, chap. 141; 1941, chap. 176.

82. Georgia State Legislature, *Session Laws*, 1937, no. 220; Idaho State Legislature, *Session Laws*, 1939, chap. 60; Arizona State Legislature, *Session Laws*, 1931, no. 331; New Mexico State Legislature, *Session Laws*, 1933, chap. 119; Colorado State Legislature, *Session Laws*, 1935, chap. 125.

83. The territory of Alaska created a restricted highway patrol in 1941 (Alaska State Legislature, *Session Laws*, 1941, chap. 65, sec.1, subsec. J). In 1947 the law was amended to give the highway patrol the powers of United States marshals (Alaska State Legislature, *Session Laws*, 1947, chap. 49). The highway patrol was abolished in 1953 and replaced with a Department of Territorial Police able to enforce all criminal laws effective in the territory (Alaska State Legislature, *Session Laws*, 1953, chap. 144). On becoming a state in 1959, Alaska created a Department of Public Safety which encompassed the territorial police (Alaska State Legislature, *Session Laws*, 1959, chap. 64, sec. 18). Hawaii has no state police per se; rather, each island has its own police force.

# Chapter 4

# The State Police
# in Historical Context

Movement to establish state-controlled police forces in the United States is primarily a product of the first two decades of the twentieth century. Although a few states (Texas, Massachusetts, Delaware, and South Carolina) created state-controlled enforcement agencies during the nineteenth century, they were small, specialized forces intended for specific purposes such as protecting frontier borders or enforcing liquor laws. These forces were exceptions, rather than the rule, and had little impact on police development during the 1800s.

During much of the nineteenth century, the United States was dominated by the ideology of republicanism, which emphasized decentralization of power and accountability to local constituents. Changing the police so that control would be in the hands of a single individual, or a small group of officials, who were removed from local authority would have provoked cries of despotism.[1] Moreover, Americans, like their British ancestors, had a long-standing animosity to any agency resembling a permanent military presence. The idea of a state-controlled police force was an unprecedented and controversial development in nineteenth-century America.[2] Nevertheless, toward the end of the century, important changes took place that would weaken these basic principles and create an environment more receptive to the concept of centralized police forces.

## CHANGING VALUES

Nineteenth-century America has been described as a society of "island communities" with each community a self-regulating unit, free to form opinion and enact its own policies. The isolation and autonomy were reinforced by a lack of communication which "restricted the interaction among these islands."[3] Following the Civil War, economic development produced fundamental changes as the country shifted from a commercial and agrarian economy to an urban and industrial society. These innovations produced a reexamination of traditional values that now seemed irrelevant in light of the events taking place.[4]

Reactions to these changes were magnified by a series of events that shook American society in the late 1800s and gave rise to fears of radicalism and a politically conscious working class. The national railroad strike in 1877 was accompanied by numerous strikes in other industries. These were followed by the Haymarket riot in 1886 and the bloody conflict between strikers and Pinkerton detectives during the strike at the Carnegie-owned Homestead steel plant. The depression of 1893 produced a number of organized marches to Washington by urban workers, while President Grover Cleveland was forced to use federal troops in 1894 to intercede in the Pullman strike in Chicago. Finally, throughout the 1890s there was continued conflict in the coal fields of Pennsylvania and Colorado.[5]

Increasingly these disturbances became associated with the "foreign" element and the problem of immigration. Americans began to attribute various problems such as vice, crime, and the general social unrest to the immigrants. Moved by both contempt and fear, natives pictured the newcomers as political subversives who were undermining American society.[6] Searching for some semblance of continuity and stability in the face of rapid change, Americans responded by striking out at perceived enemies and by cultivating an intense wave of nationalism. These emerging ideals of "Americanism," with emphasis on loyalty and hostility toward immigrants, provided the justification for mobilizing force to protect the institutional structures of American society. It was at this time that demands were placed on the federal and state governments to transform the National Guard into a repressive agency for use in future labor disturbances. In fighting to retain a society that had provided meaning to their lives, Americans began assigning greater power to government and urging a greater centralization of authority.[7]

In conjunction with these social disruptions, the American economy, during the last quarter of the nineteenth century, was being shaped by a revolution in industry, agriculture, and transportation. By the turn of the century, the United States had emerged as a world leader in agricultural and industrial production. The result was a productive economy that provided an increasingly higher standard of living for a majority of the people. But this extraordinary growth created destructive competition and monopolies on the one hand, and a magnitude of social problems—unemployment, illness, exploitation of women and children, urban poverty—on the other. In addition, individuals discovered that community political systems had also been transformed. Instead of impartial representation, many cities were controlled by political machines in a hierarchical structure characteristic of the corporate monopoly.[8]

Emerging in the midst of these massive changes was the populist crusade, a reform effort dedicated to preserving individualism and democracy in the face of industrial growth. Those involved in the populist effort clung to traditional ideals and believed that there was no conflict between local community control and the demands of an industrial technology.[9] Faced with the ever expanding industrial and urban society, however, populist reform collapsed and gave way to a contrasting effort to reform the injustices brought on by economic growth.

## PROGRESSIVISM

Where populists had maintained the ideology of individualism, the new reform effort was bureaucratic in nature, aiming to accomplish a rearrangement of economic and political relationships by systematic use of state power.[10] From the 1890s on there emerged numerous "progressive" movements addressing different, often contradictory, objectives. All, however, were attempting to "insure the survival of democracy . . . by the enlargement of governmental power to control and offset the power of private economic groups over the nation's institutions and life."[11]

Referred to as the Progressive Era, the period from the late 1890s to 1920 witnessed a variety of diverse efforts at political, social, and economic reform. It would be misleading, however, to characterize these activities as a single cohesive movement. Rather, there were different progressive reforms operating simultaneously in different sectors of society. There were the social justice activities of social workers and religious leaders to provide for the disadvantaged, a movement for political reform to end political corruption in city government, as well as progressive reform at the state and national level.[12] Whatever the issue, most reformers saw society as operating according to rational laws. They searched for that one important dysfunction which, when corrected, would bring an end to society's problems.[13] While progressive reform movements were mostly middle-class in orientation, many of the important reform efforts were "inspired, staffed and led by businessmen with very specific or special-interest objectives."[14]

The bureaucratic, rational, and business dimensions of progressive reform reflected the change in values that was taking place in American society. Throughout the nineteenth century, ideals stressing autonomy and individualism were dominant, while at the beginning of the twentieth century these traditional values were replaced by an "orientation that stressed ideals of efficiency, order, rationality, and systematic control."[15] Advances in scientific and technical methods during the progressive period provided an ideology in which reformers became enamored of the possibilities of improving society by making it more efficient.[16] The morality of nineteenth-century reform, with its emphasis on the battle between good and evil, was to be replaced by "management, control, and regulation." Reform thus became a "technical question," with an emphasis on intelligence and fact.[17]

An outgrowth of Taylor's methods of scientific management, the "cult of efficiency" was a significant component of progressive reform.[18] The emphasis was on creating a program of action without an appeal to morality—a "turning toward hard work and away from feeling, toward discipline and away from sympathy."[19] Efficiency required freedom from pressures of self-interest that could lead away from decisions required by technical knowledge; reform called for experts and elites. As Haber puts it:

> These reformers talked of social control, national guidance, and the end of laissez faire. They rejected the disorder of the uncontrolled market but often wished to preserve middle class independence through expanding the realm of "professionalism." For this segment of progressivism, scientific management had an intrinsic appeal. It developed the notion of social control into a program of planning and placed the professional expert near the top.[20]

Attempting to rise above class interests, reformers looked beyond both capital and labor and toward the state as the means for bringing needed social efficiency. In concrete terms this translated into the basic themes of urban progressive reform: a strong executive, nonpartisanship, and the separation of administration and politics.[21] However, the cult of efficiency "implied a drastic shift in the method of making public decisions and an equally drastic shift in the location of political power."[22] As Haber points out, reformers who were enthusiastic about guidance and control saw themselves as the controllers.[23]

Controlling the economy to make it more efficiently serve the needs of a changing society was only one aspect of the progressive reform effort. Other elements in society were also deemed in need of rational organization. Business especially feared the growing power of organized labor which was a factor of industrial production not easily controlled or directed. Labor opposed the cult of efficiency, as they perceived it as a threat in the form of specific factory techniques or of antilabor public opinion. Declaring collective bargaining to be illegal and un-American, business leaders became more aggressive in their struggle against labor by fighting union recognition through a number of nationwide organizations such as the National Association of Manufacturers.[24]

While business sought to bring labor under control, the native middle class continued its animosity toward the immigrant. Americans found it difficult to "separate the strangeness of the immigrant from the strangeness of industrial change; both seemed 'foreign.' "[25] The fear of foreigners was intensified during this period as the influx of immigrants drastically increased from the late 1890s to 1914. Even more threatening than sheer numbers was the fact that newer arrivals were from southern and eastern Europe and were perceived as being different and more poverty stricken than earlier immigrants from northern Europe. Prevailing sentiment toward the immigrant is caught by Hays in the following quote:

> These hordes of newcomers . . . maintained strange customs, spoke peculiar languages, dressed oddly, and practiced alien Catholic and Jewish religions; they had not the proper reverence for American values, symbols, and heroes. Moreover, they were intimately involved with the most vulgar and unpleasant features of industrial society.[26]

In addition, the immigrant was linked increasingly closer to labor disturbances and violence, creating a temper in which native Americans sought to protect their way of life by a variety of restrictive and repressive measures.[27]

## PROGRESSIVE POLICE REFORM

Within the context of massive social change during the early 1900s and the corresponding progressive response, one can locate the essential elements which brought about the emergence of the state police. The changes, fears, and desires created a sense of urgency with regard to maintaining social control. Thus, many reformers turned their attention to the police as an institution also in need of modification. Although there had been attempts to reform the police during the nineteenth century, these efforts were blocked by the republican values of community autonomy and local control over law enforcement. Progressivism, however, with its emphasis on rationality, control, and efficiency, "weakened the national dominance of the decentralized model for policing by introducing changes in the structure of politics and by organizing the various ideas about police reform into a fairly consistent intellectual position."[28]

Police reformers came from the same elements of respectable middle-class society as other progressives. They believed that scientific management, efficiency, and expert knowledge would solve a wide range of problems, including those they believed to be affecting the police—lack of uniform law enforcement, officers of inferior quality, lack of discipline, and general police inefficiency.[29] Believing that present police practices were inadequate to meet the problems of a modern, industrial society, reformers focused on the idea of administrative efficiency and evoked the drive to make police work "professional." Reflecting progressive reformers' dissatisfaction with local government, professionalism was a direct attack on the grip partisan politics had over municipal government. Police were seen not as public servants but as agents for particular political factions with only minimal commitment to the enforcement of the law.[30] Professionalizing the police—centralization of authority, improved training, and the implementation of civil service—would, according to reformers, break the link between the police and the political machines. However, city bosses were successful in their resistance to attempts at reforming the police. Professionalism, therefore, remained more an idea, a goal, than a concrete accomplishment.[31]

## EMERGENCE OF THE STATE POLICE

Thwarted at the local level, police reformers took their fight to the state and federal levels and were successful in establishing two new law enforcement agencies that "embodied the central concepts of efficiency-oriented professionalism."[32] In 1908, Attorney General Charles Joseph Bonaparte established the Bureau of Investigation (which eventually became the FBI). This was the first move in the continuing pattern of greater involvement of the federal government in law enforcement. The creation in 1905 of the Pennsylvania constabulary was the beginning of the movement to establish state police forces across the nation.

During the first decade of the twentieth century, six states created state-controlled law enforcement agencies (Arizona, Connecticut, Nevada, New Mexico, Pennsylvania, and Texas). However, only the Pennsylvania constabulary represented the ideals of progressive police reform. Embodying all the values of administrative efficiency, the Pennsylvania force was highly centralized, paramilitary, and impersonal in organization. A large force (228 officers and men), the Pennsylvania constabulary was given total police powers of search, seizure, and arrest in any part of the state. With complete authority in the hands of the superintendent, who was answerable only to the governor, the Pennsylvania force provided one of the primary objectives of progressive police reform—insulation from political influence. The fact that the force was highly mobile, recruited nationwide, and without ties to any particular communities was, by design, an effort to eliminate any sympathy between the police and the public—a move intended to reduce differential and selective enforcement of state and federal laws.[33]

Although representing the epitome of progressive police reform, the state police idea was not immediately adopted by other states. It would be twelve years before other states began to establish police forces similar in style to the Pennsylvania constabulary. Social and economic change had generated, among certain segments of the population, a desire for improved effectiveness in law enforcement. But the idea of a military-like police, controlled by the state, remained a radical and unproven departure from the traditional, accepted practice of local control over the police. Nevertheless, the existence of the Pennsylvania constabulary served as a model on which progressives would attempt to style police reform in other states during the ensuing years.

Unsuccessful attempts to enact state police legislation in a number of states took place during the prewar years. Reduction in the tensions between labor and capital, brought on by a gradual acceptance of the union movement, and the massive decline of foreign immigration in 1914 may have contributed to a climate less conducive to major police reform.[34] Nevertheless, progressive ideals had established a bureaucratic orientation toward social issues in which "the values of continuity and regularity, functionality and rationality, administration and management set the form of problems and outlined their alternative solutions."[35]

Beginning in 1917 a number of states finally passed previously defeated legislation creating Pennsylvania-style state police. The war had stimulated the reemergence of long-standing prejudices and hostilities, and the fears concerning law and order during wartime were an important factor in the move to establish state police.[36] In addition, the war provided a tremendous rationale for increased social control and suppression as public opinion mobilized to stifle all kinds of dissent. Various agencies, such as the American Defense Society and the American Protective League, spread propaganda which served only to aggravate the already heightened dangers of wartime sabotage and sedition. Various campaigns led by corporate executives, prosperous farmers, newspaper editors, and politicians attacked all manner of "radical" activity.[37]

The state police forces created in Colorado, Georgia, Maine, Michigan, and New York in 1917 were the result of the "preparedness" drive during the war. With the National Guard being mobilized for duty overseas, many businessmen and political leaders sought alternative means for controlling anticipated disturbances as the fear of riot and sabotage outweighed the fear of centralized policing. Yet, even with the distorted perceptions resulting from wartime hostility, a number of the state police forces created in 1917 were considered temporary and were to be disbanded at the end of the war. People were willing to justify the need for some form of state-controlled police during extreme emergencies such as a world war, but remained apprehensive about the idea.

Conditions following the war served only to heighten war time fears and to generate a widespread drive for improved methods of social control. As Murray states:

> In spite of the nation's desire for rapid return to peace, it was obvious the American public of 1919 was still thinking with the mind of a people at war. . . . Still in existence were the National Security League, the American Defense Society, and other such patriotic organizations which in order to live now sought to create new menaces.[38]

"Menaces" were not hard to find. The success of the bolshevik revolution in Russia and its spread into western Europe triggered a wave of hysteria in the United States. For the American people, the emergence of bolshevism was probably the most threatening aspect of the postwar era.[39] The fear of revolution in America was escalated in 1919 by a series of bomb attacks, the Seattle general strike, and numerous riots stemming from the May Day celebrations. All these events came together in the public mind and contributed to the general panic and paranoia known as the "red scare."[40]

Added to the fear of revolution was a postwar inflation that triggered a massive outbreak of labor disputes. During 1919 alone there were over 2,500 strikes involving more than four million workers.[41] Along with labor troubles, Link and Catton argue,

> There . . . were numerous other manifestations of a growth of intolerance, bigotry, and chauvinism among all classes and in all sections during the decade following the First World War. There was fear of "reds," an intensification of anti-semitism, organized campaigns against Roman Catholics, and legislation practically to end immigration from southern and eastern Europe.[42]

An indication of the state of public opinion, which placed repression and control above understanding, was the adoption, at the state level in 1919 and 1920, of laws "outlawing the display of the red flag, prohibiting memberships in organizations that advocated the violent overthrow of the government, and forbidding seditious utterances."[43] At the federal level, conservative leaders sought to enact peacetime sedition and criminal syndicalism laws to replace wartime legislation.[44]

Hostility toward foreigners reemerged as immigration in 1920 returned to prewar levels. Increases in immigration and the state of the economy had always been associated with past nativist movements, and postwar America continued that pattern.[45] Foreigners were blamed for everything from labor unrest to the increase in crime. The hatred and fear culminated in the passage of three major pieces of antiforeign legislation during the postwar period.

In 1921 Congress passed a bill placing absolute numerical limits on European immigration that would ensure that future levels would be but a small fraction of those during the prewar period. Three years later Congress enacted the Johnson-Reed Act, further restricting immigration by establishing a quota system based on national origin for Europeans and eliminating Oriental immigration altogether.[46] But probably the most significant antiforeign legislation was the passage of the Eighteenth Amendment, which created nationwide prohibition of alcoholic beverages. Regarded by many old-stock natives as the "ultimate reform," it was viewed by immigrants as the "ultimate horror." The Volstead Act was "an unprecedented attempt to regiment morality by law," and was considered by anti-liquor groups to be the crowning achievement in "their crusade to regulate behavior" thereby preserving the "American way of life."[47]

In this context of postwar hysteria, there was renewed interest in the state police as a means of dealing with the perceived threats to order and stability. Any lasting apprehensions about the threat to personal liberty from a centralized police evaporated in the face of bolshevism and the threat of a nationwide general strike. In all, fifteen states created police forces during the period from 1919 to 1921, many of which were paramilitary forces modeled after the Pennsylvania state police. Other states attempted to establish similar agencies but for various reasons were unable to get the necessary legislation enacted into law. Although the rationale for such forces was couched in terms of police protection for the rural districts, the apparent purpose was to protect the middle class from immigrants, business from organized labor, and society from revolution.

Immigration and the "foreign problem" were key factors prompting many individuals to opt for increased measures of social control. A 1921 editorial on immigrants, in a magazine promoting the state police, indicates a prevalent view on the issue:

> The immigrants of today are of a different and lower racial average than those of the olden days. . . . The certain and sure result of more immigration at present is the further congesting of our city slums and the lowering of our national standards and ideals.[48]

After a brief criticism of the "sentimentality" of the view that America should be a refuge for the unfortunate, the editorial argues for getting "rid of some of our vicious and unassimilable human material" and preventing others from entering. The writer closes with a call for a return to immigration from the "original" stock of northern Europe to bring the balance back to where it was, "before our ill-considered generosity opened the doors to the horde of low grade incomers whom we now find so poor an addition to our race."[49]

Stressing the inadequacy of the rural police, and the necessity for a state police the Bureau of State Research of the New Jersey State Chamber of Commerce wrote in 1917 that many counties were annoyed by "riff-raff" elements from the large cities and the "foreign settlements along the river." Other areas of the state had large plants located in rural areas "which employ foreigners," and many of the suburban areas had no police patrol despite their location in a section of the state "which has a peculiarly high proportion of foreigners."[50]

The importance of the state police for dealing with immigrants becomes quite clear from the remarks made by state police officers themselves. Commenting on the "peculiar labor conditions" that gave rise to the Pennsylvania state police, Deputy Superintendent George F. Lumb remarked that

> the vast mining interests and iron industries have brought into our state, thousand upon thousands of foreign laborers, many of whom are criminals, from southern Europe, and all of whom are ignorant of our laws and social conditions.[51]

The following excerpt from the general rules laid down by the superintendent of the Pennsylvania state police in 1912 explicitly underscores the emphasis placed on controlling immigrants:

> A man can be a gentleman, as well as a policeman. He must treat everybody with respect. If he starts after a criminal he must get him. He must never strike a prisoner after an arrest, and EACH CON-

STABLE MUST ALWAYS BE EQUAL TO ONE HUNDRED FOR-
EIGNERS [emphasis in original].[52]

The impact of immigration on the state police movement is suggested
by an examination of the chronological pattern of state police development. The first period of state police development corresponds to the
initial rise of immigration at the turn of the century, while the spurt in
state police forces follows the period of ever increasing rates of immigration from southern and eastern Europe. Thus, for the native-born
members of the old-stock establishment, the immigrant was a social and
political threat. Dangerous as potential voters, inefficient and imperfect
as a labor pool, and threatening to an orderly society, the foreign born
were "at best a challenge, at worst a menace."[53]

Closely aligned with the nativistic fear of the immigrant was the
increasing "problem" presented by organized labor. From the biased
perspective of industry, unchecked labor unions would cripple American
business and bring progress to a halt. Literature of the period is filled with
critical remarks concerning labor, especially their opposition to the state
police. In its report on the state police, the New Jersey State Chamber of
Commerce pointed to the "unusually high number of labor disputes"
accompanied by violence as a major problem for existing police forces.
Although quick to affirm labor's right to strike, the report made the
distinction between "strikes" and "riots," pointing out that "rioting is
illegal and the law makes mandatory the suppression of riots."[54]

Responding to charges that a state police would be a strike-breaking
force, proponents employed the rhetoric of "impartial" and "fair" law
enforcement to explain state police use during labor disputes.

State police have never interfered with the right of any man to
strike; they have merely taken the necessary measures to prevent
unwarranted and illegal interference with those who did not desire
to strike but, instead who wished to work.[55]

The issue was order, not rural crime. State police were intended to
provide increased protection for business interests as they expanded
operations into suburban and rural towns and villages. When labor
begins to organize, the argument ran, a force is needed "which has the
appearance of independence" so as to avoid the charge of taking sides,
but "which is merely there to enforce the law."[56]

Calling on the business community to "set in motion" the process for
creating the state police, Milton R. Palmer (editor of *The State Trooper*)
stated:

It is to the interests of every business man to see that state police
forces are so organized and so administered that politics shall be
excluded and the officers and troopers be allowed to act impartially
and freely that the good of the entire community may be en-
hanced.[57]

In a surprisingly forthright fashion, the New Jersey State Chamber of
Commerce flatly stated that the "particular need" which the Pennsylvania state police were created to meet was the "industrial problem" of
the state. They reiterated this point by noting that the superintendent
of the Pennsylvania state police, after a survey of the state's needs,
located the state police barracks in the mining centers of the state: "Two
of the barracks are situated in eastern Pennsylvania in the anthracite
region, only fifty miles apart; the other two are situated forty-five miles
apart, in the bituminous region of western Pennsylvania."[58] The business elite during the Progressive Era feared activist labor organizations,
and they took as their basic perspective "prevention of the emergence
of an aggressive working class."[59]

The drive to establish state police forces during the postwar period
was the result of exaggerated fears and repressive responses. When the
forces contributing to the fears dissipated, so did the pressure to create
state police. After reaching a peak in 1921, when seven states created
state law enforcement agencies, the number fell dramatically; only one
state created a police force in 1923 and only three other states followed
suit over the next five years. This decline in state police activity corre-
sponded to a "waning of American nativism" brought about by the
"ever-increasing level of economic prosperity that helped to smother
the flames of hostility and reaction of the early 1920's."[60]

The return of "prosperity" during the mid-1920s was accompanied
by a decline in the power and influence of organized labor. An aggressive "open shop" campaign and the adoption of "welfare capitalism"
combined with an increasingly conservative labor leadership produced
a notable reduction in tension between labor and capital after 1921. The
average number of strikes dropped significantly and trade union membership steadily declined from over five million in 1920 to less than three
million in 1923.[61] The decline of the labor union movement and the
reduction in immigration "undermined the need for a Pennsylvania-
style state police," as "social and industrial discipline" were no longer
crucial issues.[62]

A new problem had emerged, however, that would affect the future
development of state law enforcement—the automobile. By the 1920s
the automobile industry had become the single largest manufacturing
industry in the United States. From 4,000 automobiles in 1900, produc-

tion had reached 1.5 million by 1921, with over 300,000 workers employed by the automotive industry in 1919. The expanding use of the automobile was directly linked to the "good roads movement," which sought to increase funding and construction of hard-surfaced roads. By the 1930s county, state, and federal governments were spending nearly $2.5 billion a year for construction and maintenance of highways.[63]

Responding to the need for regulating the increased use of the automobile, states began creating "highway patrol" enforcement agencies in the late 1920s and 1930s. In fact, most of the state police forces created after 1925 were highway patrols, restricted to enforcing the motor vehicle laws. The peak for this last phase of state police development came in 1935, when ten states organized law enforcement agencies, eight of which were restricted highway patrols. Although the number of patrols created by the states during the 1930s represent, in large part, a response to the automobile, the Great Depression had an impact as well. According to Johnson, financial problems overcame political opposition to greater departmental centralization and made more qualified recruits available as police work became attractive to men from the middle class.[64] By 1941 the process begun in 1905 was complete, as all states had some form of state law enforcement agency.

## SUMMARY

At the turn of the century, the United States had emerged from its agrarian heritage as a major industrial power. The beneficiaries of these changes, the white, old-stock members of America's business and political elite, were both optimistic about the future and, at the same time, apprehensive about growing problems from below—the poor, the immigrants, the workers, and all others who appeared strange and threatening. As stated by Kolko:

> The problems that a newly industrialized society confronts by their very nature . . . look threatening, and to the established American ruling class their concerns about the possible disintegration of social life . . . seemed all the more urgent in light of the untested hordes of foreign workers entering America.[65]

Under such conditions, the climate of the times favored consensus and solidarity in political and social institutions. Political and economic leaders believed it necessary to gain greater control over society—its people, ideas, thoughts, and actions. Regulating society "gained wider currency before 1920 than in any other period of American life."[66] During the first two decades of the twentieth century, reformers experimented with different forms of social control such as scientific management and eugenics, as well as the passage of various forms of repressive legislation, for example, immigration restriction and prohibition. Within this coercive context, reform of the police became an important issue. To gain maximum benefit from repressive laws, the machinery for enforcing them also had to be refined, specifically by wresting control of the police from the immigrant-dominated political machines. As Walker makes clear, the concept of professionalism and the drive to centralize police departments were simply additional "attempts to break the power of the lower class."[67]

The creation of the state police, like other progressive reforms, was another tool for removing "the masses from politics" and satisfying leaders' desires for "rationalized and efficient" administrative agencies.[68] Couched in terms of a "modern crime problem," progressive arguments for police reform stressed that the "decentralized nature" of existing police organizations presented a "serious handicap to effective and economical" law enforcement. The idea of a state police was advanced as the best remedy for this defect as it would provide centralized and coordinated statewide police forces.[69] Rhetoric aside, the primary factors leading to the development of the state police were the increase in immigration from eastern and southern Europe and the desire to curb the growing labor movement. Along with prohibition and eugenics, centralized policing, as provided by the state police, was a product of a "social thought when challenges from below are perceived."[70]

The preceding discussion was intended to flesh out the legislative outline of state police development presented in Chapter 3. The main theme of this discussion is to argue that the state police were but one of many related reforms that emerged from the progressive attempts to deal with dramatic social change. As law enforcement reform, the state police embodied many of the basic principles of progressivism: efficiency, rationality, and centralization of authority. Nevertheless, the argument remains speculative, as it needs to be substantiated by in-depth study of concrete situations. Only then, by talking about real people addressing real concerns, can a human face be put on the abstract arguments. The next three chapters provide this information by presenting the results of research into the dynamics of state police development in Illinois and Colorado.

## NOTES

1. David R. Johnson, *American Law Enforcement: A History* (St. Louis, MO: Forum Press, 1981), p. 25.

2. Samuel Walker, *A Critical History of Police Reform* (Lexington, MA: D. C. Heath, 1977), p. 6. Discussion and analysis of the British dislike for organized police forces can be found in the works of Charles Reith, *British Police and the Democratic Ideal* (London: Oxford University Press, 1943); E. P. Thompson, *Whigs and Hunters: The Origin of the Black Act* (New York: Random House, 1975); T. A. Critchley, *A History of Police in England and Wales, 1900–1966* (London: Constable, 1967); Leon Radzinowicz, *A History of the English Criminal Law and Its Administration from 1750*, vol. 3 (New York: Macmillan, 1968); and Robert D. Storch, "The Plague of the Blue Locusts: Police Reform and Popular Resistance in Northern England, 1840–57," *International Revue of Social History* 20, part 1, (1975): 61–90.

3. Robert H. Wiebe, *The Search for Order, 1877–1920* (New York: Hill and Wang, 1967), p. xiii.

4. Gerald N. Grob and George A. Billias, *Interpretations of American History*, vol. 2, *Since 1865* (New York: Free Press, 1972), p. 159.

5. Samuel P. Hays, *The Response to Industrialism, 1885–1914* (Chicago: University of Chicago Press, 1957), p. 43; Gabriel Kolko, *Main Currents in Modern American History* (New York: Harper and Row, 1976), p. 174.

6. Hays, *Response to Industrialism*, p. 43; Wiebe, *Search for Order*, p. 54.

7. Hays, *Response to Industrialism*, p. 43; Wiebe, *Search for Order*, pp. xiii–xiv; Kolko, *Main Currents*, p. 175.

8. Arthur S. Link and William B. Catton, *American Epoch: A History of the United States since the 1890s* (New York: Alfred A. Knopf, 1963), pp. 3, 6, 81.

9. Wiebe, *Search for Order*, pp. 74–75.

10. Link and Catton, *American Epoch*, p. 70.

11. Arthur S. Link, "What Happened to the Progressive Movement in the 1920s?" *American Historical Review* 64 (July 1959): 836.

12. Link and Catton, *American Epoch*, p. 68.

13. Wiebe, *Search for Order*, p. 62.

14. Link, "What Happened," p. 836.

15. Grob and Billias, *Interpretations of American History*, p. 169.

16. Hays, *Response to Industrialism*, p. 156.

17. Samuel Haber, *Efficiency and Uplift: Scientific Management in the Progressive Era, 1890–1920* (Chicago: University of Chicago Press, 1964), p. 55.

18. David W. Noble, *The Progressive Mind, 1890–1917* (Chicago: Rand McNally, 1970), p. 38.

19. Haber, *Efficiency and Uplift*, p. ix.

20. Ibid., p. xii.

21. Ibid., pp. iii, 60.

22. Hays, *Response to Industrialism*, p. 157.

23. Haber, *Efficiency and Uplift*, p. 66.

24. Hays, *Response to Industrialism*, pp. 52–53; Haber, *Efficiency and Uplift*, p. 66.

25. Hays, *Response to Industrialism*, p. 100.

26. Ibid., p. 99.

27. Ibid., p. 100.

28. Johnson, *American Law Enforcement*, p. 68.

29. Ibid., p. 67.

30. Walker, *A Critical History*, p. 3.

31. Ibid., p. 53.

32. Ibid., p. 75.

33. Ibid., pp. 75–76.

34. Thomas A. Reppetto, *The Blue Parade* (New York: Free Press, 1978), pp. 133–134.

35. Wiebe, *Search for Order*, p. 295.

36. Walker, *A Critical History*, p. 76.

37. Robert K. Murray, *Red Scare: A Study of National Hysteria, 1919–1920* (New York: McGraw-Hill, 1955), p. 12; Paul L. Murphy, "Sources and Nature of Intolerance in the 1920s," *Journal of American History* 51 (July 1964): 63; Wiebe, *Search for Order*, p. 289.

38. Murray, *Red Scare*, pp. 14–15.

39. Ibid., p. 33; Link and Catton, *American Epoch*, p. 237.

40. Murray, *Red Scare*, p. 57.

41. Link and Catton, *American Epoch*, p. 234.

42. Ibid., p. 301.

43. Ibid., p. 239.

44. Murphy, "Sources and Nature of Intolerance," p. 64.

45. John Higham, *Strangers in the Land: Patterns of American Nativism, 1860–1925* (New Brunswick, NJ: Rutgers University Press, 1955), p. 267.

46. Ibid., pp. 308–324.

47. Ibid., p. 267; John D. Buenker, "Urban Immigrant Lawmakers and Progressive Reform in Illinois," in *Essays in Illinois History*, edited by David F. Tingley (Carbondale, IL: Southern Illinois University Press, 1968), p. 72.

48. *The State Trooper* 2, no. 10 (June 1921): 19.

49. Ibid.

50. New Jersey State Chamber of Commerce, "State Police Problem in America," in *State Research*, supplement to *New Jersey* 4, no. 4 (1917): viii.

51. F. C. Miller, "The State Police," in *Papers and Proceedings of the Third Annual Meeting of the Minnesota Academy of Social Sciences*, edited by William A. Schaper, vol. 3, no. 3 (Index Press, 1910), p. 101.

52. *New York Times*, September 15, 1912, sec. V, p. 1.

53. Kolko, *Main Currents*, p. 284.

54. New Jersey State Chamber of Commerce, "State Police Problem," p. ix.

55. Milton R. Palmer, "The State Police as an Asset," *American Industries* 23 (August 1922): 22.

56. Ian McDonald, quoted in Tony Bunyan, *The History and Practice of the Political Police in Britain* (London: Julian Friedman, 1976), p. 62.

57. Palmer, "State Police as an Asset," p. 23.

58. New Jersey State Chamber of Commerce, "State Police Problem," p. 7.

59. Kolko, *Main Currents*, p. 31.

60. Link, "What Happened," p. 842; Higham, *Strangers in the Land*, p. 329.

61. Link and Catton, *American Epoch*, pp. 309–310.

62. Johnson, *American Law Enforcement*, p. 161.

63. Hays, *Response to Industrialism*, p. 112; Link and Catton, *American Epoch*, pp. 262–263.

64. Johnson, *American Law Enforcement*, p. 117.

65. Kolko, *Main Currents*, pp. 29–30.

66. Ibid., p. 31.

67. Walker, *A Critical History*, p. 55.

68. Kolko, *Main Currents*, p. 305.

69. New Jersey State Chamber of Commerce, "State Police Problem," p. 2.

70. Kolko, *Main Currents*, p. 279.

# Chapter 5

# State Police Development in Illinois, 1917–1929

The purpose of this chapter is to describe the historical events involved in the attempts to create a state police force in Illinois. The focus of the discussion is on identifying the various individuals and organizations involved in the process and locating them in relationship to each other. Specific analysis of these facts, with an eye toward explaining the process, is presented in Chapter 6.

The first attempt to develop a state police in Illinois took place in 1917 with the introduction of two bills to the 50th General Assembly. Both bills died quietly, failing to generate much legislative or public support. But beginning in 1919, and lasting for the following ten years, state police legislation was introduced or proposed in every legislative session. The central figure in this process was Senator Henry M. Dunlap. A veteran of the legislature (having been elected for his first term in 1892), Dunlap was a wealthy fruit farmer from Savoy in central Illinois. Between 1919 and 1929, Dunlap served as the primary sponsor and advocate of state police legislation, and for this reason his name eventually became synonymous with the state police issue in Illinois. However, the efforts of Dunlap and others proved ineffective as none of their bills were successfully passed in the legislature. Primary opposition came from organized labor, particularly the Illinois State Federation of Labor, which at the time was under the control of John H. Walker, its president. With the help of Governor Len Small and prolabor legislators, Walker was able to prevent the passage of state police legislation.

Nonetheless, the Illinois legislature did manage to create two state-controlled law enforcement agencies. In 1921 a bill was passed authorizing the secretary of state to appoint a small force of "inspectors" to investigate violations of the motor vehicle act. During the same session, a second bill was passed modifying this act. The second measure authorized the Department of Public Works and Buildings to appoint "state highway patrol officers." Both bills quietly moved through the legislature, generating little media interest and virtually no opposition. During the 1923 legislative session, the "highway patrol" bill was amended to create the "Illinois highway maintenance police," a force of 100 officers intended to enforce motor vehicle laws and the weight restrictions for trucks. Dunlap and other advocates of a "state police" considered the "inspectors" and "maintenance police" nothing more than patronage forces, totally inadequate for providing rural police protection. They continued their fight for a strong state police system.

The maintenance police, which had been established in 1923, proved to be the forerunner of the present-day Illinois state police. While Dunlap was failing to gain support for his state police system, the maintenance police were gradually increased in size and eventually gained more police powers. In fact, the existence of the maintenance police proved to be a major obstacle to Dunlap's efforts to establish a state police in Illinois, since modification of the existing force could be used to undermine support for his bills. While the attempt to establish a Pennsylvania-type state police in Illinois was a failure, the analysis of this failure is crucial to an understanding of the complexities involved in the politics of police reform.

## THE FIRST ATTEMPT, 1917

Efforts to create a state police force in Illinois began in 1917 when the first bills relating to a department of state police were introduced in the Illinois General Assembly. In the House, the measure (HB no. 715) was sponsored by Representative Edwin Perkins of Lincoln, while an identical bill (SB no. 407) was introduced in the Senate by Judge John D. Turnbaugh of Mt. Carroll.[1]

As proposed, the state police department was to be managed by a board of four commissioners appointed by the governor with approval of the Senate. A majority vote of the commissioners elected a superintendent who would direct the activities of the state police force. Upon recommendation of the superintendent, the commission initially appointed ten deputies as permanent state police officers. Additional deputies could be appointed; however, their number could not exceed twenty. The superintendent and deputies were to investigate and prosecute all criminal matters. To carry out these duties, the state police were to be granted the same powers as sheriffs, which would result in the police having jurisdiction anywhere in the state.[2] Surprisingly, unlike the situation in other states which were also involved in creating state police at this time, introduction of the state police bills generated little interest among the legislators, the press, or the general public. After having been in committee for over a month, both bills died without further legislative action.[3]

Although the first attempt at creating a state police in Illinois had failed, those interested in supporting such a plan realized that future efforts would have to be better organized, especially in the area of increasing awareness among the general public regarding the "benefits" and "necessity" of a state police.

## LABOR'S VICTORY, 1919

Shortly after the General Assembly convened in January 1919, measures to create a state police were again introduced in the legislature. In the House, Howard Castle, a Republican lawyer from Barrington, introduced a bill (HB no. 38) to create a "department of state police." A similar but different measure (SB no. 43) was introduced in the Senate by Henry M. Dunlap.[4]

Castle's bill was prepared under the guidance of the War Veterans Alliance of America. Noting the "wisdom" shown by the Pennsylvania state police in recruiting most of its members from the army, the veterans' proposal stressed high salaries and called for a total force of 1,440 men.[5] Although the alliance publicly argued that a state police was necessary to provide protection for the people of Illinois, it was clear from the size of the proposed state police that the alliance was also interested in providing employment for veterans returning from World War I. When Castle introduced the bill, however, the size had been reduced to a maximum of 320 men who were to be under the direction of a superintendent appointed by the governor. The superintendent and the men were given the power to arrest, without warrant, anyone committing or attempting to commit any breach of the peace in their presence. Further powers included the ability to serve arrest or search warrants, prevent and detect crime, apprehend criminals, and cooperate with any other state departments or local authorities. The only restriction was that the state police could not be used in any city or village to suppress rioting or disorder without approval from the governor.[6]

Dunlap's Senate bill was more comprehensive and less restrictive. The superintendent had more authority to determine rules and regulations, the size of the force was made flexible—ranging from three to seven troops of sixty-five men each, and the state police were given additional powers to arrest, without warrant, anyone the state police had "reasonable cause to believe has committed a criminal offense." The force could be summoned by the following officials: the governor, the attorney general, mayors of all cities, chiefs of police, constables, sheriffs, and state's attorneys of all counties. No restrictions were placed on the state police, which meant they could operate in cities or villages without prior approval.[7]

Immediately upon introduction of the state police bills in the General Assembly, Illinois labor organizations began voicing their opposition. At a labor conference in Chicago, the secretary of the Chicago Federation of Labor, Edward Knockels, opened the attack by declaring that "if the scoundrels behind this hellish bill" manage to get it passed they would "find themselves in the hottest fight they ever had." Another spokesman for Illinois labor at the conference, Duncan McDonald, threatened to call a general strike that would "tie up every industry in the state" if the bill passed. Not wishing to have repeated in Illinois "the shame of Pennsylvania," Illinois labor leaders went on record as opposing any form of a state constabulary.[8]

The main fight against the state police issue was carried on by the Illinois State Federation of Labor, then under the leadership of President John H. Walker and Secretary-Treasurer Victor A. Olander. In a signed statement sent to all local unions affiliated or unaffiliated with the state federation, Walker charged that

> No more deadly menace to American institutions has ever crept into our government than the so-called "constabularies" that have been created in several states where the corporation interests dominate and control. They are really armed government strike-breakers, kept for the purpose of crushing the workers into submission, preventing their organizing or improving their wages, hours, conditions, or treatment, against the wishes of the despotic interests.[9]

Indicating that such a constabulary measure was now before the Illinois legislature, Walker urged Illinois workers to contact immediately the congressmen from their respective district, the governor, and the lieutenant governor and demand the withdrawal or defeat of the Dunlap-Castle state police bills.

Walker's plea was effective. During the months of February and March letters protesting against passage of the state police bills poured into the legislature. All elements of Illinois labor were represented in the protests; the United Mine Workers, the American Federation of Labor

(AFL), building trades, plumbers, painters, and electrical and railroad workers all came out against the state police.[10] In addition, labor put direct pressure on Dunlap himself. The Twin City Federation of Labor, representing labor in Dunlap's home county, wrote him a letter in which they stated their opposition to a state constabulary, arguing that a state police would

> serve the people no good, will place an added burden on them in the form of taxes, [and] is a dangerous weapon in the hands of employers endeavoring to breed strife between them and the workers. Workers are already deprived of their civil rights by injunctions and to force a barbaric state police on them is more than we can stand.[11]

They closed their letter by requesting that Dunlap withdraw his bill and work against future measures of this type.

In a lengthy reply, Dunlap charged that labor was "mistaken" and "unduly alarmed" over a bill that was intended for the purpose of "protecting the people" in rural communities from criminals of all kinds and for the "better enforcement" of all laws. He argued that while the cities had their police, the rural communities were "helpless" because the local authorities feared retaliation from the "bootlegger, the tough, and the gambler." In addition, he stated that gangs of auto thieves came from the cities to rob country stores and banks and were able to get away because there was no cooperation between the police of different cities. Dunlap refuted the charge that the state police were "barbaric" by claiming that the Pennsylvania state police had been called on by the miners and other working men to protect them from intimidation by the Industrial Workers of the World. He referred to Katherine Mayo's book *Justice to All* as the authority on this issue. Finally, he ended his reply by quoting from Theodore Roosevelt and Major General Leonard Wood, who both strongly endorsed the creation of state police forces.[12]

On February 26, the supporters and opponents of the state police confronted one another at a hearing on Dunlap's bill before the full Senate. W. W. Carroll, representing the Brotherhood of Railway Conductors, argued that Illinois had been fortunate in avoiding industrial trouble during the war and that organized labor wanted to keep it that way. Labor, he said, saw the state police bill as a "direct intimidation measure."[13] G. T. Putell, speaking for the Brotherhood of Firemen and Engineers, voiced opposition simply on the grounds that the state police could be used during industrial disturbances. Claiming that present laws had been sufficient in the past to deal with those who commit crimes during strikes, Putell argued that state police were unnecessary.[14]

Representing the Illinois State Federation of Labor, John Walker argued that the state police were just another example of the "science of camouflage" by which antilabor measures were made to appear as though they were intended to serve the common good. Walker opened his remarks with the following statement:

> The average worker feels that no matter by what name you call it and no matter what purpose you may advocate for its adoption it is nothing else and won't be used for anything else but as a strike breaking agency. . . . We know that the same arguments have been made for every constabulary bill that ever was advocated . . . the same arguments were used in its creation and the same defect came from it after it was enacted. It was used as a brutal strike breaking agency, and an agency of repression, and we feel that is exactly what it will be used for here.[15]

Stressing the importance of local control over law enforcement, Walker took the position that towns and cities could take care of their affairs through existing police agencies and through the courts of justice, thus eliminating the need for a state police.[16] The last person to speak against the state police was John L. Lewis of the United Mine Workers. Lewis gave in-depth testimony of the repressive antistrike activity of the Pennsylvania state police. He cited incidents of antilabor activity as reasons why labor organizations in Illinois and other states opposed the formation of state police forces.[17]

Anticipating labor opposition, Dunlap and Castle had written to Major John C. Groome, superintendent of the Pennsylvania state police, requesting that he come to the hearing (all expenses paid) and explain the advantages and operation of the state police.[18] Groome was unable to appear and Deputy Commissioner L. S. Pitcher was sent in his place. Pitcher told of the operation of the state police in Pennsylvania, denying charges that the constabulary had been brutal in breaking strikes in the eastern Pennsylvania coal fields. Senator Harold Kessinger of Aurora and Representative Michael Igoe of Chicago vigorously questioned Pitcher on the issues of protection for farmers, the amount of protection that could be provided by such a small force in a large state such as Pennsylvania, and the cost to the state of operating such a police force.[19]

The last person to testify at the hearings in favor of the state police was Charles Peters, the sheriff of Cook County. Peters claimed that county authorities were without real power and lacked the manpower and finances to do their work properly. Because of these handicaps, he felt a state police force would greatly improve police protection in the rural areas.[20] Although the hearing lasted for over three hours, no final decision was reached on Dunlap's bill.

The state police bills were also being debated outside the General Assembly. The state's largest and most influential newspaper, the *Chicago Tribune*, published numerous editorials arguing for the necessity of a state police. In promoting the state police, the *Tribune* editorials consistently stressed four basic themes. First, a state police force would be efficient. This point was supported by statements indicating the high number of arrests and convictions obtained by the Pennsylvania state police. Second, the mere presence of a state police, not subject to local influences, would act as a deterrent to potential criminals and hoodlums. Third, the inadequacy of existing rural police protection was illustrated by noting their lack of training and qualifications and the part-time status of their work. Fourth, the state police would provide security for isolated areas now vulnerable to "swift invasion" by criminals from the cities who used high-speed automobiles.[21]

*Tribune* editorials also attempted to refute opposing arguments, particularly those of labor groups. Editors argued that the provision requiring approval by the governor before the state police could be used during industrial disturbances was sufficient protection to alleviate labor's fears concerning possible strike-breaking activity by a state police force. Furthermore, the editorials repeated the claim that the Pennsylvania state police had been used less than 1 percent of the time on strike duty. For those who opposed the state police on the grounds that it was too expensive, the editorials pointed to the small size of the proposed force but quickly added that the small size would not impair effectiveness, as smaller forces had been efficient in both Pennsylvania and Texas.[22]

Additional public support for the state police came from the Illinois Bankers' Association, the Illinois Chamber of Commerce, the Chicago Association of Commerce, the Chicago motor clubs, and civic and business groups across the state. The Illinois Agricultural Association and its member county farm bureaus also endorsed the state police. The bureaus, claiming to represent the views of Illinois farmers, argued that the automobile had brought lawlessness into the unprotected countryside; therefore, a state police force was necessary to bring security to the rural districts.[23]

In the General Assembly, labor supporters and other opponents of the state police were working to defeat the Dunlap-Castle bills. On April 17, Senator Harold Kessinger attempted to have Dunlap's bill referred to a joint session of the Committee on Revenue and Finance. In response to this ploy, Dunlap charged that Kessinger's maneuver was designed to defeat the bill by unfair tactics; Dunlap was successful in having Kessinger's motion defeated. However, the vote on the motion was not strong, and it raised doubt among the supporters of Dunlap's bill as to the final passage of the measure.[24]

On May 13, final discussion was heard on Dunlap's state police bill. The floor debate began in the morning and continued until late in the afternoon. Leading the discussion of his bill, Dunlap charged that the present system of law enforcement was insufficient because of the lack of cooperation between city and county officials. Because the state police would not have this problem, he claimed, it would be "impossible for a criminal to escape." Arguing that his bill was a "law enforcement measure" and that farmers were demanding rural police protection, Dunlap claimed that only organized labor opposed the state police. Supporting this argument was Senator Rodney Swift of Lake Forest. Being "a farmer himself," Swift "knew" the "fear and trembling" of leaving his wife and children alone with no protection. Stating that a state police would deter rural crime by instilling "fear in the hearts of criminals," Swift favored the bill to provide the "defenseless" farmers of Illinois the "right" of police protection.[25]

Despite the arguments by Dunlap and Swift, a number of senators raised strong opposition to the measure. John Dailey of Peoria asserted that the bill was in reality a "military police" measure and feared that its passage would eventually lead to a national or international military police system. Richard Barr, a former mayor of Joliet, charged that Dunlap had, with the use of propaganda, attempted to pass a measure that nobody wanted. Claiming that Dunlap's bill did not reflect the feelings of rural residents, Barr argued that the state police represented "an autocratic form of government" that had no place in a democratic society. Defending the "sacred right" of local police power, Harold Kessinger was opposed to a state police that would be directed from the capital. He denied Dunlap's claims that the state police would be efficient, arguing instead that the existing law was more efficient, given that it permitted counties to appoint as many deputy sheriffs as needed. Echoing these sentiments was Charles Wood, a farmer and minister from southern Illinois, who resented the insinuations cast on sheriffs and constables concerning their abilities to control rural crime. Wood argued that the proper solution was to pay better wages to the present local law enforcement officials.[26]

In an attempt to appease labor opposition, Dunlap offered an amendment which provided that in cases of industrial strikes, the state police could not enter a community except by order of the governor or upon request of the sheriff with approval from the governor. The ploy failed. When Dunlap's bill was brought to a vote the result was a devastating defeat. Only sixteen senators voted in favor while thirty-one were opposed. The companion state police bill introduced in the House by Howard Castle died in committee and was never called for a vote. Organized labor, which had vigorously fought to defeat both bills, considered the final outcome a major victory.[27]

Although soundly defeated, state police proponents continued their efforts during the next five legislative sessions. During this ten-year period the cast of characters remained the same. Senator Dunlap, supported by the major business interests in the state, took the lead in pushing state police legislation. The strongest opposition continued to be John Walker and the Illinois State Federation of Labor. The outcome of each session also remained the same as each successive attempt at passage resulted in another defeat for the Dunlap state police bills. Nevertheless, each legislative session produced some interesting and noteworthy activity.

## THE HIGHWAY PATROL, 1921

Proponents of a state police in Illinois renewed their efforts in 1921. Governor Frank O. Lowden, in his final message to the legislature, argued that automobiles and improved roads had made depredation by criminals in the rural districts easier and concluded that the time had come when a rural police force was needed in Illinois. The governor urged the legislature to provide a force that would not only patrol the countryside, but that in addition would inspect roads and discover those persons who were using motor vehicles without a license, thereby bringing additional revenue into the state treasury. Five days later, however, newly elected Governor Small made no mention of a state police or highway patrol in his inaugural address to the General Assembly.[28]

As they had done in 1919, Senator Dunlap and Representative Castle introduced bills on February 9, 1921, to create the "department of Illinois state police."[29] However, unlike their "independent" efforts of 1919, Dunlap and Castle introduced identical bills in a coordinated effort. As introduced, the measures were identical to the Dunlap bill that had been defeated in 1919.[30]

Immediately upon introduction of the Dunlap-Castle bills, opponents and proponents began to prepare for the inevitable fight over the measures. Early polls indicated increased support among members of the Senate for the measure, although the attitude of the House was less assured.[31] Both sides had an opportunity to state their arguments on March 16, when both the House and Senate committees held hearings on the state police bills. Speaking against the bills were John Walker and Victor Olander of the Illinois State Federation of Labor. Arguments in support of the bills were made by C. W. Schuck, president of the Springfield Chamber of Commerce and chairman for the legislative committee of the Illinois Chamber of Commerce Association; S. H. Thompson of the legislative committee of the Illinois Agricultural Association; and M. A. Graettinger, secretary of the Illinois Bankers' Association. Graettinger presented figures concerning the increase in bank robberies in Illinois over the previous years. Claiming that local officials were incapable of dealing with the problem, Graettinger called for passage of the state police bills to provide protection for the property of the "depositors" and "stockholders."[32]

S. H. Thompson, representing the Illinois Agricultural Association, also spoke in favor of the state police. His testimony was immediately challenged by Representatives Charles Baker of Monroe Center and Lee O'Neil Browne of Ottawa. Both attacked Thompson's claim that farmers were strongly in favor of the state police. Baker, a farmer himself, stated that his county farm bureau had 1,600 members, but only 8 or 10 were present at the meeting when the resolution to support the state police was passed. If that were true of other bureaus, Baker charged, the farm bureau vote in favor of the state police was hardly significant. Lee O'Neil Browne indicated that a vote of the sixty LaSalle County supervisors, mostly rural residents, had unanimously condemned the state police.[33] The last person to speak in support of the state police was C. W. Schuck, representing the Illinois Chamber of Commerce. Schuck reported that a referendum vote among individual members had forty-nine chambers in favor of a state police, while only four were opposed. Three chambers had not voted, but Schuck was of the opinion that all three favored the state police bill.[34]

The majority of the time, however, was devoted to the testimony of the labor representatives, Walker and Olander, who opposed the state police. Walker spoke at length concerning labor's attitude toward the state police.

Every organization, state, general council, central body and local union . . . is opposed to it, and I want to say to you they are not opposed to it because of any opposition to enforcement of law and order in the state. They feel that this institution once created will mean the setting up of a military government.[35]

In the course of his remarks, Walker indicated that the farmers in Dunlap's own county had voted against the state police, and challenged the claim that the state police were intended to protect the farmers by demonstrating that with the maximum number of men allowed under Dunlap's bill it would require four officers to patrol 873 miles of highway every day. Walker also provided evidence indicating that the headquarters of the Pennsylvania state police were not located in the farming districts, but rather were in the coal fields.[36]

Walker was vigorously cross-examined by Representatives Castle and Charles W. LaPorte. LaPorte, a manufacturer from Peoria, was a strong supporter of the state police and questioned Walker on specific points of fact in what appeared to be an attempt to trick Walker into making statements that would undermine previous remarks. Walker did indicate under questioning, however, that he was not opposing "state police," but rather "military state police" which would supersede civil authorities. Also, Walker stated he had no objection to a police force that was intended to "enforce the law" and was "responsible to the will of the people."[37]

Victor Olander, on the other hand, was opposed to any form of state police. Although he was not opposed to police protection by which a community desires to maintain peace and prevent crime, he was strongly against any form of police "in which the citizens of that community have no control."[38] The remainder of Olander's testimony consisted of a critical section-by-section analysis of the state police bill and a denouncing of those who were spending large sums of money on propaganda to promote the state police.[39]

Outside of the legislature, debate on the state police issue was intensifying. As was the case in 1919, the *Chicago Tribune* was an aggressive proponent of the state police. From December 1920 through May 1921, the *Tribune* published over a dozen editorials and lead articles in support of the Dunlap-Castle state police bills.[40] Other newspapers across the state also put their support behind the state police. In addition to the standard arguments about inadequate protection for the rural districts, many of the local editorials included reports of recent bank robberies in which the robbers were able to get away by outdistancing local peace officers. This "proof" was used to illustrate the need for a mobile and efficient state police force.[41]

An interesting development centered around the Illinois Manufacturers' association. One of the strongest and most vocal proponents of state police, the association took a different position this time. At a meeting of the directors held in late January, the state police bills were discussed. Of special interest was Dunlap's modification which would prevent the proposed state police from entering any city or town for the purpose of policing a strike except by order of the governor. Mr. Llewellyn moved that John Glenn, secretary of the association, notify the associations represented in the Illinois Industrial Council "that the directors could not concur in the proposed amendment and that they favored the striking out of the provision entirely."[42]

Speaking before the Winnetka Men's Club, Glenn attacked the state police bill as a "goldbrick," arguing that the limits placed on the jurisdiction of the police made the force "a tool for privileged classes." Glenn charged that passing a law beneficial to only some of the people of Illinois would be "contrary to every principle of liberty" and that the limitation placed on the police was the result of politics. Glenn even went so far as to suggest that should the bill pass in its present form, Illinois manufacturers should move their plants "to Pennsylvania or some other state where they can get a square deal."[43]

Such action by the Manufacturers' Association created an embarrassing situation for sponsors of the state police. Dunlap and Castle, as well as the major newspapers, had made a special point to argue that the state police would not be a strike-breaking force as was being charged by labor. The position of the manufacturers, however, gave credibility to labor's claim, a point angrily made clear in a *Tribune* editorial attacking the manufacturers' opposition.

> The manufacturers who want a body of men to use in labor controversy will kill this needed bill. . . . to object to it is to say that the object is the creation of a special body of men to handle labor troubles. That is particularly stupid. It is setting up the ideas and desires of a small class against the good of the entire state. . . . Employers who try to get a Cossack bill should be sat upon.[44]

Obviously enjoying dissension among proponents of the state police, labor nevertheless intensified its fight to kill the Dunlap-Castle bills. John Walker and Victor Olander took every opportunity to speak against the state police before civic and social organizations. Labor also stated its position through articles and editorials in various labor publications such as the *Twin City Review* and the *Illinois State Federation of Labor Weekly Newsletter*. Labor leaders charged that claims that farmers favored a state police designed to patrol the rural districts were a "smoke screen" to cover the "real" purposes of the state police—the creation of a "military police" to be used against labor in strike situations. Walker argued that the state police were being promoted by the "big predatory corporations and financial interests" as a "strike-breaking adjunct" to the court injunctions against strikes in a concerted effort to "devitalize the trade union movement."[45]

Senator Dunlap had deferred final action on his bill for almost two months. In part, the delay was because of the addition of a minor amendment, but primarily it occurred because Dunlap was waiting for a time when all those who favored the bill would be present for the vote.[46] Finally, on May 24, Dunlap called his bill for a vote. However,

John Dailey moved that consideration of Dunlap's bill be postponed until action was taken on the Castle bill in the House. The vote to postpone further action on the Dunlap bill subsequently passed 27 to 21.[47] Following the Senate action, the House Committee on Efficiency and Economy voted 10 to 8 to recommend that the Castle police bill should not pass. On June 1 the House voted to sustain the committee report, and Castle's bill died on the House floor without further action.[48] Dunlap, however, had not given up on his police bill. The House action killing the Castle bill freed Dunlap's measure for further consideration, and on June 7 it was called for a final vote. The bill was again defeated, by a vote of 24 to 21, two votes short of the necessary constitutional majority for passage.[49] Labor and other opponents of the state police were once more able to prevent passage of a measure backed by the most powerful interests in the state.

The second defeat of the Dunlap-Castle state police bills was only part of the legislative story in 1921. Without much publicity or discussion, two bills of significance did pass the legislature and become law. On February 9, 1921, James A. Watson of Elizabethtown introduced a bill in the House (HB no. 115) to amend the motor vehicle act of 1919. The major portion of the bill pertained to regulations concerning the manufacture and sale of automobiles within the state of Illinois. However, in the last paragraph of the bill, the secretary of state was given authority to appoint, without regard to civil service requirement, a number of "inspectors." These men were intended to investigate and report violations of the motor vehicle act, and were also given the power to arrest without warrant anywhere in the state.[50]

The Watson bill quickly moved through the legislature. On April 28, the Senate gave it overwhelming approval as only one senator, Frank P. Sadler from Chicago, voted against the bill.[51] Governor Small signed the Watson bill on May 28, giving the Secretary of State sole charge of enforcing the state automobile laws. This measure received no attention from the press and failed to generate any excitement in the General Assembly. One small newspaper notice about the bill's approval by the governor was the only media publicity it received.[52]

In addition to the Watson bill, a second measure designed to amend the motor vehicle act was introduced in the House. On May 18, Representative Homer Tice of Greenview submitted a bill (HB no. 817) to the House regulating weight of motor vehicles and length of trailers and outlawing metal-wheeled vehicles from the roads. It seems the intention was to prevent damage to the new, paved highways that were being built throughout the state. But Tice's bill added a section to the motor vehicle act that authorized the Department of Public Works and Buildings to appoint "a significant number of State Highway Patrol Officers."[53] On June 9, the Tice highway patrol bill came to a vote in the House. As with Watson's bill, the Tice measure was overwhelmingly approved, by a vote of 100 to 8.[54] In the Senate, the Tice bill moved quickly and quietly through the Judiciary Committee with only minor changes. The Senate adopted the committee recommendation that the bill pass. No further amendments were proposed during the second reading, and the bill was approved for a vote. On June 18 the Tice bill unanimously passed the Senate.[55] Illinois had inconspicuously established state-controlled law enforcement in the form of two small, loosely structured "highway patrols."

Given the intensity of the debate surrounding the Dunlap-Castle state police bills, the ease with which the highway patrol bills moved through the legislature is intriguing. No publicity surrounded their introduction and no public hearings were called. Both bills failed to generate debate or discussion. None of the groups or individuals pushing the Dunlap bills showed any interest, and labor, the most vociferous opponent of state police, raised no objections whatsoever. The fact that the bills were amendments to the motor vehicle act may have camouflaged their enforcement aspects.

## THE HIGHWAY MAINTENANCE POLICE , 1923

In 1923, supporters of the state police began their drive for passage of the Dunlap police bill on February 8, at the annual banquet of the Peoria Manufacturers and Merchants Association. Among the three hundred who attended were John Glenn (secretary of the Illinois Manufacturers' Association), Lieutenant Governor Fred E. Sterling, fifteen members of the state legislature, representatives of the Illinois Industrial Council, and various women's clubs. The main attraction, however, was a speech by Captain George P. Dutton, deputy superintendent of the New York state police. Efficiency, effectiveness, and enthusiastic public support were the key elements in Dutton's talk concerning the operation of his department. Believing that chances for creating a state police were never as good, state police advocates freely predicted its passage, proclaiming that Illinois farmers had "awakened" to the need of a state police and were beginning to demand police protection. The lieutenant governor entered a note of caution into the proceedings, however, indicating that while there was obviously a growing sentiment for a state police in Illinois, he could not indicate how the bill would fare in the General Assembly.[56]

As in the past, Senator Dunlap was the sponsor of the state police bill. In an effort to maximize its chances of passing, it was to be introduced only in the Senate. This move was the result of opposition tactics of playing the previous bills against one another, as well as the belief that the Senate was more favorable to the state police than the House was.[57] The bill was identical to the one Dunlap had introduced in previous sessions, with one significant exception—the clause which prevented the use of state police during strikes had been removed.[58]

On February 20, the Senate Committee on Military Affairs held a hearing on the Dunlap police bill. Senator Dunlap opened the debate by stating that state police were necessary due to the inadequacy of rural law enforcement and the fact that "more highways" were creating "more lawbreakers." Primary opposition came from organized labor, which was represented by John Walker, Victor Olander, and William Collins, an organizer for the AFL from New York. In addition, Representative John W. McCarthy, a lawyer from Lemont, spoke against the bill. Those speaking in behalf of the measure included E. C. Heidrich, president of the Illinois Manufacturers' Association; Royal M. Allen, representative of the Chicago Motor Club; Major E. E. Crabtree, President of the Illinois Bankers' Association; C. W. Olson, operator of a stock insurance company in Chicago; and E. P. Imboden, a farmer from Decatur representing the farm bureaus.[59]

The most interesting development of the hearing surrounded the appearance of Charles H. Dayton. Appearing in uniform, Dayton claimed to be a captain on leave of absence from the Colorado Rangers who was speaking throughout the state on behalf of the state police bill. In explaining activities of the force in Colorado, he stated that "65 percent of the crimes were committed by aliens, of which 45 percent were foreign born."[60] Anticipating Dayton's appearance at the hearing, John Walker had wired John E. Gross, secretary of the Colorado Federation of Labor, and Senator J. Frank Coss of the Colorado legislature requesting information concerning Dayton's credentials.[61] In response, both Coss and Gross indicated that the Colorado Rangers were no longer in operation, having been disbanded by the governor earlier that month. Gross further reported that Dayton had never been a captain in the rangers. Rather, he had served at the rank of private doing investigative work during strikes, was alleged to be crooked by former rangers, and was now a professional lobbyist for state police laws.[62] Walker brought this information to the attention of the committee, but Dayton denied the charges and claimed the telegrams sent to Walker were false.[63] In point of fact, the Colorado Rangers *had* been disbanded on February 1 by Governor William E. Sweet. (See Chapter 7 for a discussion of the Colorado Rangers.)

Confident that he could get Senate approval of his bill, Dunlap delayed calling a vote for several weeks, waiting until all those who were friendly to the bill were present. But before he could get a vote, a new complication confronted the senator. On April 10, Senator Richard Meents, a banker from Ashkum, introduced a bill (SB no. 311) to create a "state road maintenance police." Under the provisions of this bill the director of the Department of Public Works and Buildings was authorized to appoint one maintenance policeman for each twenty miles of state highway. The maintenance police were given statewide powers identical to those possessed by city police to enforce the provisions of the motor vehicle act.[64] The *Chicago Tribune*, portraying Meents as a political crony of Governor Small, charged that the introduction of the maintenance police bill was in anticipation of the failure of the Dunlap bill. Noting that the Meents proposal would give the governor an initial force of 200 men, the *Tribune* lamented the introduction of politics into the state police issue and argued that "Dunlap's bill is the real measure and should not be put aside in the interest of Governor Small."[65]

On April 25, Dunlap called his bill for final passage. Debate on the measure lasted over five hours before the vote was taken. Dunlap opened the discussion by announcing that he would not be a candidate for reelection and that he hoped the bill would become law to serve as the "crowning achievement" to his legislative career. Indicating that one-third of all the bank robberies in the United States occurred in Illinois, Dunlap charged that "the country communities are helpless" and that "country banks want and demand protection."[66]

Unmoved by Dunlap's passionate appeal, opponents of the bill spent most of the time denouncing the measure. Senator William S. Jewell of Lewistown, a former constable, asserted that the bill did not represent the popular demand of the people, and deplored the amount of money that had been spent to influence Senate votes. Charging that any bill possessing merit did not require such excessive lobbying, Jewell argued that the proposed state police would cost a half-million dollars a year, and strictly opposed the creation of an additional state department.[67] In explaining his opposition to the bill, Senator Earl B. Searcy of Springfield stated that the expense of a state police would place an excessive burden on the taxpayers. Senator Richard Barr of Joliet claimed that the bill "was sailing under false pretenses" and was intended not as protection for the farmer but was rather to be used in industrial difficulties.[68] Defending his connection with organized labor, Senator W. J. Sneed, a miner from Herrin, strongly denounced the bill.[69] Finally, Senator E. D. Telford of Salem claimed that creation of a state police was not favored by his constituents and charged that the Dunlap bill was "vicious," resembling the policies of "continental Europe, where military oppression reigns." Telford then proceeded to introduce a motion to postpone further consideration of the bill until June 30. The motion, however, was defeated.[70]

Upon close of the debate, a vote was taken on the Dunlap state police bill. The measure was defeated by three votes.[71] In an editorial, the *Tribune* held organized labor responsible for the defeat of the state police bill. Believing that labor opposition was based on a misunderstanding which would eventually be cleared up, the *Tribune* predicted the eventual creation of a state police in Illinois.[72] A quite different assessment, however, was to be found in an editorial from the *Illinois State Journal* of Springfield. The *Journal* believed the arguments against the state police bill were of little influence when compared to the fact that state police "meant a further centralization in state government of powers which the people have been used to considering their own." The *Journal* called on those in the General Assembly to continue opposing measures designed to surrender the authority of local governments to the state.[73]

With defeat of the Dunlap state police bill, attention turned to the bill introduced earlier by Senator Meents. Denying that his bill was a substitute for the Dunlap measure, Meents claimed that the maintenance police were intended to provide protection along paved highways and to inspect both the roads and trucks to prevent violation of the highway laws. The senator's arguments aside, no action was taken on the maintenance police measure until after Dunlap's bill had been defeated.[74]

On May 16, the maintenance police bill was reported out of committee with amendments and a recommendation that the bill pass. The committee version of the bill eliminated the section restricting the size of the force to one officer per twenty miles of highway. With this clause removed, the director of the Department of Public Works and Buildings could appoint as many men as he thought necessary. When the bill was taken up in the Senate, however, it was further amended. Defeated in his attempt to gain approval of his police bill, Dunlap took this opportunity to expand the powers and authority of the maintenance police by amending the bill to allow the police to enforce all state laws rather than simply the motor vehicle act. In addition, believing that the Meents bill was designed to give Governor Small a patronage army, Dunlap also changed the bill to restrict the size of the force to no more than 125 persons.[75]

Senator Meents called for a vote and his bill overwhelmingly passed with fifteen of those who had opposed the Dunlap state police bill voting for the maintenance police. The two negative votes present an interesting contrast. Senator John J. Boehm of Chicago, a staunch labor advocate and opponent of the state police, joined with Senator Dunlap to vote against the maintenance police measure.[76] When the bill was then sent to the House, where antistate police sentiment was strong, it was amended to reduce the size of the force to 100 men. An additional House amendment required that those appointed must meet the physical and mental qualifications for enlistment in the United States Army. The amended version passed easily and was returned to the Senate, where all senators present, including Dunlap, voted unanimously to accept the House version of the bill.[77]

Illinois had finally created a state police force, although its structure was not what the proponents of a military-like state police had in mind. Restricted to enforcing motor vehicle laws and checking for overweight trucks, the new maintenance police were far more limited in scope and authority than the force proposed by Dunlap's legislation. For this reason the fight for a "real" state police would last another five years.

## THE STATE POLICE BATTLE CONTINUES, 1925–1929

The creation of the highway maintenance police had finally given Illinois a statewide and state-controlled law enforcement agency. But proponents of a "real" state police remained dissatisfied and renewed their efforts in 1925. As in previous efforts, the same cast of characters was involved. The bill was introduced by Senator Dunlap and supported by the Illinois Manufacturers' Association, the Illinois Bankers' Association, the Illinois Chamber of Commerce, and the Farm Bureau. Again, primary opposition came from organized labor, represented by John Walker.

Although initially optimistic, state police proponents again encountered a major obstacle in the form of an alternative police bill. Senator Richard Barr introduced a bill (SB no. 250), endorsed by Governor Small, to amend the existing highway patrol law by removing the limitation restricting the force to a maximum of 100 officers. Barr, president pro tem of the Senate, was able to have the bill referred to the Committee on Roads, which was being chaired by Senator William Jewell, another staunch supporter of the governor.[78] Backers of the Dunlap bill charged that the Barr measure was a "smoke screen" intended as a political ploy to weaken support for the Dunlap state police measure. The *Chicago Evening Post* called the Barr bill a "vicious, political measure" designed to give Governor Small an opportunity to make hundreds of political appointments by creating a statewide patronage army. The Barr bill, backed by the administration and half-heartedly endorsed by the *Tribune* as being better than no state police, moved quickly through committee and was recommended for passage.[79]

The Dunlap bill was not so fortunate. After representatives of the Illinois Chamber of Commerce, the Illinois Bankers' Association, and the Illinois Agricultural Association had argued for the bill and John Walker had denounced it, the Committee on Military Affairs refused to give the bill a favorable recommendation.[80] Although his bill had been sidetracked, Dunlap continued the fight for a state police. During the all-day session on the Barr bill, Dunlap attempted to substitute portions of his bill for sections of Barr's measure. After this move failed, Senator Rodney Swift offered the complete Dunlap bill as a substitute. While this move also proved to be unsuccessful, a number of amendments were approved. The number of men to be appointed was limited to 750, and the force was given the power to enforce all laws. With these amendments, the Barr bill easily passed the Senate by a vote of 34 to 9.[81]

Taking only three weeks to move through the Senate, the Barr bill came to an abrupt halt upon being sent to the House. Robert Scholes, Speaker of the House (and a supporter of Governor Small), referred the Barr bill to the Committee on Public Utilities, which was being chaired by Reubin G. Soderstrom of Streator. Soderstrom (also a Small supporter) was one of the most outspoken sponsors of organized labor in the General Assembly. Once in Soderstrom's committee, the Barr bill sat without consideration for over a month.[82] Angered at the inaction on the Barr measure, Dunlap revived his original bill and attached a referendum clause, thus submitting the state police issue to a vote of the people should the bill be approved. Brought to a vote, the Dunlap bill was on its way to another defeat when Senator Kessinger moved to postpone further consideration. Ten days later, a second vote was taken and this time the Dunlap state police bill passed the Senate by 28 to 8.[83]

Faced with the successful passage of the Dunlap police bill in the Senate, opponents of the measure renewed their efforts in the House. Governor Small, after conferring with John Walker and other labor leaders, notified Speaker Scholes and floor leader Reed F. Cutler of Lewistown to kill the Dunlap bill. Plans were made to send Dunlap's bill to the Committee on Public Utilities, where chairman Soderstrom could be trusted to sit on it for the remaining two weeks of the session. However, Representative Charles LaPorte, a state police supporter and an opponent of organized labor, attempted to undermine the plan by having the Dunlap bill taken out of its regular order and advanced for final passage. Representative Lee O'Neil Browne moved to table LaPorte's motion and demanded a roll call vote. Browne's motion passed 88 to 50, thus preventing consideration of the Dunlap bill. An hour later, Representative Arthur J. Rutshaw of Chicago successfully moved that all Senate bills on order of second reading be stricken from the calendar, in effect killing the Dunlap state police bill.[84]

Optimistic after their partial success in 1925, state police proponents continued the fight in 1927. But after two months without any action, Dunlap suddenly withdrew his bill from the Senate calendar. Aware of labor's influence in the General Assembly (particularly in the House) and Governor Small's expected veto should the bill pass, Dunlap decided to forgo the fight this time.[85]

In 1929 proponents for a state police renewed the fight with heightened optimism. Governor Small, politically allied with labor and opposed to the state police, had been defeated by Louis Emmerson, an avowed advocate of improved law enforcement. In his inaugural address Emmerson stressed the "need for new legislation to strengthen the hands of law enforcement officials" and called for the creation of a statewide force which would be larger and more efficient than the existing "inadequate highway patrol system."[86]

Senator Dunlap once again introduced his state police bill. Having learned from past defeats, he took special precautions to reduce potential opposition. Rather than a state police bill, Dunlap introduced a measure to amend the Civil Administration Code of Illinois by creating a new department under the governor—the Department of Public Safety. The new department would take over all of the duties of the present state highway patrol and would be given full police power to enforce all criminal laws. Cognizant of labor's past objections, Dunlap stipulated that the force would not be allowed to operate in cities with populations in excess of ten thousand except upon orders by the governor. In addition, members of the public safety department were to be placed under civil service to counter objections of political interference in state police activities.[87]

The public safety bill moved quickly through the Committee on Roads and Highway Transportation. Success relied, in part, on Dunlap's position as committee chair as well as his "failure" to notify labor representatives about the hearings, which prevented them from having the opportunity to voice objections.[88] But the initial optimism of those favoring state police was quickly dashed when Dunlap's public safety bill was soundly defeated. The margin of defeat was the worst Dunlap had suffered in his attempts to pass a state police bill, and even the opposition was surprised by the outcome. After the defeat Dunlap told the Senate that it was evident that he was not the one to get a state police for Illinois because attaching his name to such legislation was tantamount to "waving a red flag at a bull."[89]

Failure of the public safety bill was a function not of Dunlap's sponsorship but of a lack of administrative support. Governor Emmerson had favored two bills that amended the highway patrol act of 1923 by providing for an increase in the number of officers from 100 to 300. Organized labor did not enthusiastically support these bills, but they made no concerted effort to fight them as they had the Dunlap bills.[90] This pattern continued throughout the 1930s as attempts at developing the state police in Illinois consisted of amending existing law by increasing the size of the highway patrol and granting it greater powers of arrest and jurisdiction.

## SUMMARY

Beginning in 1917, eight successive attempts were made to create a paramilitary state police force in Illinois—and all failed. Although the legislatures of 1921 and 1923 did establish "highway patrol" forces, these were small organizations restricted to enforcing traffic and highway maintenance laws. These forces were quite unlike the powerful state police forces of Pennsylvania, New York, or Michigan sought by Dunlap in his legislation. Given the strength and influence of various groups such as the Chicago and Illinois Chambers of Commerce, the Illinois Bankers' Association, the Illinois Farm Bureau, and the powerful Illinois Manufacturers' Association—all supporting the drive for a state police—the failure to enact such legislation is surprising.

To understand fully the failure of state police legislation in Illinois, one must take into consideration such factors as the political strength of organized labor, the impact of ethnic divisions within the political establishment, the debate between "wets" and "drys" over prohibition, the relationship between downstate and Chicago, as well as the complicated political arrangements in both the city of Chicago and Cook County in general. These and other important factors will be discussed in Chapter 6 in an attempt to provide some analysis and interpretation of the facts presented in this chapter on efforts to establish a state police in Illinois.

## NOTES

1. *Journal of the House*, 50th sess., 1917, p. 429; *Journal of the Senate*, 50th sess., 1917, p. 519.

2. *Illinois State Journal*, March 23, 1917, p. 11; Senate Bill no. 407, 50th sess., 1917; House Bill no. 715, 50th sess., 1917.

3. *Journal of the House*, 50th sess., 1917, p. 584; *Journal of the Senate*, 50th sess., 1917, p. 519.

4. *Journal of the House*, 51st sess., 1919, p. 47; *Journal of the Senate*, 51st sess., 1919, p. 298.

5. *Chicago Tribune*, January 18, 1919; Copy of bill (no number or date), John Fitzpatrick Papers, box 8, folder 59, Chicago Historical Society, Chicago.

6. House Bill no. 38, 51st sess., 1919.

7. Senate Bill no. 43, 51st sess., 1919.

8. *Chicago Tribune*, February 11, 1919, p. 16.

9. *Illinois State Journal*, February 14, 1919, p. 18.

10. *Journal of the Senate*, 51st sess., 1919, pp. 397, 417, 463, 480, 495, 525, 570.

11. *Champaign Daily-News*, February 26, 1919.

12. Ibid.

13. Senate Debates, February 26, 1919, pp. 157–158. Copy in Henry M. Dunlap Papers, box 3, file: State Police Bill 1919—Arguments and Debates, University of Illinois Archives, Champaign, Illinois (hereafter referred to as HMD).

14. Ibid., p. 158.

15. Ibid., p. 159.

16. Ibid.

17. Ibid., pp. 165–167.

18. H. M. Dunlap and H. P. Castle to J. C. Groome, February 12, 1919, HMD, box 2, file: D-G 1919.

19. Senate Debates, February 26, 1919, pp. 168–180.

20. Ibid., pp. 181–183.

21. See, for example, *Chicago Tribune*, February 1, 1919; April 9, 1919; April 20, 1919; May 8, 1919; and May 15, 1919.

22. *Chicago Tribune*, April 13, 1919, part 7 p. 4; April 23, 1919, p. 8.

23. *Illinois State Journal*, April 17, 1919, p. 3.

24. *Journal of the Senate*, 51st sess., 1919, pp. 705–706; *Illinois State Journal*, April 18, 1919, p. 4.

25. *Illinois State Journal*, May 14, 1919, p. 16.

26. Ibid.

27. *Journal of the Senate*, 51st sess., 1919, pp. 934–935; *Journal of the House*, 51st sess., 1919, p. 909; *Illinois State Journal*, May 14, 1919, p. 16.

28. *Journal of the House*, 52nd sess., 1921, pp. 30, 48–56.

29. *Journal of the Senate*, 52nd sess., 1921, p. 362; *Journal of the House*, 52nd sess., 1921, p. 103.

30. Senate Bill no. 55, 52nd sess., 1921; House Bill no. 116, 52nd sess., 1921.

31. *Chicago Tribune*, March 12, 1921, p. 3.

32. Stenographic Report of Hearing on House Bill #116, pp. 10–12, HMD, box 3, file: State Police Bill 1921 Legislative Hearings.

33. Ibid., pp. 16–21.

34. Ibid., p. 27.

35. Ibid., pp. 28–29.

36. Ibid., pp. 33–38.

37. Ibid., pp. 53–56.

38. Ibid., p. 79.

39. Ibid., pp. 80–105.

40. *Chicago Tribune*, December 17, 1920, p. 21; December 18, 1920, p. 15; December 19, 1920, p. 5; December 28, 1920, p. 6; January 6, 1921, p. 6; February 8, 1921, p. 8; March 13, 1921, part 2, p. 6; May 13, 1921, p. 8.

41. *The Peoria Star*, April 2, 1921; *The Peoria Journal*, April 16, 1921; *Urbana Courier*, December 5, 1920; and the numerous clippings in HMD, box 3, file: State Police Bill 1921 Support #4.

42. Illinois Manufacturers' Association, Minutes of directors' meetings, Book 2, January 25, 1921, p. 1628, Chicago Historical Society, Chicago.

43. "State Police Called Goldbrick," HMD, box 3, file: State Police Bill 1921 Support #4.

44. *Chicago Tribune*, February 8, 1921, p. 8.

45. *Illinois State Federation of Labor Weekly Newsletter* (ISFLN), February 12, 1921, p. 1; *Twin-City Review*, February 25, 1921, p. 1; *Illinois State Journal*, February 26, 1921, p.

3; *Springfield Register*, March 13, 1921, p. 1; "Illinois Labor Oppose Mounted Police Bill," HMD, box 3, file: State Police Bill 1921—Illinois Editorials and Articles.

46. *Chicago Tribune*, May 25, 1921, p. 6; *Illinois State Journal*, May 29, 1921, p. 1.

47. See note 46 above.

48. *Journal of the House*, 52nd sess., 1921, pp. 872–873; *Illinois State Journal*, May 26, 1921, p. 21.

49. *Journal of the Senate*, 52nd sess., 1921, pp. 1185–1186; *Illinois State Journal*, June 8, 1921, p. 1.

50. *Journal of the House*, 52nd sess., 1921, p. 103; House Bill no. 115, 52nd sess., 1921.

51. *Journal of the Senate*, 52nd sess., 1921, pp. 659, 749, 806, 840.

52. *Illinois State Journal*, May 29, 1921, p. 27.

53. *Journal of the House*, 52nd sess., 1921, p. 763; House Bill no. 817, 52nd sess., 1921.

54. *Journal of the House*, 52nd sess., 1921, p. 1077.

55. *Journal of the Senate*, 52nd sess., 1921, pp. 1314, 1350, 1360, 1399, 1565.

56. *Chicago Tribune*, February 9, 1923, p. 1.

57. *Chicago Tribune*, January 29, 1923, p. 9.

58. Senate Bill no. 49, 53rd sess., 1923; *Illinois State Journal*, February 1, 1923, p. 13.

59. *Illinois State Journal*, February 21, 1923, p. 16; *Chicago Tribune*, February 21, 1923, p. 12.

60. *Illinois State Journal*, February 21, 1923, p. 16.

61. J. H. Walker to J. E. Gross, February 19, 1923, John Hunter Walker Papers, box 15, file 141, item 47, Illinois Historical Survey, University of Illinois Library, Champaign, Illinois (hereafter referred to as JHW).

62. J. E. Gross to J. H. Walker, February 19, 1923, JHW, box 15, file 141, item 48; J. F. Coss to J. H. Walker, February 19, 1923, JHW, box 15, file 141, item 51.

63. *Illinois State Journal*, February 21, 1923, p. 16.

64. *Journal of the Senate*, 53rd sess., 1923, p. 555; Senate Bill no. 311, 53rd sess., 1923.

65. *Chicago Tribune*, April 14, 1923, p. 6.

66. *Illinois State Journal*, April 26, 1923, p. 1.

67. *Illinois State Journal*, April 26, 1923, p. 1; *Journal of the Senate*, 53rd sess., 1923, p. 679.

68. See note 67 above.

69. See note 67 above.

70. See note 67 above.

71. *Journal of the Senate*, 53rd sess., 1923, p. 679.

72. *Chicago Tribune*, April 27, 1923, p. 8.

73. *Illinois State Journal*, April 28, 1923, p. 6.

74. *Illinois State Journal*, April 29, 1923, sec. 5, p. 1.

75. *Journal of the Senate*, 53rd sess., 1923, pp. 865, 992–993.

76. *Journal of the Senate*, 53rd sess., 1923, p. 1023.

77. *Journal of the House*, 53rd sess., 1923, pp. 1066, 1114, 1205–1206, 1319–1320; *Journal of the Senate*, 53rd sess., 1923, pp. 1392–1393.

78. *Illinois State Journal*, March 25, 1925, p. 12; *Chicago Tribune*, March 25, 1925, p. 13.

79. *Chicago Evening Post*, April 10, 1925; *Chicago Tribune*, April 9, 1925, p. 8; Illinois Chamber of Commerce, *Legislative Review*, no. 14, April 10, 1925.

80. *Illinois State Journal*, April 2, 1925, p. 4; ISFLN, vol. 11, no. 1, April 4, 1925, p. 2.

81 *Illinois State Journal*, April 15, 1925, p. 1; *Chicago Tribune*, April 17, 1925, p. 5.

82. *Chicago Tribune*, May 24, 1925, part 1, p. 24.

83. *Journal of the Senate*, 54th sess., 1925, pp. 1003–1004, 1096; *Illinois State Journal*, May 31, 1925, part 1, p. 5; June 3, 1925.

84. *Chicago Tribune*, June 18, 1925, p. 4; June 19, 1925, p. 6; ISFLN, vol. 11, no. 14, July 4, 1925, p. 3; *Journal of the House*, 54th sess., 1925, pp. 1094, 1101.

85. *Illinois State Journal*, June 17, 1927; ISFLN, vol. 13, no. 17, July 23, 1927, p. 1; no. 24, September 10, 1927, p. 7.

86. *Journal of the Senate*, 56th sess., 1929, pp. 110–111.

87. *Journal of the Senate*, 56th sess., 1929, p. 313; *Chicago Tribune*, January 31, 1929, p. 7; *Illinois State Journal*, January 31, 1929, p. 1; *Chicago Daily News*, January 30, 1929.

88. *Journal of the Senate*, 56th sess., 1929, pp. 394–395; ISFLN, vol. 14, no. 49, March 9, 1929.

89. *Journal of the Senate*, 56th sess., 1929, p. 579; *Illinois State Journal*, March 28, 1929, p. 3; *Illinois State Register*, March 27, 1929, p. 1.

90. *Journal of the Senate*, 56th sess., 1929, pp. 797, 953, 1158–1159; *Illinois State Journal*, April 6, 1929, p. 2; May 18, 1929, p. 7; ISFLN, vol. 15, no. 7, May 18, 1929, p. 3; no. 9, June 1, 1929, p. 1.

*Chapter 6*

# The State Police Movement in Illinois

The previous chapter set forth the facts and events concerning the process of creating state-controlled law enforcement agencies in Illinois. This chapter presents an analysis and interpretation of that process by going behind the events to examine the interaction patterns of those groups and individuals involved in the state police issue. Specifically, an explanation will be offered for why proponents of a military-like state police failed in their attempts to create such an organization.

## PROPONENTS AND SUPPORTERS OF THE STATE POLICE

Over eighty groups and organizations went on record in support of the Dunlap state police bills. Obviously, many more organizations could be included if local branches of such umbrella groups as the Illinois Bankers' Association and the Illinois Chamber of Commerce were counted. On the surface, it appeared that there was widespread and diverse support for the state police among the various civic, commercial, and manufacturing organizations of the state. However, this broad-based support was more apparent than real. Support for the state police was the product of a well-organized campaign of public relations, subtle coercion and propaganda carried out by a small cooperative group of individuals. These people formed the nucleus of the "state police movement" in Illinois.

The most prominent individual in the drive to secure a state police was Senator Henry M. Dunlap. The sponsor of all of the state police bills introduced in the Senate between 1919 and 1929, he received most of the public notoriety on the state police issue. Elected to the Senate for the first time in 1892, Dunlap was described in his official Senate biography as a farmer and fruit grower from the small town of Savoy.[1] He was not, however, just an ordinary farmer but a prominent and wealthy agribusinessman.[2] Dunlap lived on a large farm on the edge of Champaign, near the University of Illinois campus, and owned over 1,500 acres of orchards in four counties. He was also president of the Illinois Orchard Company, a member of the International Appleshippers' Association, and a participant in the Illinois State Horticultural Society. With such credentials it makes little sense to classify Dunlap as simply a "farmer."[3]

As principal sponsor of the legislation, Dunlap received most of the public attention on the state police issue. From his records, it would appear that the campaign to establish a state police was his primary concern during the 1920s. His correspondence and legislative notes provide a sense of the motives that drove him to fight vigorously for a state police force. A member of the old-stock middle class, Dunlap espoused the rhetoric that America should not recognize the existence of classes, as doing so causes trouble by setting class against class. Instead, Dunlap affirmed the great opportunities for mobility in American society. Given this orientation, Dunlap saw legislation, such as the state police bills, as efforts to protect the conditions that gave rise to these opportunities. In other words, the state must provide sufficient authority for the "full enforcement" of the law to protect life and property in every section of the state. Stressing that all types of crimes were occurring in the rural areas with "little or no protection" available, Dunlap believed that a state police would cooperate with the sheriffs and other local officials in an "organized effort to provide for a better enforcement of the laws through the length and breadth of the state."[4]

An important issue to reformers such as Dunlap was the principle of efficiency. Dunlap believed that local law enforcement officials were outdated and notoriously incompetent. Because sheriffs and small-town police chiefs were elected officials and too familiar with local residents, Dunlap felt they were incapable of maintaining order and often overlooked violations of the law as "eccentricities to be deplored and not punished."[5]

Issues of inadequate law enforcement and American values aside, Dunlap was probably motivated more by two personal issues—his business and prohibition. Since he owned farm property in four counties and was heavily involved in the interstate marketing of produce, it is not surprising to find that Dunlap was a major backer of the hard-roads program designed to improve Illinois highways. However, the development of paved roads did present two major problems for rural businessmen like Dunlap. First was the problem of the road construction gangs:

> Some of these men will be uneducated vicious characters from the cities, or foreigners. These men when they find themselves in rural communities miles removed from the large city with no police force in hailing distance are going to throw restraint to the wind and indulge their vile passions and vicious natures.[6]

Second, although the new paved roads would make it easier and cheaper for Dunlap and other farmers to move their products to the markets in Chicago and St. Louis, they feared these same roads would also give big-city criminals easy access to banks and merchants of small rural towns. While Dunlap sometimes may have been speaking for rural Illinois in general, it appears he was also acting in his own self-interest.

Another issue of personal interest to Dunlap was prohibition. He was a committed "dry" and had consistently voted in favor of prohibition legislation and against "wet" laws designed to modify prohibition restrictions or weaken their enforcement.[7] A state police force would be an effective agency to enforce the "dry" laws because it would not be hampered by local influence and "would do more to enforce the prohibition laws of the state than all other measures combined."[8]

Dunlap worked hard to promote support for the state police. He used every opportunity to push his bills by speaking to various civic, business, and local organizations, as well as to labor groups. But Dunlap's primary goal was to generate support for the state police among farmers and rural businessmen. Using his contacts in the various agricultural organizations and the farm-oriented press, Dunlap created "support" for his legislation. The major farm papers such as *The Illinois Farmer*, *The Prairie Farmer*, and *The Orange Judd Farmer* were asked to print favorable editorials in support of the state police idea. Along with these requests, Dunlap would provide the editors with all types of propaganda material to use in their articles.[9] In one instance, Dunlap apologized that the material he had sent was "not more sensational so as to attract attention," and gave the editor the option to modify the material "to make it more interesting."[10]

Dunlap's most effective method of generating support for the state police was winning favor from county farm agents of the agricultural extension service (the farm bureaus). Working with Eugene Davenport, dean of the College of Agriculture at the University of Illinois, Dunlap was able to secure the cooperation of the county agents in support of his state police legislation. Davenport would contact the agents concerning the state police bills and suggest that they write the senator for further information. Upon receiving the requests, Dunlap would write the agents a letter indicating the reasons why Illinois needed a state police and would enclose copies of the bill for distribution among the local farmers. In addition, Dunlap would request that the county agent "secure a number of letters and telegrams from influential farmers" to be sent to their local legislator to help "convince him that the farmers are very much in earnest about the passage" of the state police bills.[11]

The state organization of the county farm bureaus, the Illinois Agricultural Association, also came out in support of the state police. Relying on propaganda supplied by Dunlap, they sent out fliers across the state presenting the "Facts versus the False Prophets" of the state police issue. An important component of their propaganda was to stress that the Farm Bureau represented the views of Illinois farmers. This tact is illustrated by a paragraph taken from one of their fliers:

Many of the Farm Bureaus of Illinois, through definite resolution of the directors, have recorded their support . . . for a state police in Illinois. These directors are *truly representative* of the farm people of the state. For each county, the Board of Directors of the county farm bureau can be said to *represent a real cross-section* of the thought and the feeling of the farm people of the county. The fact that they are supporting the legislative committee of their state association in its position relative to the state police bills, *means that the farmers of the state are officially for enactment* of the necessary legislation [emphasis added].[12]

Such propaganda was necessary because the county agents often were unsuccessful in generating a sufficient quantity of support from individual farmers to have an impact on the local legislator. It was therefore important to stress that the county agent and, more important, the Illinois Agricultural Association spoke on behalf of the farmer.

Leaving no stone unturned, Dunlap even courted the favor of Richard J. O'Halloren. In 1925, O'Halloren, a member of the United Mine Workers Local 45, was running against John H. Walker for the presidential candidacy of the Illinois State Federation of Labor. Dunlap requested a meeting with O'Halloren to discuss the state police issue and asked him to appear at a public hearing to speak in favor of the bill.[13] Attempting to win over O'Halloren, Dunlap wrote:

I am in hopes the labor unions, or at least some of them will take a sane view of this matter of law enforcement and favor the bill. If we could show the members here that one or two unions had the good judgment and good sense to favor this bill, it would remove what is now considered the unanimous opposition of labor against the bill.[14]

Superficially, the movement to establish the state police appeared to be the sole effort of one wealthy farmer and his friends in the agricultural community to secure police protection for their growing agribusiness concerns. In fact, Dunlap attempted to promote this very idea. In a letter to O'Halloren, he writes: "My occupation is that of farmer. I am not connected in any way with employers associations or manufacturers or any other associations, and am acting entirely independently in this matter."[15] In fact, Dunlap was not working independently, but was in collaboration with other groups on the state police issue. Dunlap states in a letter to W. H. White, a bank president, that he has "been working closely with the state bankers' association, the Illinois Chamber of Commerce, and the Illinois Agricultural Association."[16]

Available data indicate that one of the primary centers of the state police movement in Illinois was that of the "state police committees" of the Illinois Chamber of Commerce and the Industrial Club of Chicago. The members of these two committees coordinated a program composed of propaganda, speakers, media coverage, and lobbying efforts designed to gain favorable public and legislative support for the state police bills. The most prominent members of these committees were Joseph T. Ryerson and Joseph C. Belden, who served as chairmen of the Industrial Club committee. (Ryerson also served for a time as chairman of the Chamber committee.)

Both Ryerson and Belden were members of Chicago's elite. Ryerson was president of a wholesale iron, steel, and machinery company bearing his name and served on the board of directors of two Chicago banks. He was a member of the city's most prominent social clubs and lived in Chicago's "Gold Coast," an elite residential neighborhood along the shore of Lake Michigan. Belden, a member of the same clubs, was president of a large electrical wire and cable manufacturing firm. Although not a resident of the "Gold Coast," he did have a home in the exclusive northern suburb of Lake Forest.[17]

Using the vast resources of their organizations, these committees engaged in a multifaceted program of propaganda. Ryerson and Belden, along with George H. Stephens, manager of the legislative bureau of the Illinois Chamber of Commerce, made hundreds of public appearances across the state promoting the state police. In addition to the speaking tours, the committee would take out full-page ads in newspapers across the state stating the reasons why Illinois needed a state police. The ads also included a listing of the "many different" groups backing the state police bills, thus giving the impression that practically every civic, business, and agricultural organization in the state favored a state police.[18]

The official publication of the Illinois Chamber of Commerce, the *Illinois Journal of Commerce*, was also used as a forum for promoting the state police. Mostly written by the editor, Frank Barth, and carrying such titles as "Why Illinois Should Have a State Police Force," "Increasing Crime Demands State Police," and "Crime Victims Pleading," the articles presented a picture of increasing crime and lawlessness that could not be controlled by the "poorly trained" local officials in the rural sections of the state. Explaining that the state police idea was not new, having been "successful" in many other states, the articles claimed that the cost of the police would be offset by both revenue collected from fines and the recovery of stolen property. One article was accompanied by a cartoon in which a "bootlegger" and a "highwayman" were agreeing that Illinois did not need a state police. The caption read, "State police would spoil business for some folks."[19]

Finally, the committees were instrumental in bringing officials from already existing state police forces to speak at special sessions in different cities of the state. At one such hearing held in Springfield, two officials were brought in to speak. George P. Dutton, deputy superintendent of the New York state police, and Captain Caesar J. Scardardia of the Michigan state police, told about the operation of their respective forces. In the course of his remarks, Dutton argued that "the friendliest relations and cooperation" existed between his force and the county sheriffs and local police officials. Scardardia spoke on the issue of cost, claiming that for only $350,000 the Michigan state police were now doing the work of four previous departments "that formerly cost $561,370." He went on to state that his force actually made money for the state and had recently "turned in $180,000" to the state treasury. Both men attempted to undermine labor opposition by arguing that in their states, labor was "friendly" toward the state police and had actually requested that state police, instead of the National Guard or federal troops, be assigned to strike situations. Scardardia added that "the labor men in the Michigan legislature were in favor of the police and voted for it."[20]

The members of the Illinois Chamber of Commerce state police committee were especially well suited for coordinating a mass propaganda campaign. The committee included Frank Barth, editor of the *Illinois Journal of Commerce*; Royal N. Allen from the Chicago Motor Club; E. P. Imboden, a representative of the Illinois Agricultural Association; and M. A. Graettinger of the Illinois Bankers' Association. Using their positions of influence within these organizations they were able to mobilize their respective members to become active in the state police campaign. Members of the state police committees would individually appear at legislative hearings claiming to represent farmers, bankers, or simply themselves as concerned citizens and businessmen. The immediate perception was that of broad-based and diverse support of the state police. The emphasis on appearances was a crucial element of the state police movement. State police advocates believed it was necessary to garner favorable public opinion for the state police and felt a picture of broad support from diverse organizations had to be created. Ryerson, in an internal memo to the Industrial Club, made reference to this issue:

Through the activities of the Illinois Chamber of Commerce and members of the Industrial Club ... sufficient pressure has been brought throughout the state *to make it very apparent* that the citizens of the state demand some kind of state police legislation [emphasis added].[21]

Dunlap's relationship with the Chamber and Industrial Club state police committees was essentially that of an "agent," not a full participating member. His primary role was to make public appearances at Chamber-sponsored programs about the state police issue and keep the committees informed of the legislative activity concerning the state police bills. Undoubtedly, Dunlap's most important function was to be publicly identified as the primary sponsor or "father" of the state police issue in Illinois. This tactic was intended to prevent the state police idea from being depicted as a business-backed measure. The Chamber and other organizations could then make a public appearance of "supporting" Dunlap in "his" efforts.[22] This issue became a major concern after continued defeat of the Dunlap bills. During the 1929 drive, it was recommended by the Industrial Club's state police committee that neither the Illinois Chamber of Commerce nor the Illinois Manufacturers' Association "should appear at Springfield as sponsor of a state police bill because it immediately would be branded as an employers' measure."[23] Moreover, Dunlap's role in drafting the state police legislation appears to have been limited. His agent status is indicated in a report to the executive committee of the Industrial Club:

Certain changes in the form of the bill and in the manner of presentation will be made next year and our efforts should be successful. ... As soon as our new bill is drafted and in some preliminary form the state police committee of the Industrial Club will be called together and the bill submitted to the committee for approval or such changes as the members of the committee suggest.[24]

Dunlap was also closely connected with another state police advocate—the State Police Auxiliary Committee (SPAC). Located in Chicago, the SPAC was an organization of three or four men who devoted all of their time to generating public sentiment in favor of the state police. Although scattered references can be found in press reports, transcripts of legislative committee hearings, and the personal correspondence of Dunlap, little information is available on the SPAC. In fact, it appears that little was known about this committee by its contemporaries, since many of the references remark on the "mysterious" nature of the organization.

According to their own publications, the SPAC was directed by Frank L. Mather as "general superintendent," with Bliss W. Boering, Alpheus Stewert, and Frank A. Collins as "deputies." Incorporated in 1907 as the Information Bureau of American Municipalities, the group changed its name to the SPAC in 1919. The SPAC was a propaganda organization which engaged in a wide range of activities promoting public sentiment in favor of the state police. Primary attention was directed at "educating" the rural residents about the benefits of a state police and at undermining labor opposition. After the first defeat in 1919, Dunlap wrote Mather indicating a greater need for

propaganda ... so as to bring [the state police to] the attention of the people of the state. To secure this, we must get the information to the country people. ... It is only by strong sentiment and by proper education of the people to favor law enforcement, that such a bill can be passed, and it is up to those who believe in the measure to keep up this propaganda.[25]

The propaganda efforts of the SPAC took many different forms. Concentrating on the rural sections of the state, they placed full-page ads in hundreds of local newspapers and prepared special packets of "information" containing

a hundred reasons why farmers desire and need a state police. ... copies will be sent to each county advisor, asking how many they can send out with their regular bulletins and other literature. These folders will be furnished free of cost, and will serve as the first lessons to the farmers in our campaign of education.[26]

Civic and social clubs were shown movies about the training facilities of the New York and Pennsylvania state police forces, and officers from these organizations were brought for weeks at a time to speak at special programs throughout Illinois. But, in all probability, the most crucial dimension of the SPAC campaign was its publication of the *State Police Book* (*SPB*).

The first volume of the *SPB* was published in March 1919, and an issue appeared every month thereafter for at least the next six years.[27] A sophisticated and high-quality publication, the *SPB* carried the SPAC message on every page. Each article, speech transcript, news item, or editorial was designed to convince its readers of the absolute necessity of a state police for Illinois. The authors were unabashed at explicitly stating their aims; the following item from an early issue clearly indicates the purpose of the *SPB*:

The propaganda in which the Police Book is engaged is one of enlightenment and education as to a state police force. It feels satisfied that once the people of Illinois KNOW about a state police that the bill will go through the next session, all "reds," radicals, Socialists, lawbreakers, disturbers, I.W.W.'s, Bolsheviki and labor misleaders to the contrary notwithstanding.[28]

Toward this end the *SPB* was distributed throughout the state free of charge and was mailed to paying subscribers. Regardless of the form the propaganda took, the message was always the same: state police would protect outlying districts through constant patrol, protect suburban localities which lacked an adequate police force, enforce the liquor laws and suppress illegal resorts, provide additional revenue through the collection of fines, and give Illinois better and more comprehensive protection by providing a highly trained force which was both flexible in operation and a deterrent to crime.[29]

Dunlap's personal correspondence indicates that from 1919 to 1932 he had a close working relationship with the SPAC. The interaction between the two appears to have been one of reciprocity, with both Dunlap and the SPAC supplying each other with information and suggestions for promotional activity. One such activity was the "Citizen's Protective Club." Intended to generate public support for state police, the club was to be made up of

victims of highwaymen, bandits, burglars, sneak thieves, kidnappers, assailants of women and girls, in fact those who have been wronged by the horde of underworld forces operating in various parts of the state, committing crimes of all kinds and escaping over the new state system of highways.[30]

At the club's organizational meeting held in Springfield on March 11, 1925 the "crime sufferers" heard talks about their experiences at the hands of criminals, as well as an address from Major Lynn Adams, commander of the Pennsylvania state police, who spoke about the benefits of statewide policing. After planning their lobbying efforts, the club passed a resolution endorsing the Dunlap state police bill and demanded its passage by the General Assembly. Although the club promoted itself as being composed of "citizens" from all walks of life, in reality the membership was primarily composed of bankers.[31] Letters reveal that the "crime sufferers' club," which eventually was organized by the Illinois Chamber of Commerce, and the referendum clause added to the 1925 bill that successfully passed the Senate were both original ideas of Frank Mather.[32]

The actual nature of the overall relationship between Dunlap, Mather, and the state police committees of the Chamber of Commerce and the Industrial Club remains a mystery. The Illinois Chamber of Commerce publicly declined to endorse SPAC activities because Mather refused to reveal the sources and use of collected funds. But the fact that Dunlap worked closely with both the Chamber and the SPAC suggests a "cooperative" effort if not an intimate one.[33]

Another important proponent of the state police was the Illinois Manufacturers' Association (IMA). Formed in 1893, the IMA was one of the most outspoken opponents of organized labor in the state. Under the uncompromising leadership of its secretary, John M. Glenn, the "cause" of the IMA was directed toward resisting the "menace" of organized labor.[34] Although the IMA strongly supported the state police concept, its position in relation to other organizations was marginal. The extreme position taken by the IMA on the state police only served to alienate it from more reform-minded groups such as the Illinois Chamber of Commerce and the agricultural associations. On at least two occasions, Glenn provoked the wrath of potential allies by the manner in which he handled activities related to state police legislation.

In 1921, Glenn and the directors of the IMA took the position that the association was "strongly favorable" to Dunlap's police bill, but "damnably opposed the measure in its present form."[35] Glenn objected to Dunlap's clause restricting the authority of the state police during strikes. Intended to reduce the opposition of labor groups, the clause read as follows:

But within any incorporated city, village, or town, the Illinois state police shall not enter upon duty for the purpose of policing a strike except by order of the Governor, or upon the request of the mayor of a city or the sheriff of a county, approved by the Governor.[36]

A promotional flier was sent by the directors to IMA members across the state. The flier claimed that the offensive clause made the bill "class legislation" and "discriminatory" against industrial interests. Stating the bill as written would afford no protection for the manufacturers of the state, the flier cited the following situation as an example of the bill's inadequacy:

Suppose that a mob of strikers, led by lawless radicals, after beating up some independent workers, marches upon a factory to put it to the torch. Under the bill now being considered, a squad of state police, if stationed in the town where the violence was threatened, could not act without authority of the governor. It would be too late to save possible loss of life and damage to property.[37]

It was just this type of inflammatory, antilabor posture that the other state police advocates wanted to avoid. Organized labor was attacking the Dunlap police bills for creating nothing more than a state-controlled, strike-breaking force, and the response of the IMA served to reinforce labor's argument. Not only did supporters of the state police denounce Glenn's position, but some members of the IMA strongly disapproved of Glenn for singling out the restrictive clause as a basis for his opposition to the state police measure.[38]

During the 1923 legislative session, Glenn further incurred the wrath of state police advocates by requesting IMA members to "use their influence" to force an immediate adjournment of the legislature.[39] Critics of Glenn's actions charged that he was motivated by the possibility that the eight-hour bill for women would pass if the legislature stayed in session and that the Senate had already defeated the state police bill which Glenn wanted passed. Representative Castle charged that the failure of the state police bill was due to "bungling support" by Glenn and stated that Glenn was "a liability to the Illinois Manufacturers' Association" and should be replaced for "the better of the association and the legislature both."[40] Glenn's dogmatic influence kept the IMA on the fringe of the state police movement in Illinois. A close association by the other state police proponents with the IMA would have identified them with the antilabor views of Glenn, further weakening their efforts to win public support for the state police.

The principal state police advocates were members of the state's social and economic elite, representing the most powerful organizations in the Midwest. Yet, even with money, power, and the ability to organize and finance a massive, ten-year public relations campaign of propaganda and legislative lobbying, the state police advocates failed to meet their ultimate goal—the establishment of a strong, military-like state police similar to the forces in New York and Pennsylvania. Partial under-standing of this failure can be found in the opposition they encountered to this type of state-controlled police system.

## OPPONENTS OF THE STATE POLICE

Opposition to the establishment of a military-like state police in Illinois came from three sources: local law enforcement officials, tax-payer groups, and organized labor. Although local sheriffs feared that a state police would threaten their jobs, they did little in the way of active campaigning against the state police bills. Nonetheless, local sheriffs did have some impact. A report of the Industrial Club state police committee states, "The Illinois State Sheriffs' Association has quietly but effectively opposed state police bills believing that it interfered with their preroga-tives."[41] Also opposed to the Dunlap police bills were those who be-lieved a state police would increase taxes. Loosely organized taxpayer groups would often appear at legislative hearings to voice their oppo-sition to what they felt was an extravagant and unnecessary use of state money. Most of the farmers and other rural residents who expressed opposition to the state police based their position on the issue of cost and taxes. Neither the sheriffs nor the taxpayer groups, however, pre-sented a hurdle to Dunlap, the Chamber of Commerce, or the other powerful state police advocates.

Instead, the most formidable opposition to the state police was organ-ized labor, specifically the Illinois State Federation of Labor (ISFL), under the leadership of John H. Walker. Walker was born in Scotland to a family of textile workers and coal miners who had been active in the Scottish unionization movement. At the age of seven he came to Illinois with his parents and began working in the mines of Coal City. He became an official of District 12, which was the largest district in the United Mine Workers of America and the state's most powerful and progressive union. He was president of the Illinois State Federation of Labor for all but one year from 1913 to 1930. As a political activist and the state's leading official of the AFL, Walker was at the forefront of legislative debate on important labor issues.[42]

An idealist and romantic, Walker had views that were in direct conflict with the expansion favored by industry, the centralizing of power in the hands of union officials, and the conservatism of the AFL. His philosophy won him recognition and power during the first two decades of the twentieth century, but proved to be a handicap in the industry-dominated period of the 1920s.[43] Nevertheless, Walker was an effective and tireless lobbyist who worked to gain the passage of such labor legislation as the anti-injunction bill (passed in 1925), convict-labor legislation, and bills promoting free textbooks and mine safety, while he also fought a ten-year battle against the Dunlap state police measures. To aid in these efforts Walker founded the *Illinois State Federation of Labor Weekly Newsletter* in 1915. With him as its editor, the newsletter reflected Walker's point of view and served as the major vehicle for labor propaganda within the state.[44]

Eugene Staley, in his history of the Illinois State Federation of Labor, maintains that the effort to resist the establishment of a state police was "the hardest defensive battle waged by the [federation] in the legislature."[45] Declaring its opposition to a state police in 1918, the federation, under Walker's leadership, spent the next twelve years fighting these measures. Walker strongly believed a state-controlled police, of the type proposed in the Dunlap bills, was inherently un-American and in violation of the basic principles of the Constitution: "The men who founded our government knew that a military police was the most cruel and effective weapon that a ruthless despotism could have at its disposal to crush the common people into submission so that they might be exploited like animals."[46] Walker argued that law enforcement had been intentionally placed under local control and made subject to the vote of the people so that Americans would not suffer the abuses of a military type of police system. But, Walker continued, this "sort of constabulary does not serve the purpose of the predatory interests of our country who want to crush and enslave and exploit the people hence they want the military police."[47]

Organized labor continually stressed that they were in favor of law enforcement and that police were a "necessary part of every community," but that police officers should be members of the community and directly responsible to the public. The issue of using the state police during strikes was incidental to the question of "liberty." Victor Olander, the federation's secretary, argued that unionized labor's principal opposition to the state police bills was due to the measure's "dangerous centralization of political power." For labor, the basic issue underlying the state police was the principle of "self-government."[48]

The tactics Walker and organized labor used to fight the Dunlap bills were quite similar to those employed by the state police proponents. Although lacking the resources available to the advocates of a state police system, Illinois labor was not completely without the means with which to carry on an effective propaganda campaign of its own. In addition to the ISFL newsletter, there were fifteen other weekly labor papers in the state plus the International Labor News Service— all of which presented labor's views to the public. The ISFL offices were located in the state capital, which allowed Walker to observe legislative developments and be in constant contact with key politicians.

As ISFL president, Walker could maintain close contact with federations in other states and with AFL leadership. He used these contacts to collect information concerning the operation of state police forces in other states and to develop propaganda strategies. For example, after consulting with Samuel Gompers (AFL president), Walker decided to focus the campaign on rural residents and farmers. The plan was to point out the high cost of state police and the possible interference with municipal forces.[49] By giving the farmers the "facts" about the state police, Walker believed it would be possible to prevent such laws from being enacted. According to Walker, "real farmers" were being misled by the agricultural organizations, which he characterized as being run by "banker landlords and money lenders" who were associated in a reciprocal manner with anti-union corporations.[50]

Besides the contacts and resources available to him in his capacity as ISFL president, Walker was a confidant of Governor Len Small; this relationship was an asset which proved invaluable in the fight against the state police bills. Walker kept Small informed of labor's position on legislative matters by providing him with detailed analyses of proposed bills and noting features that would be objectionable to labor.[51] Without the support of Governor Small, the ISFL would have been in a weaker position in its fight to prevent passage of the Dunlap state police bills.[52] The right combination of resources—media access, AFL support, and cooperation from the Small administration—proved quite beneficial in labor's successful opposition to the state police.

The defeat of state police legislation in Illinois was not solely a function of labor opposition. Organized labor, even with support in the legislature and a friendly governor in the state house, was ineffective in its overall legislative agenda. Business groups successfully opposed most labor-sponsored bills. In his study of the IMA, Kelly stresses this point when he notes that "between 1911 and 1929 but one statute (the anti-injunction bill of 1925) to which the association had decided objections became law."[53] Also, many of the votes on Dunlap's police bills were close; often only one or two votes prevented passage. Obviously, factors besides the political contacts of Walker or the power of organized labor were at work. Regardless of the tactics employed by the proponents and opponents of the state police, the final outcome was determined in the General Assembly. It was in the committees and on the floor of the House and Senate that the crucial battles took place.

## LEGISLATIVE VOTING ON THE STATE POLICE

Reflecting the national political trend of the time, an average of 65 percent of the seats in the Illinois legislature were held by Republicans.

Therefore, the Republicans were in a position to pass or defeat any measure brought for a vote. However, very few issues were strictly partisan. As was the case with most state political systems of the time, political parties in Illinois contained rival factions organized around a political "boss." During the early 1900s, Illinois Republicans were split three ways into the Lorimer-Thompson-Lundin, Deneen, and Busse-Brundage factions, while the Democrats were split between the Harrison-Dunne and Sullivan-Brennan groups.[54] Despite differences among themselves, Democrats were able to maintain party unity when crucial votes or elections were at stake. On the other hand, rival Republican factions were unable to surmount internal feuds, which made it difficult for them to act as a unified party. This lack of unification is apparent in the voting patterns on the Dunlap state police bills.

Between 1919 and 1929 there were six final votes taken on the Dunlap state police bills—five in the Senate and one in the House. Analysis of the voting patterns (see Table 6.1) illustrates that Democrats were unified in their opposition to the state police while the Republican vote was split. This split prevented passage of the state police bills. Looking at the legislative voting in more detail, the final outcome on the state police issue was determined by three closely related factors that contributed to the factionalism of Illinois politics: urban/rural differences, prohibition, and immigration.

**Table 6.1**
**Political Party and the State Police Vote**

|  |  | Republican | | Democrat | |
|---|---|---|---|---|---|
|  |  | *No.* | *Percent* | *No.* | *Percent* |
| 1919 | For | 16 | (48) | 0 | (0) |
|  | Against | 17 | (52) | 14 | (100) |
| 1921 | For | 24 | (62) | 0 | (0) |
|  | Against | 15 | (38) | 6 | (100) |
| 1923 | For | 23 | (58) | 0 | (0) |
|  | Against | 17 | (42) | 8 | (100) |
| 1925 | For | 21 | (75) | 6 | (75) |
| Senate | Against | 7 | (25) | 2 | (25) |
| 1925 | For | 41 | (49) | 9 | (17) |
| House | Against | 43 | (51) | 43 | (83) |
| 1929 | For | 8 | (23) | 0 | (0) |
|  | Against | 26 | (77) | 9 | (100) |

With one-third of Illinois's population living in Chicago, there was bound to be a rivalry with the rest of the state. This classic Illinois political battle was apparent in the state police issue as Chicago legislators voted against the Dunlap bills while those from rural districts voted in favor (see Table 6.2). Given the arguments of state police proponents concerning the need for better police protection in rural areas, the urban/rural split in the vote is not surprising. However, these voting patterns can be misleading. Opposition to the state police by Chicago legislators reflects party opinion rather than an urban lack of interest in rural problems. Although Democrats were in the minority in the General Assembly, most of them represented Chicago legislative districts. For the Republicans, the expected urban/rural split is reversed. Chicago Republicans voted for the state police but Republicans representing downstate districts were more likely to hold negative opinions of the state police. An important trend that is also illustrated in Table 6.2 is the increasing percentage of downstate senators (42 percent in 1919, 75 percent in 1925) who voted in favor of the state police bills. This may reflect the impact of the propaganda campaigns directed at rural residents.

One of the most important issues facing Illinois and the nation during the 1920s was prohibition. The Woman's Christian Temperance Union and the Anti-Saloon League were active in Illinois, and prior to the ratification of the Eighteenth Amendment, they had been successful in passing a number of local prohibition measures. However, opponents of prohibition attempted to modify alcohol restrictions through legislation placing limitations on enforcement. From 1919 to 1929 there were a number of votes concerning prohibition which made it possible to classify legislators as either "wet" (against prohibition) or "dry" (in favor of prohibition). On the issue of the state police it is clear that "wets" overwhelmingly opposed the state police idea, while the "drys" favored it (see Table 6.3). Again, the major difference is revealed in the Republican Party. As a whole, Democrats tended to oppose prohibition measures. However, the Republican split over the state police issue is clearly linked to the question of prohibition as "wet" Republicans joined with Democrats in voting against the state police.

Party factions, urban/rural differences, and prohibition reflect another important feature of Illinois politics at this time—immigration. Outside of New York, Illinois had the second highest percentage of immigrants in the United States. In 1920, Chicago was over 70 percent first generation, with over 30 percent foreign born. Immigrants tended to concentrate in specific neighborhoods and many political wards in the city had foreign populations in excess of 90 percent. Within these wards, immigrants had considerable political power and were able to elect representatives who were sympathetic to immigrant values. These

Table 6.2
Urban/Rural Differences and the State Police Vote

| | | Chicago | | | | | | Downstate | | | | | |
|---|---|---|---|---|---|---|---|---|---|---|---|---|---|
| | | Total | | Democrat | | Republican | | Total | | Democrat | | Republican | |
| | | No. | Percent | No. | Percent | No. | Percent | No. | Percent | No. | Percent | No. | Percent |
| 1919 | For | 6 | (35) | 0 | (0) | 6 | (67) | 10 | (33) | 0 | (0) | 10 | (42) |
| | Against | 11 | (65) | 8 | (100) | 3 | (33) | 20 | (67) | 6 | (100) | 14 | (58) |
| 1921 | For | 7 | (44) | 0 | (0) | 7 | (70) | 17 | (59) | 0 | (0) | 17 | (59) |
| | Against | 9 | (56) | 6 | (100) | 3 | (30) | 12 | (41) | 0 | (0) | 12 | (41) |
| 1923 | For | 5 | (31) | 0 | (0) | 5 | (50) | 18 | (56) | 0 | (0) | 18 | (60) |
| | Against | 11 | (69) | 6 | (100) | 5 | (50) | 14 | (44) | 2 | (100) | 12 | (40) |
| 1925 Senate | For | 9 | (75) | 3 | (60) | 6 | (86) | 19 | (79) | 4 | (100) | 15 | (75) |
| | Against | 3 | (25) | 2 | (40) | 1 | (14) | 5 | (21) | 0 | (0) | 5 | (25) |
| 1925 House | For | 10 | (22) | 0 | (0) | 10 | (43) | 40 | (44) | 9 | (31) | 31 | (51) |
| | Against | 36 | (78) | 23 | (100) | 13 | (57) | 50 | (56) | 20 | (69) | 30 | (49) |
| 1929 | For | 4 | (25) | 0 | (0) | 4 | (40) | 4 | (15) | 0 | (0) | 4 | (17) |
| | Against | 12 | (75) | 6 | (100) | 6 | (60) | 23 | (85) | 3 | (100) | 20 | (83) |

Table 6.3
Prohibition and the State Police Vote

| | | "Wet" | | | | | | "Dry" | | | | | |
| | | Total | | Democrat | | Republican | | Total | | Democrat | | Republican | |
| | | No. | Percent | No. | Percent | No. | Percent | No. | Percent | No. | Percent | No. | Percent |
|---|---|---|---|---|---|---|---|---|---|---|---|---|---|
| 1919 | For | 1 | (6) | 0 | (0) | 1 | (14) | 15 | (54) | 0 | (0) | 15 | (60) |
| | Against | 16 | (94) | 10 | (100) | 6 | (86) | 13 | (46) | 3 | (100) | 10 | (40) |
| 1921 | For | 2 | (14) | 0 | (0) | 2 | (25) | 22 | (73) | 0 | (0) | 22 | (73) |
| | Against | 14 | (86) | 8 | (100) | 6 | (75) | 8 | (27) | 0 | (0) | 8 | (27) |
| 1923 | For | 0 | (0) | 0 | (0) | 0 | (0) | 23 | (68) | 0 | (0) | 23 | (70) |
| | Against | 14 | (100) | 7 | (100) | 7 | (100) | 11 | (32) | 1 | (100) | 10 | (30) |
| 1925 Senate | For | 7 | (64) | 4 | (67) | 3 | (60) | 21 | (84) | 3 | (100) | 18 | (82) |
| | Against | 4 | (36) | 2 | (33) | 2 | (40) | 4 | (16) | 0 | (0) | 4 | (18) |
| 1925 House | For | 3 | (5) | 0 | (0) | 3 | (12) | 44 | (65) | 7 | (58) | 37 | (66) |
| | Against | 53 | (95) | 32 | (100) | 21 | (88) | 24 | (35) | 5 | (42) | 19 | (34) |
| 1929 | For | 1 | (6) | 0 | (0) | 1 | (11) | 6 | (24) | 0 | (0) | 6 | (25) |
| | Against | 16 | (94) | 8 | (100) | 8 | (89) | 19 | (76) | 1 | (100) | 18 | (75) |

representatives, often immigrants themselves, opposed legislation such as prohibition as being detrimental to immigrant interests. Voting on the state police bills follows this pattern (see Table 6.4). Although the differences are not great, legislators from immigrant districts tended to oppose the state police bills, while legislators from nonimmigrant districts favored the idea of a state police.[55]

Given these characteristics of the legislative voting patterns on the state police issue in Illinois, the complexity of the situation becomes more obvious. While labor opposition was an important factor, so were party politics, ethnic-immigrant values, and the controversy over prohibition. Legislators who consistently voted in favor of the state police were usually Republicans from nonimmigrant districts who favored prohibition and opposed labor legislation. Those legislators who consistently voted against the state police were likely to be Democrats from immigrant districts who opposed prohibition and tended to vote in favor of labor legislation.

## SUMMARY

The activity surrounding efforts to establish a state police in Illinois appeared on the surface to represent a concern for law enforcement and improved police protection for rural areas of the state. Given the character of the public debate over the state police issue, in which the

**Table 6.4**
**Immigrant Districts and the State Police Vote**

|  |  | Immigrant | | Nonimmigrant | |
|---|---|---|---|---|---|
|  |  | No. | Percent | No. | Percent |
| 1919 | For | 5 | (31) | 11 | (33) |
|  | Against | 11 | (69) | 22 | (67) |
| 1921 | For | 5 | (38) | 19 | (61) |
|  | Against | 8 | (62) | 12 | (39) |
| 1923 | For | 4 | (29) | 20 | (59) |
|  | Against | 10 | (71) | 14 | (41) |
| 1925 | For | 6 | (67) | 22 | (81) |
| Senate | Against | 3 | (33) | 5 | (19) |
| 1925 | For | 4 | (15) | 46 | (42) |
| House | Against | 22 | (85) | 64 | (58) |
| 1929 | For | 1 | (8) | 6 | (21) |
|  | Against | 11 | (92) | 23 | (79) |

criterion of law enforcement was stressed over all other factors, such an interpretation would not be unexpected. Law enforcement, however, was only one dimension of a larger issue which included not only the state police, but also politics and conflicting value systems.

That law enforcement was not the critical issue is evident in the reactions to the various highway patrol bills that came before the General Assembly. These measures provided statewide police protection for the new hard roads and increased police presence in the rural areas. Three highway patrol bills, which easily passed both the House and Senate, were signed by the governor and were unopposed by organized labor. Yet they were opposed by Dunlap, Mather and the SPAC, the Illinois Chamber of Commerce, and other organizations backing the Dunlap bills. If the issue had been strictly law enforcement, opposition from state police advocates would appear out of character with their professed desires. Also, if law enforcement was the principal goal, why did the IMA buck the other state police advocates and refuse to support state police legislation that prohibited the force from interfering in industrial disturbances and strikes? The question was not one of law enforcement per se, but rather one of a particular type of law enforcement. The type of state police desired by the powerful interests in Illinois gives a clue regarding the political and cultural dimensions involved.

Dunlap, Mather, and the others wanted not just a state police, but a "military state police." Enamored of the Canadian mounted police and the state forces in Pennsylvania, New York, and Michigan, state police supporters in Illinois would settle for nothing short of a force of similar design. Characterized by military structure—a system of officers and enlisted personnel, organized in platoons, living in barracks, mounted on horses, and heavily armed—the police proposed in Dunlap's bills were to be completely autonomous from political interference (the superintendent was appointed for life) and were to be given total police power to arrest, search, and seize anywhere in the state.

It was just these features, however, that opponents such as organized labor considered objectionable. Although the possibility of such a force being used against strikers was a constant theme of their attack, underlying their arguments was the basic desire to protect local control and responsibility over the police. Indicating that Dunlap's bills provided military regulations and military qualifications for the personnel but made no mention of police experience or training, labor charged that an "army," not a police force, was being created. That labor was not opposed to law enforcement in general is evident in its neutral, if not mildly favorable, position toward the highway patrol bills.

The state police issue in Illinois was, in reality, a debate concerning local control versus centralization of the police. Dunlap and the other state police advocates attempted to create a police force free from "political" corruption, free from local influences, and willing to enforce all laws anywhere in the state. Opponents, on the other hand, saw local control of police as the only protection for liberty and personal freedom.

These same issues are also evident in the debate over prohibition. For more than ten years prior to the ratification of the Eighteenth Amendment, the question of prohibition had provided a major element of activity in the Illinois General Assembly. On the surface it would have appeared as either a partisan issue, with the relatively "wet" Democrats against the relatively "dry" Republicans, or as an urban/rural battle, with "wet" Chicago opposed to "dry" downstate. The prohibition question in Illinois, however, was essentially "a cultural struggle . . . which pitted the state's old-stock, traditionally Protestant populace against her new-stock, largely non-Protestant group."[56]

Illinois immigrants distrusted the social reformer and used any available political means to preserve cultural values and protect personal liberty. Immigrants and their leaders preferred decentralized arrangements which conserved local immigrant life-styles, and they were strongly opposed to "enforced conformity."[57] This cultural conflict would occasionally surface during debates in the General Assembly. John Boehm, a Bohemian Catholic immigrant and Democratic senator from Chicago, charged prohibitionists with "trying to take away 'his religion and his god,' " while Senator Henry Austin, an old-stock Baptist, responded "that his religion taught him that liquor was evil."[58]

These very same value conflicts were embedded in the debate over the state police bills.[59] Old-stock reformers were looking for a police force to aid them in their crusade against liquor and corruption, and the Dunlap police bills provided exactly what they wanted—centralized control, efficiency, and freedom from local influences. Immigrants, on the other hand, viewed a centralized police as a threat to local control and as a means to force them to conform to the values of the old-stock reformers. The reformers, however, viewed the state police as the best method available for enforcing the law everywhere, thus breaking immigrant control over local officials who would enforce the law selectively.

Other states, such as Pennsylvania, New York, and Michigan, were successful in their reform attempts to create centralized military-like police forces. Illinois, however, presented a different situation, as both the immigrant political organizations and the strong labor organizations were powerful enough to thwart the efforts of business and reform-minded elites. If not for this combination of labor and immigrant political influence, in all probability, Illinois would have established a Pennsylvania-style state police force during the early 1920s.

The facts presented on the efforts to establish a state police in Illinois have indicated a distinct pattern of interest group involvement. Illinois, however, was but one of many states during this time period to engage in the process of creating a state police force. The process in other states—its initiation, the interests involved, and the final outcome— may have been quite different from that described above. To address this issue, a similar analysis of state police development was carried out using Colorado as the comparison state. The results of that research are presented in the following chapter.

## NOTES

1. Illinois, *Blue Book of the State of Illinois, 1923–1924* (Springfield, 1923), p. 184.

2. As of December 1916, records indicate Dunlap had on hand total cash deposits of $124,000 in checking accounts at two Champaign banks. Henry M. Dunlap Papers, box 2, file: Personal Accounts 1906–1917, University of Illinois Archives, Champaign, Illinois (hereafter referred to as HMD).

3. HMD, box 2; file: D-C 1919.

4. "The State Police Bill S.B. 43," HMD, box 3, file: State Police 1919—Dunlap's Arguments and Legislative Debates.

5. "The State Constabulary Bill," HMD, box 2, file: A-C 1919; H. M. Dunlap to A. E. Jones, April 9, 1925, HMD, box 4, file: H-M 1925.

6. "The State Police Bill S.B. 43," pp.7–8.

7. H. M. Dunlap to Champaign County Woman's Christian Temperance Union, January 10, 1931, HMD, box 7, file: H-K 1931.

8. H. M. Dunlap to S. N. Madden, June 5, 1919, HMD, box 2, file: M-S 1919.

9. A. M. Augustine to H. M. Dunlap, April 23, 1919, HMD, box 2, file: A-C 1919; H. M. Dunlap to C. V. Gregory, June 9, 1925, and H. M. Dunlap to C. E. Page, June 9, 1925, HMD, box 4, file: N-S 1925.

10. H. M. Dunlap to F. L. Petty, May 2, 1929, HMD, box 5, file: L-R 1929.

11. E. W. Rusk to E. Davenport, April 7, 1919; H. M. Dunlap to C. G. Starr, May 2, 1919; H. M. Dunlap to O. Snyder, May 2, 1919, HMD, box 2, file: M-S 1919.

12. "The State Police Bills," n.d., HMD, box 3, file: State Police Bill—Dunlap's Arguments, Bills, Supporting Documents.

13. H. M. Dunlap to R. J. O'Halloren, March 19, 1925, and March 24, 1925, HMD, box 4, file: N-S 1925.

14. H. M. Dunlap to R. J. O'Halloren, March 12, 1925, HMD, box 4, file: N-S 1925.

15. Ibid.

16. H. M. Dunlap to W. H. White, April 26, 1925, HMD, box 4, file: T-Z 1925.

17. *Who's Who in Chicago: The Book of Chicagoans, 1926*, pp. 77, 758, Chicago Historical Society, Chicago.

18. *Peoria Journal*, February 2, 1925; "Illinois State Police," scrapbook of clippings, letters, and reports concerning legislative activity to create a state police in Illinois, Chicago Historical Society, Chicago (hereafter referred to as ISP).

19. *Illinois Journal of Commerce*, 4 (August 1922): 7, 30, 32; 5 (March 1923): 11; 6 (February 1924): 13, 28; 8 (March 1925): 7.

20. *Chicago Tribune*, March 9, 1923, p. 15; *Illinois State Journal*, March 9, 1923, p. 12.

21. "To the Members of the Industrial Club," May 11, 1925, p. 1, ISP.

22. See the many letters between H. M. Dunlap and J. C. Belden, HMD, boxes 4 and 5.

23. Report of the state police committee of the Industrial Club of Chicago, January 17, 1929, ISP.

24. Report of Ryerson to the Executive Committee, September 23, 1926, ISP.

25. H. M. Dunlap to SPAC, May 20, 1919, HMD, box 2, file: M-S 1919.

26. *State Police Book*, 1 (January 1920): 8.

27. Because research failed to locate a complete collection of the *SPB*, it was impossible to determine how many issues actually were published. The issues in the University of Illinois Library were used in this research.

28. *State Police Book*, 10 (December 1919): 10.

29. *State Police Book*, any issue.

30. *Illinois State Journal*, March 1, 1925, part 1, p. 7.

31. *Illinois State Journal*, March 9, 1925, p. 9; March 11, 1925, p. 6; March 12, 1925, pp.1–2; *Chicago Tribune*, March 11, 1925, p. 6.

32. H. M. Dunlap to F. L. Mather, March 12, 1925, HMD, box 4, file: H-M 1925; F. L. Mather to H. M. Dunlap, April 24, 1925, HMD, box 4, file: H-M 1925.

33. Illinois Chamber of Commerce, letter no. 6, Rockford, Illinois, February 6, 1926, ISP.

34. Alfred H. Kelly, *A History of the Illinois Manufacturers' Association* (Chicago: University of Chicago Libraries, 1940), pp. 5–6.

35. IMA Minutes, Directors' Meetings, book 2, May 2, 1921, pp. 1665–1666, Chicago Historical Society, Chicago.

36. Senate Bill, no. 55, 52nd sess., 1921, sec. 6, par.(e).

37. "No 'Ifs' or 'Buts,' " January 5, 1921, HMD, box 3, file: State Police Bill 1921 Opposition.

38. IMA Minutes, Directors' Meetings, book 2, March 8, 1921, p. 1640, Chicago Historical Society, Chicago.

39. *Illinois State Journal*, May 1, 1923, p. 4.

40. *Chicago Tribune*, May 4, 1923, p. 19.

41. Report of the state police committee of the Industrial Club of Chicago, January 29, 1929, ISP.

42. John H. Keiser, "John H. Walker: Labor Leader from Illinois," in *Essays in Illinois History in Honor of Glenn Huron Seymour*, edited by Donald F. Tingley (Carbondale, IL: Southern Illinois University Press, 1968).

43. Ibid., p. 78.

44. Ibid., p. 95.

45. Eugene Staley, "State Constabulary or Military Police," in *History of the Illinois State Federation of Labor* (Chicago: University of Chicago Press, 1930), p. 512.

46. *Illinois State Federation of Labor Weekly Newsletter* (ISFLN), February 12, 1921, p. 1.

47. Ibid.

48. ISFLN, vol. 11, no. 22, August 29, 1925, p. 4; vol. 14, no.16, July 21, 1928, p. 2.

49. S. Gompers to J. H. Walker, January 11, 1923, John Hunter Walker Papers, Box 15, file 138, item 12, Illinois Historical Survey, University of Illinois Library, Champaign, Illinois (hereafter referred to as JHW).

50. J. H. Walker to S. Gompers, January 16, 1923, JHW, box 15, file 139, item 3.

51. J. H. Walker to L. Small, April 18, 1925, JHW, box 20, file 186, item 42.

52. Staley, *History of the Illinois State Federation of Labor*, p. 519.

53. Kelly, *History of the Illinois Manufacturers' Association*, p. 14.

54. Charles E. Merriam, *Chicago: A More Intimate View of Urban Politics* (New York: Macmillan, 1929); Alex Gottfried, *Boss Cermak of Chicago: A Study of Political Leadership* (Seattle: University of Washington Press, 1962); John M. Allswang, *A House for All Peoples: Ethnic Politics in Chicago, 1890–1936* (Lexington: University Press of Kentucky, 1971).

55. Using census data it was possible to reconstruct the ratio of immigrant to nonimmigrant voters for each legislative district. Those districts having 60 percent or more immigrant voters were classified as immigrant, while those with less than 60 percent were classified as nonimmigrant. U.S. Department of Justice, *Fourteenth Census of the United States, 1920*, vol. 3 (Washington, DC: Government Printing Office, 1923), pp. 251–264.

56. John D. Buenker, "The Illinois Legislature and Prohibition, 1907–1919," *Journal of the Illinois Historical Society* 62 (Winter 1969): 363.

57. John D. Buenker, "Urban Immigrant Lawmakers and Progressive Reform in Illinois," in *Essays in Illinois History*, edited by David F. Tingley (Carbondale IL: Southern Illinois University Press, 1968), p. 73; Joel A. Tarr, *A Study in Boss Politics: William Lorimer of Chicago* (Urbana: University of Illinois Press, 1971), p. 306.

58. John D. Buenker, *Urban Liberalism and Progressive Reform* (New York: W. W. Norton, 1973), p. 188.

59. The close relationship between prohibition and the state police can be indicated statistically. By computing Lambda coefficients for predicting roll call response, it was found that a legislator's stand on prohibition was the best predictor of his stand on the state police in four out of the six votes on the state police bills [1919-(.125); 1921-(.54); 1923-(.52); 1925 House-(.21)].

Chapter 7

# Creating the State Police
# in Colorado

By the turn of the century, Colorado was an important industrial state, with coal and hard-metal mining, the smelting of ore, and the refining of beet sugar as its primary economic concerns. Along with the industrial states of the Northeast, Colorado had more than its share of labor disputes and related violence. From 1890 to 1914 the state experienced numerous strikes, lockouts, violence, the implementation of martial law, and the use of federal troops to restore order. The violence associated with these labor disputes culminated in 1914 with the infamous Ludlow Massacre.[1]

Throughout the period, local officials, such as the municipal police and county sheriffs, attempted to maintain order. More often than not, however, state militia and federal troops had to be called to control the disturbances associated with labor disputes. In addition, mine and refinery owners employed private police to guard their property and provide protection for strike breakers. Although effective in controlling the working class, the militia and private police increased worker hostility toward employers and the state government and generated middle-class sympathy for the workers by the brutality and violence used in suppressing strikes. Searching for a solution to the dilemma of maintaining order without offending the middle class, government officials and business leaders concluded that a state-controlled police force would be the best response.

## THE STATE DEPARTMENT OF SAFETY, 1917

The first effort to organize a state police in Colorado came in January 1917, when Representative Alphonse P. Ardourel, a mine developer from Boulder, introduced a bill creating a department of state police. Influenced by the paramilitary structure of the Pennsylvania constabulary and its reputation for being effective in policing labor disturbances, the Ardourel bill was a word-for-word copy of the law that established the Pennsylvania state police in 1905. However, as had been the experience in Illinois, this first attempt failed to generate much support as the bill died in committee and no other state police bills were introduced that year.[2]

Shortly after Congress declared war on Germany in April 1917, plans were instituted for mobilizing the various state National Guard units for active military service. Colorado Governor Julius C. Gunter worried that there would be no force to guard the state's tunnels, bridges, and reservoirs or quell any labor disturbances after the National Guard was to be mustered into federal service that coming August. In response, the governor appointed a "state war council" composed of prominent citizens to deal with the problem. Two different proposals were considered: a "home guard," similar in structure to the National Guard and manned by those who would be least likely to be called for military duty, and a constabulary organization similar to the Texas Rangers. The governor and the war council were to decide which model would provide the best protection and recommend this to the special session of the legislature which was to begin on July 18.[3]

Prior to the special session, the attorney general's office, in consultation with Governor Gunter and the war council, prepared bills for regulating food and revenue and for establishing a home guard and a state police. The home guard bill provided for a three-member nonpartisan commission responsible for appointing the superintendent and assistant superintendent of the force. The organization was to consist of eight companies of fifty men and, if necessary, twenty companies, or one thousand men. The members of the guard were granted absolute police power, superseding both sheriffs and municipal police authorities, and could be equipped as a mounted constabulary.[4]

Hopes that the special session would be non-partisan, reflecting the patriotism and seriousness of the times, were quickly dispelled in the first days of deliberation. Not wishing to be bound to the support of the administration's measures, Republican members of the Senate refused to sponsor any of the bills prepared by the governor and the war council.[5] Some legislators had definite opinions on the issues and were not willing to submit to the administration's proposals without being convinced that they were the best measures for the state. Nor were they swayed by charges in the press to the effect that any legislator who would oppose passage of the administration's home guard law should be considered a traitor.[6]

As if party partisanship were not enough, the governor introduced a note of confusion when, on the second day of the special session, he apparently changed his mind on the home guard issue. Originally backing a constabulary type of force, the governor now directed the adjutant general to recruit a squadron of cavalry under the existing National Guard laws to be used as a home guard. This major shift in policy reflected the governor's fear that the original police bill would not pass because of anticipated opposition by organized labor, which was claiming that the law would establish a state constabulary, not a home guard.[7]

During the second week of the session, the House Committee on Indian and Military Affairs debated several measures creating a state police force. The committee finally agreed on a compromise bill calling for the creation of a "state department of safety" consisting of six companies of twenty-five men each. They were to repress any uprising, strike, or other emergency that might arise and were given general police powers for this purpose. The force was to be stationed in Denver under the direction of the governor and a general superintendent.[8] Upon favorable committee recommendation, the state police bill was amended to require that all companies of the state police would be disbanded within thirty days of the return of the National Guard, and that within sixty days of the guard's return, all provisions of the act would become null and void. This change was intended to prevent the state police from becoming permanent, an indication that many legislators believed law enforcement should remain in the hands of local officials. On July 27, the bill was called for a vote and received the necessary majority to pass.[9]

Opposition to the "state guard department" began to surface almost immediately following the passage of the state police bill in the House. Local peace officers were apprehensive about the provision giving the state police power to supersede their authority in local matters. Believing that such power was unwise and dangerous, county sheriffs appeared at the state capital to protest the passage of the state police bill.[10]

Protest also came from organized labor. On July 28, representatives of twenty-three coal miners' unions, employed by the Colorado Fuel and Iron Company, presented formal protests to the Senate. John McLennan, a member of the miners' committee making the protest, stated the unions' views on the matter:

Organized labor is not opposed to the state militia doing its duty in time of trouble. True, the National Guard is to be called into federal service. The miners' unions believe that the civil authorities are able to cope with any situation that might arise. They are absolutely opposed to a constabulary, and in my opinion the passage of such a bill would invite fresh trouble. Gunmen would be put to guard the properties of large corporations. All the constabulary bills mix civil and military authority, and that is a dangerous thing to do.[11]

During Senate consideration of the bill, numerous amendments were adopted. The major change was the elimination of the clause disbanding the force upon return of the National Guard. The number of men in each company was increased from twenty-five to forty-five, the force was given authority to supersede civil authorities, and the funds to pay the department's expenses were to come from National Defense Bonds rather than the state treasury.[12] Led by supporters of the governor, the Senate had succeeded in amending the bill back to its original form.[13]

The amended bill was passed by the Senate and returned to the House for approval.[14] A motion was introduced in the House to accept the Senate amendments to the state police bill. The vote produced only one affirmative response, that of Alphonse Ardourel, an original sponsor of the bill. The remaining five sponsors, along with fifty-seven members of the House, voted to refuse the bill as amended by the Senate. A second motion was introduced asking the Senate to recede from its amendments. This motion passed 36 to 26. Upon receiving notice that the House had refused to agree to the amendments, Senator Siewers Fincher of Breckenridge moved that the Senate insist upon its amendments and ask for a conference.[15]

Three days before the National Guard was to be mobilized to leave the state, the House and Senate were deadlocked over the proper apparatus to replace them. The Senate, in support of the governor, favored a large, permanent constabulary force with authority over local peace officers. The House favored a smaller, temporary force with normal police powers. Governor Gunter responded to the deadlock by threatening to keep the legislature in session until they had complied with the requirements of his war program. Unshaken, opponents of the state police had not been swayed by the governor's threats and continued to oppose any constabulary measure. They took the position that a constabulary force would be in direct conflict with the civil authority vested in county officials, and predicted dire consequences if these forces were placed in opposition to one another.[16]

After much political posturing and procedural delay, the House finally agreed to a conference to work out the differences between the two versions of the state police bill. The final bill, as amended by the conference committee, reduced the control of the state police over civil authorities, cut the number of companies from six to four, set the initial appropriation at $650,000, and contained the provision that "within ninety days after conclusion of peace between the United States and . . . Germany all companies formed under this act shall be disbanded."[17] Accepted by the House, the amended bill was debated in the Senate for more than an hour. Led by Senator Agnes Riddle of Denver, opposition focused on the provision disbanding the force ninety days after the war ended. Unlike the original bill, there was no provision that the law would become null and void when the constabulary was disbanded. It was argued that this "joker" made the constabulary a permanent apparatus of the state government. Nevertheless, the Senate eventually passed the state police bill.[18]

Statements by Senator Riddle characterize the sentiments of those legislators who were opposed to the state police bill. Denouncing the legislature for not passing measures regulating the price of food and coal, she stated:

We have passed a bill for a state constabulary. . . . It is a victory for capital over labor. We came here ostensibly to help the general public. What have we done for them but to give them bullets instead of food and shelter. Every measure for their benefit has been defeated and yet we speak of law and order.[19]

Similar criticism was leveled at the legislature by the *Denver Post*. The press, however, placed most of the blame on Governor Gunter and the vested interests of his close advisors. The governor was chided for representing the wishes of such men as Cass Herrington of the Colorado Fuel and Iron Company, J. K. Millen, head of the milling and flour trust, and Fred Johnson, agent for the packing trust. The *Post* stated:

Instead of concentrating on an adequate home guard . . . the governor insisted on a state police. The state police are given the right to arrest without warrant of law any suspected person, and presents the Democratic party with a machine building implement that in its most ambitious moments it could not hope to possess. The state is saddled with a constabulary, demanded by the interests, which seem to have taken a mortgage on the . . . governor.[20]

Governor Gunter signed the constabulary bill creating the "department of safety" on August 7, 1917. Immediately rumors began as to whom the governor would appoint as superintendent of the new state police force. The names most frequently mentioned in the press were General Sherman Bell and Felic O'Neill, the latter of whom had been chief of the Denver police department. The governor eventually named Frank Adams, former president of the Denver Fire and Police Board. The appointment of the superintendent was seen as further evidence of the governor's ties to special interests, as Adams was also the president of the Colorado Ice and Cold Storage Company.[21]

## TO DISBAND OR NOT?

By law, the Department of Safety was to be disbanded ninety days after the end of World War I. However, before determination could be made on this matter, the General Assembly in April 1919, passed an appropriation bill that cut off funds for the state police as of July 15, 1919. A number of key individuals in the state government and the Colorado business community, however, wanted the state police to remain in operation. Foremost among these persons were Oliver Shoup, the newly elected governor, and Harry F. Allen, superintendent of the Department of Safety. The governor argued that the constabulary was a military organization and must exist even if there were no funds available for its operation. Following this line of reasoning, Superintendent Allen believed that the members of the department were subject to the call of the governor in the same manner as the National Guard. Contending that the legislature had not disbanded the department, but merely stopped its funds, Allen requested the attorney general to render a decision on the legality of the Department of Safety retaining its employees after July 15.[22] Anticipating that the attorney general would rule against him, Allen made preparations for reducing the force to a minimum.[23]

The obvious desire and intention of the governor to keep the Department of Safety operating after July 15 can be taken from the questions he asked in a letter to the attorney general. The governor wanted to know if the state police automatically went out of existence at the conclusion of peace between the United States and Germany. The attorney general indicated that the act expressly provided that the department be disbanded, although the law had not been repealed and some question regarding the exact status of the department remained. In anticipation of this response, the governor asked if, after the department was disbanded, the companies of men would be subject to the call of the governor. The attorney general responded that when disbanded, the companies would cease to exist and therefore would no longer be subject to the call of the governor. The governor then asked whether, if a surplus of state funds were on hand, it could be used to operate the state police beyond the cutoff date. Again the attorney general stated that any balance of state money must be returned to the general fund, where it would become unappropriated money and would be unavailable for specific expenditures such as the Department of Safety.[24] Ultimately, the attorney general ruled against Shoup and Allen, stating unequivocally that no state funds could be used to run the Department of Safety after July 15, 1919. On receiving this decision, Governor Shoup requested that Allen immediately reduce the force to ten employees and on June 1 dispose of the force completely.[25]

Shoup and Allen had lost their bid legally to keep the state police running. But despite the attorney general's ruling and the cutoff of funds on July 15, the Department of Safety continued to function on a limited basis. With a reduction of the department to a skeleton force, there was an excess of equipment on hand. Clifton H. Wilder, the newly appointed superintendent, sold the surplus equipment and used the proceeds to pay the salaries of the men.[26]

Superintendent Wilder was able to raise approximately $8,000 from the equipment sale but no account of the proceeds was made to the state auditor. The money was deposited by Wilder into a special account under his name. Claiming he had been guided by department precedent and to his knowledge had not violated the law, Wilder indicated that the sale was sanctioned by the governor. Governor Shoup acknowledged this fact, stating that, as commander-in-chief of the department, he authorized Wilder to dispose of the surplus equipment. By not depositing the money in the state treasury, Shoup and Wilder were able to circumvent the attorney general's ruling that no "state" funds could be used by the state police.[27]

As details of the equipment sale and use of the funds became public, state finance officers and the legislature began to take an interest in the matter. The Colorado Federation of Labor, which had unsuccessfully worked to repeal the state police law in the last legislative session, now pressured for a complete investigation in the hope of ending all activities of the Department of Safety.[28] Early in December 1919, at a special session of the legislature, Democratic senators who had opposed the department from the beginning introduced a resolution calling for the appointment of a committee to investigate the state police. The committee would look into the circumstances surrounding the continued existence of the Department of Safety, as well as the manner in which it was being financed.[29] The resolution passed unanimously in the Senate, but the House, under the control of the Republicans, declined to support the Senate resolution. No further action was taken, but the Democratic senators were satisfied with having the Republicans being the ones on record opposing the investigation of the state police.[30]

The state treasurer had become interested in the matter and requested a thorough audit of the state police department's records. But opponents of the Department of Safety received another setback when on January 13, 1920, the state police department was given a clean bill of health by Arthur M. Stong, the state auditor. In a report sent to the governor, Stong indicated that all moneys appropriated for the department by the legislature, and all moneys obtained from the sale of excess equipment, had been accounted for. The only irregularity the auditor could find was that during the time that Harry F. Allen was superintendent, six thousand pints of confiscated whiskey had disappeared.[31]

Surviving one crisis, the state police soon faced a new problem—it was running out of money. Although the equipment sale had netted $8,000, by November 1919 only $2,500 remained, and the force had to be cut to a minimum of personnel and activities. However, existing records fail to indicate if and when the Department of Safety ever stopped functioning due to lack of funds. Regardless of the financial situation, since the original statute remained in effect, the governor could revive the state police anytime funds became available.

### THE COLORADO RANGERS

Claiming that it was the state's duty to preserve law and order, and that Colorado could not continue to rely on federal troops for this purpose, Governor Shoup decided in September 1920 to reorganize the state police. A long-time friend of the governor and commander of the 157th Infantry during World War I, Patrick J. Hamrock was selected by Shoup to command the new force.[32] Not wanting the public to confuse the new police force with the old Department of Safety, Shoup and Hamrock named the new organization the Colorado Rangers.[33] The ranger force was to consist of four companies of fifty men each, including a full complement of commissioned and noncommissioned officers. The officers were to be on duty at all times and receive regular pay; the enlisted men could continue their regular occupations but were subject to immediate call to duty. The only condition imposed on the force was that every person accepted for service must be an ex-military man who had been overseas and had an honorable discharge. The rangers were to be trained by Colonel Hamrock and an officer supplied by the Pennsylvania state police.[34]

The name had been changed, but the legal basis for establishing the ranger force was the 1917 statute creating the Department of Safety. Since that law had not been repealed, the governor used the powers under that law to organize the new police force. The only obstacle facing Hamrock and the governor was finding funds to pay the rangers' operating expenses. Not wishing to invite the negative publicity that had surrounded the earlier attempt to fund the state police through the sale of departmental equipment, Shoup followed the legal path and authorized the state to incur an indebtedness of $50,000. By executive order, certificates of indebtedness were issued for purchase by Colorado citizens. The certificates were to be redeemed by a request for funds from the next General Assembly.[35]

Underwriting of the certificates was handled by soliciting subscriptions for the Colorado Ranger Fund, set up at the International Trust Company of Denver. By mid-December 1920, the fund had a total of $294,450 obtained from 278 Colorado "citizens." A 20 percent payment on the subscriptions generated $58,890, of which $14,750 had been spent as of December 14, 1920.[36] Eighty-one of the 278 subscribers had pledged a total of $243,700, or approximately 83 percent of the total, with an average subscription of $3,000. The other 197 subscribers accounted for the remaining $50,750, at an average pledge of $260. More important than the amounts, however, are the occupations of the subscribers themselves. The secondary subscribers (less than $1,000) were small-business operators, such as car dealers, grocery, furniture, and clothing store owners, and small manufacturers. The notable contributors ($3,000 or more), on the other hand, were owners or managers of the largest mining, manufacturing, and business concerns in the state; they represented a veritable who's who of Colorado's business elite (see Table 7.1). Although the average subscription among this elite group was about $3,000, such firms as the Rockefeller-owned Colorado Fuel and Iron Company, Great Western Sugar Company, Holly Sugar Company, and Midwest Refining Company pledged $10,000 each to the ranger fund.[37]

As soon as the General Assembly convened in 1921, Governor Shoup recommended the continuation of the ranger force. Citing serious industrial disturbances during the past two years, Shoup argued that a state police was the most effective means available for controlling such situations and was the surest and most economical agency for protecting "life and property" in Colorado. Having justified reviving the state police, the governor requested that the legislature provide adequate funds for maintaining the rangers and a change in the law to make them permanent.[38]

Within a week of the governor's request, two bills were introduced in the General Assembly. Both measures provided for a complete reorganization of the old Department of Safety along lines already established in the new ranger force. Bert M. Lake, a Republican from Denver, introduced a bill in the House that appropriated funds for the continued operation of the rangers and amended the original 1917 law. An identi-

**Table 7.1**
**Subscribers to the Colorado Rangers Fund ($3,000 or more)**

| Subscriber | Location | Amount of Pledge |
|---|---|---|
| J. S. Brown Mercantile Co. | Denver | $5,000 |
| Colorado Fuel and Iron Co. | Denver | $10,000 |
| Denver Bond Dealers Association | Denver | $5,000 |
| Denver Clearing House Association | Denver | $50,000 |
| Denver Gas and Electric Co. | Denver | $5,000 |
| Denver Post | Denver | $5,000 |
| Denver Rock Drill Mfg. Co. | Denver | $5,000 |
| John Evans | Denver | $3,000 |
| Great Western Sugar Co. | Denver | $10,000 |
| Hallack & Howard Lumber Co. | Denver | $3,000 |
| Edwin B. Hendrie | Denver | $5,000 |
| Holly Sugar Corporation | Denver | $10,000 |
| McPhee & McGinnity Co. | Denver | $5,000 |
| Midwest Refining Co. | Denver | $10,000 |
| J. C. Mitchell | Denver | $3,000 |
| Morey Mercantile Co. | Denver | $5,000 |
| Moutain States Telephone Co. | Denver | $5,000 |
| L. C. Phipps, Sr. L. C. Phipps, Jr. | Denver | $5,000 |
| Oliver H. Shoup | Denver | $3,000 |

*Source:* Shoup Papers, box 9921, file: Department of Safety, Colorado State Archives, Denver.

cal bill was introduced in the Senate by M. E. Bashor, a Republican farmer from Ordway.[39] Both bills increased the size of the present ranger force by allowing the recruitment of one or more troops of fifty men and provided $550,000 from National Defense Bonds to operate the force until January 1, 1923. The rangers were placed under the direction of the governor and the adjutant general, who was to be the ex officio superintendent. The superintendent was authorized to establish headquarters at various points in the state and was permitted to use the armories, arms, and equipment of the National Guard. To further assist the rangers the bills authorized the creation of an information bureau to investigate "any and all impending or suspected violations of the laws of this state and the United States."[40]

Governor Shoup appeared before groups of legislators and government officials to generate support for the ranger bills. Claiming that using the National Guard to police the state was too expensive, Shoup threatened to veto the measure if it did not provide enough men and money to do the work for which the force was created.[41] Failing to be intimidated, the House reduced the appropriation from $550,000 to $290,000 and then easily passed the bill when it was brought to a vote.[42] The Senate passed the measure after amending the legislation by restricting the force to one troop of fifty rangers. On April 2, 1921, the House approved the amended ranger bill by an overwhelming margin, and the Colorado Rangers became a legitimate and permanent feature of the state government.[43]

## ABOLISHING THE RANGERS

For eighteen months the rangers policed the state receiving both praise and condemnation. Much of their activity during this period was centered around two big coal strikes in southern Colorado. The policy of using the rangers in strike situations, and the manner in which they went about their policing activities, became an issue in the elections of 1922. Although the ranger issue was only one aspect of the campaign, it generated a high degree of emotion, dividing the electorate into those favoring "law and order" and those "advocating liberty under the Bill of Rights."[44]

Shoup had declined to run for reelection, and the Republicans nominated Benjamin Griffith, former state attorney and a follower of Theodore Roosevelt in the Progressive Party. A supporter of big business, Griffith indicated his position on the rangers by stating that "law and order will be the issue at the polls. . . . I favor the Rangers as a law enforcement organization, and I am backing them in my platform."[45] Griffith's opponent was William E. Sweet, whose nomination as the Democratic candidate for governor is an interesting story in itself. A wealthy member of the Denver business elite, Sweet held ideals of social welfare that led him to join the ranks of the liberal Democrats. Although respecting him for his financial success and philanthropic ideals, many members of Denver's business and financial community could neither understand nor accept his views regarding the desires of organized labor and other disadvantaged groups. Sweet openly declared he was in favor of the principles of organized labor and collective bargaining, and he actively sought support among the various trade unions of the state—something no past candidate for governor had dared to do.[46] Sweet's announcement as a candidate for governor shocked and frightened Colorado's business establishment. Branding him a traitor to his class, they feared that, unlike the rantings of a wild-eyed radical, his attacks on the social system would be listened to by the average voter.

Opposed by the conservative element within his own party, Sweet took his campaign to the people and easily won the primary to become the Democratic candidate for governor. More important, the Democratic voter turnout was larger than the Republican—a fact that sent shock waves through the Republican Party and its wealthy business supporters. As Williams points out, "Never in any state campaign in this country has the line been more closely drawn between human rights and property rights—between wealth and privilege on one side and social welfare on the other."[47] To Republicans and the business elite of Colorado, Sweet posed a threat to their position and interests. He was viciously attacked in the press as a socialist, and his followers were labeled bolsheviks and he himself a follower of Lenin and Trotsky. The election was close, and it wasn't until ballots from the rural areas had been counted that Sweet could be declared the winner. His victory was striking considering the influential backers opposed to his candidacy and Colorado's predominantly Republican electorate.[48]

In his farewell address to the General Assembly, Governor Shoup argued that during the short time in which the ranger system had been tried, it had proven to be "essential to the welfare of the state."[49] Contending that Colorado's decline of industrial disturbances compared with other states was due to the existence of the ranger force, the governor strongly recommended that the rangers be continued.[50] Four days later, Governor Sweet delivered his message to the General Assembly. Continuing the theme of his campaign in which he was critical of the rangers, Sweet restated his philosophy that the constitution placed responsibility for the enforcement of law and order in the hands of local county an d city officials, and he strongly urged repeal of the ranger law to restore the proper distribution of authority and to save the state money.[51]

The battle over the rangers began in the General Assembly. Senator J. Frank Cross of Walsenburg, a strong opponent of the rangers, and Representative Robert D. Elder of Ledville both introduced measures to repeal the ranger law of 1921 and the Department of Safety act of 1917. But Republican domination prevented favorable action and the bills died in committee. On the other hand, Republican supporters of the rangers introduced bills providing an appropriation for payment of salaries and continued operation of the force. The introduction of the appropriation measures was an attempt to put resolution of the ranger issue up to the governor and force him to make good on his campaign pledge to abolish the rangers—in this case by a veto of the appropriation bills.[52] Governor Sweet took the initiative, however, and on January 29, 1923, signed an executive order abolishing the ranger force. In a letter to Colonel Paul Newlon, adjutant general and head of the rangers, Sweet directed that all rangers be discharged as of February 1, 1923, ordered all equipment stored and inventoried, and indicated he would refuse to sign a bill, introduced at the insistence of Colonel Newlon, that would make available $50,000 from the sale of National Defense Bonds to pay ranger salaries.[53] On February 1, 1923, the Colorado Rangers ceased to function as an agency of the state government.

## REPEAL OF THE RANGER LAW

The rangers reemerged as a political issue in the 1926 campaign for governor. The Democratic candidate, William H. Adams, a rancher and cattleman, ran a campaign centered on repeal of the ranger law. Citing past experience with the rangers as an indication of their failure, Adams argued that "the danger that a governor may call that system into existence again should be permanently removed by repeal of the law."[54] Adams's concern about a revived ranger force was not intended as mere campaign rhetoric, but was directed squarely at his opponent. Running against Adams as the Republican candidate for governor was none other than Oliver Shoup—the former governor who had worked to bring the rangers into existence. During the campaign there were rumors that should Shoup be elected, his first official act would be to revive the ranger force.[55] The state police laws remained in the statutes and only required the word of the governor to make the force operative. Adams won the election and in his inaugural address to the General Assembly he stated that "the state ranger act should be speedily repealed" as it was "useless, unnecessary, and a source of irritation."[56]

Early in the legislative session, two bills were introduced to repeal the ranger law. In the House, Representatives Edwin C. Johnson of Craig and J. E. Martinez of Trinidad offered a measure that would abolish the Department of Safety. An identical bill was introduced by Senators Samuel Freudenthal of Trinidad and P. M. Hudson of Gardner.[57] The House bill moved quickly through committee, emerging a week after its introduction with a recommendation that it pass. The House immediately approved the bill on second reading without amendment and on the following day unanimously passed the bill to abolish the rangers.[58] In the Senate, on the other hand, two months passed before the measure emerged from committee with a favorable recommendation.

The bill then quickly moved to final consideration without amendment and easily passed 26 to 11.[59] Governor Adams signed the ranger repeal bill on April 1, 1927, removing from the statutes the law creating a "temporary" state police force passed a decade earlier. As they had done in the past, organized labor vigorously supported the adoption of the repeal measure, and representatives of various labor organizations were present when the governor signed the bill.[60] Colorado would not have another state-controlled law enforcement agency until 1935, when the "highway courtesy patrol" was established.

## THE STATE POLICE MOVEMENT IN COLORADO

From the very beginning, the state police issue in Colorado was primarily a political phenomenon. Emerging as a compromise between partisan factions, the Department of Safety was intended as a "temporary" force to protect the state for the duration of World War I in the absence of the National Guard. The force was kept in operation, however, through questionable administrative actions, and eventually emerged as the Colorado Rangers. The rangers became the focal point of two heated gubernatorial campaigns, which resulted in the disbanding of the force and finally the repeal of the enabling legislation.

The political nature of the state police issue in Colorado is illustrated in the voting activity of the state legislature. The process of creating and abolishing the state police resulted in nine recorded roll call votes in the Colorado General Assembly. Only eight of these votes are useful, however, as the 1927 vote to repeal the state police statutes was unanimous in both the House and the Senate. Table 7.2 shows the partisan nature of the voting on the state police measures. Generally, Republicans favored the state police while Democrats opposed the idea. Although the demands of World War I tempered opposition to the Department of Safety in 1917, Democratic opposition was evident. Once the war was over and the department had been kept in operation, the political divisions became acute. Beginning in 1919, with a Democratic bill to repeal the state police legislation, and in 1921, with the bill to fund and reorganize the rangers, the Democrats unanimously opposed the state police idea, while Republicans backed it even more strongly than they had in 1917. Decimated in the 1920 elections, the Democrats lacked the votes to counter the Republican domination of the General Assembly.

Although not one Democrat voted for the ranger bill, it was not entirely a partisan issue, as a number of Republicans also disapproved. In fact, Republican Paul Godsman of Burlington attempted to kill the bill before the vote by moving that it be sent back to committee. Godsman was opposed to the appropriation carried by the bill, as well as to the provision

**Table 7.2**
**Political Party and the State Police Vote**

| | | Democrat | | Republican | |
|---|---|---|---|---|---|
| | | *No.* | *Percent* | *No.* | *Percent* |
| 1917 (HB 28) | For | 14 | (37) | 18 | (75) |
| House | Against | 24 | (63) | 6 | (25) |
| 1917 (HB 28) | For | 8 | (50) | 15 | (88) |
| Senate | Against | 8 | (50) | 2 | (12) |
| 1917 (HB 28) | For | 26 | (67) | 19 | (86) |
| House | Against | 13 | (33) | 3 | (14) |
| 1917 (HB 28) | For | 8 | (50) | 13 | (76) |
| Senate | Against | 8 | (50) | 4 | (24) |
| 1919 (SB 74) | For* | 18 | (90) | 0 | (0) |
| Senate | Against | 2 | (10) | 14 | (100) |
| 1921 (HB 110) | For | 0 | (0) | 43 | (80) |
| House | Against | 6 | (100) | 11 | (20) |
| 1921 (HB 110) | For | 0 | (0) | 24 | (100) |
| Senate | Against | 11 | (100) | 0 | (0) |
| 1921 (HB 110) | For | 0 | (0) | 51 | (88) |
| House | Against | 5 | (100) | 7 | (12) |

* Repeal measure—yes vote indicates opposition to the state police.

that would permit the recruitment of former servicemen. Republican Iver H. Daily of Le Veta, however, defended the bill against charges that it was an antilabor measure by asserting that since he came from a strong union labor community, he knew that the "better elements" of organized labor were in favor of the enforcement of law and order.[61]

The Senate further amended the bill by restricting the force to one troop of fifty rangers and passed the measure 24 to 11. The partisan split over the ranger issue was again in evidence as all of the Republicans voted in favor while all of the Democrats voted against it.[62]

The political nature of the state police issue in Colorado is reinforced by the fact that party affiliation was the only variable to show any major difference in the voting on the state police bills. Information available on residence and occupation of legislators failed to reveal any particular pattern as both rural and urban legislators, as well as lawyers, merchants, and farmers, favored or opposed the state police in equal numbers. The only occupation to show a consistent voting record on the state police issue was banking; the banker legislators voted unanimously in favor of the state police. The only other variable related to voting on the state police was the residence of individual legislators. Although the differences were small, those who lived in the south central and southwestern parts of the state were more likely to vote against the state police, while those from the northeast and northwest tended to vote in favor of the state police. This reflects the fact that most of the mines were located in the southern part of the state, and legislators from districts with a large number of mine workers tended to support labor's opposition to the state police.

Information on other factors that could have provided deeper insight into the state police voting, such as votes on prohibition and labor legislation, was not available. During the period covered by the important votes on the state police (1917–1921), all labor legislation was buried in committee while only one prohibition measure was introduced, and this bill was also killed in committee.

Various groups were involved in the debate surrounding the state police issue in Colorado. Local peace officers were opposed as they saw the state police as a threat to their authority and power in the community. Middle-class liberals, those supporting the ideals of freedom and justice, also opposed the state police. In their view, centralized policing was a means of subverting the principles of constitutional protections and distribution of authority. Clearly, the two main groups in conflict over the state police were organized labor and the corporate elite.

Mine owners, manufacturers, and the business community as a whole were strong advocates and supporters of the state police in Colorado. Fearing that the mobilization of the National Guard for the war would leave them without any means of protection, Colorado's industrial elite used their influence in the legislature and the state administration to create a substitute—the Department of Safety. Postwar red scare hysteria and increased labor aggressiveness convinced the state's dominant interests that state police were necessary, even with the return of the National Guard. So important was the state police, that when the force ran out of money, it was kept operating through contributions to the ranger fund. The list of fund subscribers leaves little doubt as to the interests involved in supporting the operation of a state police in Colorado.

During the coal strikes of 1922, business interests were quick to praise the impact of the rangers. William B. Lewis, president of the Oakdale Coal Company, wrote the governor and thanked him for "the safe conduct" the company enjoyed from the administration, and pledged to cooperate with the governor in the "conservation of our mutual interests."[63] Stronger words are found in a letter to the governor from F. R. Wood, president of the Temple Fuel Company—located in the heart of the strike activity, at Trinidad. Wood wrote:

I want to express to you my gratitude and endorsement of the able manner in which you have handled the strike difficulty in this section of the state. . . . I was also pleased to hear . . . that you expect to let the rangers remain in this vicinity until the trouble is entirely wiped out. I feel that something drastic should be done to avoid this continued trouble and it seems to me . . . that there should be some way of *eliminating this organization of United Mine Workers from our midst* [emphasis added].[64]

The principal opposition came from labor groups, primarily the Colorado State Federation of Labor and the United Mine Workers. Previous labor troubles in Colorado, including the imposition of martial law and the Ludlow Massacre, had created a deep fear among labor groups and an antipathy to any centralized, state-controlled force, whether police or military. Labor unions, which had been fighting the state police issue for years, used an incident in which the rangers prevented a group of United Mine Workers from holding a meeting to open another attack on the state police.[65] Although labor opposed the state police from the very beginning, their lack of a strong and coordinated organization allowed the business and industry leaders to have their way. Criticism of the rangers also came from individuals not directly linked to labor organizations. A contractor from Durango, B. L. Gilbert, wrote a scathing letter to the governor, charging that his use of the rangers was a further indication of the administration's ties to the Rockefeller-owned Colorado Fuel and Iron Company.[66]

With the election of liberal Governor Sweet in 1923, labor and the other opponents of the state police finally had an ally in the state house. Continuing the theme of his campaign, in which he favored repeal of the ranger law, Sweet stated in a message to the General Assembly:

I believe the existence of the rangers for police purposes and their use to supplant civil officers is wrong, because it deprives our people of the right of local self-government. The ranger law had created an overlapping of duty, a divided assumption of authority, which has resulted in friction, an absence of cooperation, a lack of efficiency and a heavy burden upon our already overburdened taxpayers.[67]

As one of his first official acts, Sweet abolished the ranger force. Nevertheless, the General Assembly was firmly under the control of the Republican Party, and as representatives of the mining and sugar interests they were able to prevent passage of legislation intended to repeal the ranger and safety department laws. Not until 1927, when legislation backed by labor passed the General Assembly, were these laws finally repealed.

## SUMMARY

Formally called the Department of Safety, the Colorado state police were created as a war emergency measure by an act of the 21st General Assembly during a special session in the summer of 1917. The bill passed on August 4, 1917, and received the governor's approval three days later. The force consisted of four companies of forty-five men and five officers each. Heading the department were a superintendent and a deputy superintendent, both appointed by the governor. Unrestricted as to powers and authority, the state police could act anywhere in the state and arrest without warrant violators of any state or federal law.[68]

Since the Department of Safety was explicitly a war measure intended to protect the state in the absence of the National Guard, the law creating the force specified that it was to be disbanded at the end of the war. Nevertheless, powerful interests, including the governor, were able to keep the state police in operation and expand its activities. But the manner in which the state police went about their work generated negative and hostile attitudes among the citizens, and by 1922 public opinion had soured on the state police. The fate of the force became a political issue during the 1922 gubernatorial campaign, and shortly after taking office in 1923, Governor Sweet quickly acted to disband the Department of Safety.

The original law, however, remained in the statutes and was subject to reactivation at any time a governor so desired. This fact became a central campaign issue in 1926, and when Governor Adams took office in 1927 he actively sought legislation to repeal the state police laws. Such a bill eventually passed the legislature and on April 1, 1927, the governor signed the act repealing the 1917 law creating the Department of Safety. Colorado did not have another state law enforcement agency until 1935 when a highway patrol, restricted to enforcing traffic laws, was established.

## NOTES

1. In late September 1913, the United Mine Workers called a strike at the Ludlow coal mine in Colorado. Having been evicted from their company houses, the miners and their families were living in a tent colony set up by the union. Months of harassment by private guards and troops of the Colorado National Guard culminated on April 20, 1914, when a small unit of guardsmen opened fire on the tent colony with machine guns, killing six people. The guardsmen then proceeded to set the tents on fire killing eleven children and two women. In response, the miners organized an

armed counter attack on the mines. By the time President Wilson sent in Federal troops nine days later, seventy-four people had been killed. See Richard Hofstadter and Michael Wallace, *American Violence: A Documentary History* (New York: Random House/Vintage Books, 1970), pp. 160–161. For excellent discussions of the labor troubles in Colorado and other western states, see, for example, Melvyn Dubofsky, "The Origins of Western Working Class Radicalism, 1890–1905," *Labor History* 7 (Spring 1966): 131–154; George G. Suggs, *Colorado's War on Militant Unionism: James H. Peabody and the Western Federation of Miners* (Detroit: Wayne State University Press, 1972); Richard Peterson, "Conflict and Consensus: Labor Relations in Western Mining," *Journal of the West* 12 (January 1973): 1–17; and Merle W. Wells, "The Western Federation of Miners," *Journal of the West* 12 (January 1973): 18–35. For interesting contemporary accounts of the conflict between the Western Federation of Miners and the industry-dominated Citizen Alliances in Colorado, see Ray S. Baker, "The Reign of Lawlessness: Anarchy and Despotism in Colorado," *McClure's Magazine* 23 (May 1904): 43–57; and J. Warner Mills, "The Economic Struggle in Colorado: Dominant Trusts and Corporations," *The Arena* 35 (February 1906): 150–158.

2. *Journal of the House*, 1917, pp. 347–348; House Bill no. 336, 1917, Colorado State Archives, Denver.

3. *Denver Post*, June 12, 1917, p. 1.

4. *Denver Post*, July 17, 1917, p. 2.

5. *Denver Post*, July 20, 1917, pp. 8–9.

6. *Denver Post*, July 16, 1917, p. 4; July 17, 1917, pp. 1–2.

7. *Denver Post*, July 20, 1917, p. 9.

8. *Rocky Mountain News*, July 25, 1917, p. 5.

9. *Journal of the House*, special sess., 1917, pp. 78–80.

10. *Denver Post*, July 27, 1917, p. 11.

11. *Rocky Mountain News*, July 29, 1917, p. 5.

12. *Journal of the Senate*, special sess., 1917, pp. 136–140.

13. *Rocky Mountain News*, July 31, 1917, p. 7.

14. *Journal of the Senate*, special sess., 1917, pp. 165–166.

15. *Journal of the House*, special sess., 1917, p. 179; *Journal of the Senate*, special sess., 1917, pp. 181–182.

16. *Rocky Mountain News*, August 3, 1917, p. 1.

17. *Journal of the House*, special sess., 1917, pp. 213–214; *Journal of the Senate*, special sess., 1917, pp. 219–220.

18. *Journal of the House*, special sess., 1917, p. 221; *Journal of the Senate*, special sess., 1917, p. 215; *Denver Post*, August 4, 1917, p. 2.

19. *Denver Post*, August 5, 1917, sec. 1, p. 8.

20. Ibid.

21. *Denver Post*, August 4, 1917, p. 4; August 9, 1917, p. 3; August 23, 1917, p. 10.

22. *Rocky Mountain News*, April 12, 1919, p. 3.

23. *Rocky Mountain News*, April 26, 1919, p. 9.

24. V. E. Keyes to O. H. Shoup, May 5, 1919, Shoup papers, box 9921, file: Department of Safety, Colorado State Archives, Denver (hereafter referred to as SP).

25. O. H. Shoup to H. F. Allen, May 3, 1919, SP, box 9921, file: Department of Safety.

26. *Rocky Mountain News*, November 30, 1919, pp. 1, 7.

27. Ibid.

28. *Rocky Mountain News*, December 9, 1919, p. 2; December 12, 1919, pp. 1, 4.

29. *Journal of the Senate*, special sess., 1919, pp. 45–46.

30. *Journal of the House*, special sess., 1919, pp. 51–52; *Denver Post*, December 12, 1919, p. 1.

31. *Denver Post*, January 13, 1920, p. 1.

32. Patrick J. Hamrock also has the "distinction" of being the commanding officer leading the troops responsible for the Ludlow Massacre in 1914.

33. *Denver Post*, September 4, 1920, p. 1; September 9, 1920, p. 16.

34. *Denver Post*, September 4, 1920, p. 1.

35. Executive Order, September 28, 1920, SP, box 9921, file: Department of Safety; *Denver Post*, September 4, 1920, p. 1.

36. Memo, W. A. Horner to account subscribers, December 14, 1920, SP, box 9921, file: Department of Safety.

37. W. M. Bond to O. H. Shoup, October 18, 1920, SP, box 9921, file: Department of Safety (includes a complete list of subscribers to the ranger fund).

38. *Denver Post*, January 7, 1921, p. 8.

39. *Journal of the House*, 1921, p. 78; *Journal of the Senate*, 1921, p. 2.

40. Senate Bill no. 97, 1921, Colorado State Archives, Denver.

41. *Journal of the House*, 1921, p. 803.

42. *Denver Post*, February 9, 1921, p. 4; *Journal of the House*, 1921, pp. 867–868.

43. *Journal of the House*, 1921, pp. 1428–1429.

44. Wayne C. Williams, *Sweet of Colorado* (New York: Fleming H. Revell, 1943), p. 63.

45. Ibid.

46. Ibid., pp. 54–59

47. Ibid., pp. 60–61

48. Ibid., pp. 64–68

49. *Denver Post*, January 5, 1923, p. 21.

50. *Journal of the House*, 1923, pp. 33–34.

51. *Journal of the House*, 1923, p. 113; *Denver Post*, January 9, 1923, p. 1.

52. *Journal of the House*, 1923, pp. 159, 163, 277–278; *Denver Post*, January 5, 1923, p. 21; *Denver Post*, January 17, 1923, p. 15.

53. *Denver Post*, January 29, 1923, pp. 1, 4; *Rocky Mountain News*, January 30, 1923, p. 3.

54. *Rocky Mountain News*, October 12, 1926, p. 3.

55. Ibid.

56. *Journal of the House*, 1927, p. 83.

57. *Journal of the House*, 1927, p. 98; *Journal of the Senate*, 1927, pp. 63–64.

58. *Journal of the House*, 1927, pp. 245, 253–254, 260–261.

59. *Journal of the Senate*, 1927, pp. 765, 867–868, 891.

60. *Denver Post*, April 1, 1927, p. 18.

61. *Journal of the House*, 1921, pp. 842, 866; *Denver Post*, March 5, 1921, p. 5.

62. *Journal of the Senate*, 1921, pp. 911, 1041–1042, 1080–1081.

63. W. B. Lewis to O. H. Shoup, January 6, 1922, SP, box 9921, file: Coal Strikes.

64. F. R. Wood to O. H. Shoup, December 15, 1921, SP, box 9921, file: Coal Strikes.

65. *Rocky Mountain News*, June 1, 1922, pp. 1–2; *Denver Post*, June 1, 1922, p. 8.

66. B. L. Gilbert to O. H. Shoup, February 1, 1922, SP, box 9921, file: Department of Safety.

67. *Journal of the House*, 1923, p. 105.

68. Colorado State Legislature, *Session Laws*, 1917, chap. 12.

*Chapter 8*

# Analysis of the State Police Movement

The patterns of activity identified in the previous discussion of the state police creation process in Illinois and Colorado provide support for my argument that the emergence of the state police was a product of the unique combination of events occurring during the first two decades of the twentieth century. Social and economic change, urban growth, immigration, labor troubles, and a world war created a climate in which different interests—business, reformers, and politicians—favored changes in traditional patterns of social control. Most of the state police forces created between 1905 and 1925 fall into this category. However, the discussion of state police developments in Colorado and Illinois illustrates differences in the creation process that require further analysis. Comparative study of the unique differences between these two similar responses to a common problem provides deeper insight into the process itself. Moreover, this type of analysis is made easier given the legislative nature of state police development as stated at the outset. This dimension of state police development affords the opportunity to analyze and evaluate their emergence as a case of lawmaking.

Study of the law creation process is firmly anchored in the "law in action" tradition within the sociology of law and has produced a number of important works. The most well-known are Hall's analysis of the Carrier's Case and the resulting theft laws, and the study of vagrancy laws by Chambliss.[1] In addition, other studies of specific laws such as prohibition, marijuana and heroin legislation, prostitution statutes, and federal ransom kidnapping laws have contributed significant insight into the law creation process.[2]

The central argument of these various studies is that rather than being an expression of societal consensus, law is the reflection of "cultural difference, value clashes, and social conflict."[3] The conflicts may be expressed

> in violent confrontations between social classes or more genteelly in the form of institutionalized dispute-settling procedures. Regardless of the form the conflict takes, in the end it is the existence of the structurally induced conflicts between groups in the society that determines the form and content of the . . . law.[4]

As these studies suggest, the form and content of law represent the interests of those individuals and groups who have the power to shape public policy. Yet while agreement exists on this basic tenet of law creation, there are differences of opinion regarding the specific nature of the interests involved in lawmaking.

The studies of Hall, Chambliss, Hay et al., and Thompson suggest that material economic interests and elites determine the character of law.[5] Gusfield argues that status-based class conflict is the prime factor in lawmaking.[6] On the other hand, Becker, Lindesmith, and Duster favor the impact of morally based bureaucratic interests in shaping legislation.[7] Finally, Lemert, Akers, Roby, and Alix point to the activity of pragmatic vested interests among organizations, agencies, and professionals for affecting the content of law.[8] Such differences indicate that any analysis of law creation must be able to account for a range of possible interests and not be restricted to one particular type.

Drawing from this diverse body of research, a basic set of questions can be framed for identifying and comparing the elements of social conflict involved in creating the state police in Illinois and Colorado. The first element that needs to be identified is the interaction pattern—who are the individuals and groups that are in conflict over the state police issue? Second, the specific aspects that influence the interaction need to be established—why are the individuals and groups in conflict over the idea of creating a state police? Third, the relative conditions of power available to each party involved in the conflict become the focus of study—what resources do those involved in the debate over the state police bring with them to the conflict? Fourth, the specific policies, programs, and procedures of each party need to be described—how are the resources used by those in the conflict? And fifth, the outcome of the conflict for each party needs to be established—what are the final results of the conflict over the state police, that is, who won and why?

## THE INTERACTION PATTERN

This dimension of the process concerns the various individuals, groups, and organizations that were involved in the legislative activity on the state police. Clearly, a consistent pattern of interest group activity is evident. The primary proponents of the state police, those individuals and groups who actively worked to get state police laws introduced and passed, were the most powerful business interests in each state. In Illinois, state police proponents included the state Chamber of Commerce, the Illinois Manufacturers' Association, the state bankers' association, and the Illinois Agricultural Association. In Colorado, it was the mining interests, the sugar producers, and the bankers who supported the state police effort. In both states, the principal opposition to the state police came from organized labor, especially the respective state federations of labor and the United Mine Workers.

There were other groups involved in the state police issue, but they were of minor significance as their impact on the legislation was barely noticeable. Women's groups, individual small-business owners, car clubs, and local civic and fraternal organizations all endorsed the idea of a state police. Joining organized labor in opposition to the state police were various taxpayer groups who feared an increase in state taxes to pay for the new police force, and numerous local enforcement agencies (sheriffs and constables) who believed a state police would reduce their role and force them out of work. Nevertheless, the primary interests in conflict over the state police in both Illinois and Colorado were organized labor and the large economic concerns of business and industry. Evidence from other states suggests this as the common interaction pattern of the state police movement nationwide.[9]

## FACTORS INFLUENCING INTERACTION

Crucial for explaining the state police issue is an understanding of the reasons for conflict between the proponents and opponents of state police legislation. A key factor was a basic difference in values concerning the proper role of law enforcement within society. In Illinois, the business community was interested in reforming all police agencies to make them more efficient. Applying the model of the corporation to police organization, business leaders desired a centralized structure that removed control from local officials and placed it in the hands of "neutral" state officials. Along with "professionalism," centralization was believed to be the most important reform for improving the effectiveness of the police.

Illinois labor groups, on the other hand, had a different view of the police. Believing that the removal of local control was an unprecedented change in the constituted structure of American government, labor leaders vehemently opposed centralization, favoring instead local control of the police. Labor groups were quick to make the point that they were not opposed to police or law enforcement, only to the *type* of police embodied in the paramilitary organizations being proposed. The best form of law enforcement, from labor's point of view, was a locally controlled police responsive to community needs and interests.

Although the data were less clear on this issue for the state of Colorado, it would appear that a similar difference of opinion was involved. However, proponents of the state police in Colorado were more open in their hostility to organized labor, with a number of individuals explicitly stating their desire for a force that could be used against labor groups during strikes. Because of long-standing animosities dating back to the 1890s, relations between business and labor in Colorado were akin to a situation of undeclared warfare. In such a context, the idea of a state police was viewed more as an additional weapon than as a law enforcement measure; this perception was shared by both business and labor groups alike.

## CONDITIONS OF POWER

Those involved in conflict over an issue generally have access to various resources that can be used in their fight to influence the final outcome. In both Illinois and Colorado, state police proponents, owing to their dominant economic position, had large financial resources that were used to promote a favorable decision on the state police bills. This was especially true in Illinois, where the wealthiest business and agricultural concerns financed a twelve-year battle to establish a state police. In Colorado, passage of the state police legislation was easily accomplished, but financial support was readily available when state money ran out and private funds were sought to keep the state police in operation.

In addition to money, state police proponents had the help of major newspapers in their drive for state police laws. Owned and operated by wealthy individuals, papers such as the *Denver Post* and the *Chicago Tribune* tended to be sympathetic to the interests of the economic elite and thus provided editorial support for the state police idea, although they couched it in the neutral terms of rural police protection. Also, the Farm Bureau in Illinois was able to use its position in the agricultural community to bring a "nonbusiness" voice to bear on the situation. Using the statewide network of local farm bureaus, the Illinois Agricultural Association was able to direct formidable lobbying efforts in support of state police legislation by claiming to represent the voice of the Illinois farmer.

Labor groups, although lacking the financial resources of the larger business and industrial concerns, had the advantage of an effective local and national organizational structure that could be coordinated in a strong counterlobbying effort in opposition to the state police. In Illinois, labor also had the advantage of political influence as the state administration of Governor Small was favorable to labor opinion. In addition, many Illinois state legislators were strong supporters of organized labor, with a few being union members. Colorado labor groups lacked these resources and it hampered their efforts to fight the drive for a state police. The effect of this type of support was underscored when Governor Sweet was elected in 1923. A supporter of labor interests, Sweet quickly moved to disband the state police in Colorado.

## POLICIES AND PROCEDURES

In their use of resources, proponents and opponents of the state police operated in a similar fashion—both attempted to influence directly the voting on the state police bills, as well as to manipulate public opinion in their favor. State police advocates in Illinois used their financial strength to support a massive propaganda campaign designed to promote the idea that a state police was necessary because existing rural law enforcement was incapable of dealing with modern forms of crime and lawlessness. Newspaper ads, flyers, public speakers, and motion pictures were used in a statewide effort to convince the public that a state police was a desirable addition to the state's law enforcement apparatus. First generating and then playing on the fear of rural crime, state police proponents would continually report all acts of lawlessness, no matter how minor, that occurred in the rural areas, and then point to the lack or reduction of such acts in those states that had an "efficient" state police force.

Supporters of the state police in Colorado, being more successful in their efforts to create a state police, were less involved in attempts to generate public support. Most of their activity was directed toward undermining labor opposition to the state police by promoting the idea that Colorado labor organizations were bent on revolution and lawlessness. A past history of labor unrest and involvement by the Industrial Workers of the World made it easy to portray the intentions of labor groups in a negative fashion.

Labor groups attempted to influence public opinion in the opposite direction by claiming that a state police was nothing more than a standing army and a direct threat to individual liberty and freedom. At every opportunity, labor leaders would report stories of violence and repressive actions committed by members of the state police in New York and Pennsylvania in an effort to present the "other side" of the state police issue. By means of the labor press and public appearances, labor views on the state police were circulated throughout the state of Illinois, and to a lesser degree in Colorado. In essence, the fight over the state police in both states was an ideological conflict, involving propaganda campaigns on both sides of the issue.

## THE FINAL OUTCOME

The process surrounding the legislative activity pertaining to the state police was similar in both Illinois and Colorado with regard to the groups involved, the reasons for their involvement, the resources available, and the respective policies for promoting their specific interests. However, the final outcome was different in each state. Colorado easily established a state police in 1917 and was able to keep it in operation until it was disbanded in 1923. Illinois, on the other hand, was never able to establish a military-like state police during the period from 1917 to 1929. Instead, only a small restricted highway patrol emerged from the legislative conflict.[10] Since major dimensions of the process were the same in each state, why was there a difference in the final outcome? Two factors appear to provide an explanation—labor strength and population characteristics.

Illinois and Colorado present striking contrasts with regard to the demographic characteristics of their respective populations. In 1920, Illinois was the third most populous state in the nation, with 6,500,000 inhabitants. Colorado, on the other hand, was considerably smaller, with a total population in 1920 of 940,000. In addition, Chicago was the nation's second largest city, with 2,700,000 inhabitants in 1920—two and a half million more than Colorado's largest city of Denver, which numbered only 257,000.[11] While these figures point to some basic differences in the aggregate populations of the two states, the specific characteristics of the respective state populations provide a better explanation for the difference on the state police issue.

Colorado's population was primarily rural and old-stock native. In 1920, 52 percent of its inhabitants resided in rural areas, while 65 percent of the white population was of native parentage. In sharp contrast, Illinois was more urban in character as only 32 percent of its population lived in rural areas. Furthermore, Illinois had a distinct foreign influence as 52 percent of the population was either foreign born or of foreign parentage. The ethnic differences between the two states can be more clearly illustrated by comparing the populations of Chicago and Denver. Denver's white population in 1920 was 58 percent native and 42 percent foreign, while Chicago had the country's second largest concentration of immigrants, as 75 percent of the population was either foreign born or of foreign-born parentage.[12]

The strong foreign element in Illinois provided a diversity of values and life-styles which often were at odds with the sentiments of old-stock natives. Immigrants viewed laws such as Sunday closing restrictions and prohibition as policies aimed solely at them and their values. Isolated within the larger society, immigrants turned to the "boss" and political machines for protection and support. By 1920, the size of the immigrant population in Illinois and its emerging organization gave them considerable political influence. With many legislative districts in Chicago having foreign populations approaching 90 percent, politicians could ill afford to ignore immigrant demands.

Colorado, with its smaller, predominantly old-stock population, lacked a strong immigrant presence in its social and political environment. Legislators were mostly representative of the native white populations and felt little pressure to heed the demands of immigrants in their respective districts. In addition, the character of the immigrant population in Colorado was somewhat different from that of Illinois. Colorado's foreign population was composed primarily of immigrants from northwestern Europe (England, Belgium, and Sweden), with only 24 percent coming from eastern and southern European countries such as Poland, Czechoslovakia, and Italy. In Illinois, however, eastern and southern Europeans accounted for 40 percent of the immigrant population. Thus, differences in values between the native and the immigrant were more pronounced in Illinois, while in Colorado cultural differences were less severe.[13]

Colorado and Illinois also differed in the characteristics of their respective labor populations. Illinois was a principal industrial state ranking fifth in the number of employed wage earners in manufacturing and third in the value of its industrial production. In comparison, Colorado ranked thirty-sixth and thirty-fourth, respectively. Not surprisingly, wage earners accounted for a larger percentage of Illinois's population. Combined, manufacturing and mining wage earners in Illinois made up 17 percent of the population between the ages of fifteen and sixty-five, while in Colorado the comparable figure was only 8 percent.[14]

The large number of wage earners in Illinois provided a potent force that had a measure of political influence. Politically organized under an aggressive leadership, labor in Illinois actively worked to promote legislation supportive of its interests and campaigned for legislators sympathetic to its views. In districts with a large number of wage earners labor had considerable influence and was often able to elect union members to the General Assembly. Labor in Colorado was much less of a political force. Although labor groups attempted to make an impact on important issues, they lacked the leadership and organization of their Illinois counterparts. Labor in Colorado was, therefore, a marginal participant in legislative activity dominated mostly by ranchers and businessmen.

The differences between Colorado and Illinois with regard to labor and immigrants provide an explanation for the respective outcomes on the state police issue. Immigrants and organized labor viewed attempts to reform police by centralization in the same context as blue laws, prohibition, strike injunctions, and yellow-dog contracts—repressive attempts by the native white businessmen and professionals to preserve their privileged position in society. The idea of a state police was seen as a tactic to eliminate local control of the police and give the middle and upper class greater control of law enforcement. For this reason, labor opposed the state police on grounds that it would be used as a state-controlled army to aid the industrialists in breaking strikes, while immigrant groups opposed the state police in the belief that it was intended as a mechanism for enforcing prohibition and other unpopular laws favored by the old-stock elite.

The combined strength of labor and immigrant groups in Illinois proved to be a formidable opponent, able to prevent passage of state police laws for over twelve years. But for these two factors, Illinois in all probability would have created a Pennsylvania-style state police in the early 1920s. Colorado, on the other hand, lacked the influence of strong labor and immigrant groups, making it much easier for state police proponents to pass the ranger legislation in 1917. It took repressive and illegal excesses and scandal to end the state police when a liberal governor, backed by labor and the middle class, abolished an agency that had gone beyond the bounds of culturally permissible activity.

In general, the state police issue was a conflict between groups having fundamentally opposed views on the direction and scope of social control in American society. The established elite (business, industry, and the old-stock middle and upper classes) favored professionalism and centralization to make the police more efficient and more responsive to the needs of a "business"-oriented society. Labor and the immigrant favored the retention of locally controlled police forces that were more in tune with community needs and desires concerning the enforcement of the law. Both sides, however, were responding to a perceived threat. The established elite feared the growing power of organized labor and the "dangerous classes" of the foreign immigrant. The wage earner and the foreign born, more often than not one and the same, already felt threatened by strike injunctions and laws aimed at imposing middle-class values on the immigrant; the state police would only make the struggle that much more difficult. Given the resources of the established elite, they were by and large successful in their attempts to establish state police forces. Where opposition was strong, well organized, and politically influential, the outcome was less certain. The history of state police development in Colorado and Illinois supports this conclusion.

## WHY POLICE?—THE DEBATE

This book began with the goal of providing a descriptive analysis of the interest structure surrounding the development of the state police in the United States. The topic was introduced by noting the deficiency of scholarly attention given to social-historical dimensions of the American police system. The lack of a comprehensive body of data on police development in the United States has created a void in which competing explanations have emerged in the literature. Social disorganization, political process, and Marxist perspectives each claim to provide the "correct" explanation for the rise and transformation of the American police. But with limited historical material available on the American police, these perspectives remain plausible alternatives, each with its own unique explanation for police development. It might prove useful to use the data on state police development to further examine the potential validity of these models of police development.

From a social disorganization perspective, the state police would appear as a necessary and logical reform for bringing the existing law enforcement apparatus in line with the changed conditions of the twentieth century. Economic expansion and industrial growth, which had been aided by developments in transportation and communication, had begun to "urbanize" the countryside and bring the city crime problem to the rural districts. But owing to their local affiliations, limited jurisdiction, and lack of training, the old-fashioned and decentralized system of sheriffs, constables, and town marshals was inadequate for dealing with the increased demands of modern crime control. This theme of social disorganization, that social change produced increased disorder which in turn prompted community leaders to reform the police, was a key component of the arguments used by early proponents of the state police.

A social disorganization perspective may provide an appreciation for the impact social change had on desires to reform mechanisms of social control but is too "mechanical" in its portrayal of this process. Aside from introducing the element of change, social disorganization does not offer an explanation of why a *state* police was necessary. Why not reform existing agencies by granting more powers, improving training, or simply hiring more police? An adequate explanation would require an investigation into the political considerations involved in decisions to focus on certain kinds of disorder, and the efforts to reorganize the police in a specific way. Apart from cataloging a variety of disparate influences, social disorganization fails to establish the precise linkages between changing political, social, and economic circumstances and changes in the apparatus of formal social control. Rather, analysis is limited to describing certain events and suggesting possible correlations between the events and police reform.[15]

A response to the social disorganization argument can be found in the political process perspective. From this point of view, social change is seen as affecting group conflict within the political arena, eventually bringing about changes in methods of social control. Competing political factions sought to use the police in efforts to advance their specific interests.[16] The state police, it could be argued, represented another development in the process of manipulating law enforcement for political gain. Progressive reformers, threatened and challenged by the ethnic-dominated political machines, desired to break machine control of the police. The reformers wanted to have greater influence over the police so as to redefine the concept of law and order to coincide with their values. Locked out of the urban political arena, reformers looked to the state legislature and its dominance by conservative rural legislators for sympathetic support in their efforts to professionalize the police and eliminate inefficiency and corruption.

State police would be the ideal agency since they were free from machine control and were able to go anywhere in the state to enforce all state and federal laws. Thus, the state police embodied the elements of reform sought by the middle and upper classes, as well as giving them a measure of control over its operation. By creating an agency of control that could supersede municipal and county officials and enforce all laws, police reformers were able to break the grip of urban political machines over law enforcement and increase their level of political control within the urban community.[17]

Although an improvement over the social disorganization approach, the political process model also seems inadequate in the light of the present research. Other than vague references to "organized" and "unorganized" groups fighting for control of the police, there is a lack of specificity in identifying the particular groups involved or describing the nature of their interactive relationships in working to bring about the desired reforms.

In contrast to both the social disorganization and political process explanations, proponents of a Marxist interpretation of police development argue that the genesis and transformation of organized police must be examined within the changing class relations accompanying the rise of industrial capitalism. Stressing the relationship between police and the political economy, Marxists see the emergence of the police as the first of many "ruling-class" reforms as a means to enforce class, social, and cultural oppression of the worker and maintain the privileged position of the industrial class. The police are an integral component of the coercive apparatus of the state which serves not as "protectors of democracy, but the protectors of the interests of the dominant class."[18]

From a Marxist perspective, state police would be explained as an expected continuation of the ruling-class search for better methods of social control. Owing to major changes taking place in the political economy at the turn of the century, earlier methods of social control (municipal and private police and the National Guard) were beginning to show signs of weakness the ruling class wished to correct. The ideal solution would be a police system which had no jurisdictional restrictions, would be paid for out of the state treasury, would provide constant patrol, and could not be linked to ruling-class interests as they would simply be the "neutral" agents of the state.

The role of the ruling class and the political economy of capitalism are of crucial importance in understanding the emergence and transformation of the police. But, as Schur cautions,

> We must be wary of purported explanations that attribute . . . control . . . or exploitation by the "ruling elite." Such assertions gloss over several important factors: . . . the multiplicity of group interests and social forces that may come into play; the mixed or ambiguous interests that some groups may have; the inevitable limitations on absolute control that confront . . . the ruling elite even in situations where they might seek to exert it.[19]

By concentrating exclusively on the control needs of the ruling class, and posing a simplistic, instrumental relationship between elite interests and police development, the Marxist approach necessarily devaluates the significance of other factors which accompanied the development of policing agencies.[20] The complexities of the state police movement demand a more sophisticated explanation than that offered by an instrumental class analysis. The roles played by the middle-class reformer, nativism, 100 percent Americanism, racism, and fundamentalist religion indicate more at work than mere desires for a force to break strikes. Combining the more salient arguments of the various perspectives seems a more reasoned approach for understanding the creation of the state police. According to Levett, four dimensions of political activity can be associated with police reform movements.[21] First, the arrival of "strangers" is perceived as a threat by locals who mobilize against them (increased immigration and aggressive labor are seen as a threat by the old-stock middle class and business leaders). Second, those groups who feel threatened attempt to strengthen the police for added protection and as a means to limit the challenge posed by the other groups (state police, because of their authority to act anywhere in the state, would weaken the hold immigrants and labor had over local officials). Third, efforts to use the police for partisan interests provoke countermobilization actions on the part of those groups whose activities are being threatened by police reform (immigrants and labor oppose the state police). Finally, out of the conflict emerges a police policy that determines the size and strength of the new force, as well as the kinds of action and people it will be directed to control (various states succeed or fail in passing state police laws, and various forms of state-controlled police are created, that is, the restricted highway patrol versus the military-like constabulary).

## SUMMARY

Creation of the state police in the United States represents another variation on the efforts of dominant groups in society to maintain social order. Changing patterns of immigration and the emergence of an aggressive labor movement presented a situation in which a certain type of formal social control was deemed appropriate and necessary. Leaders of the various civic, business, and professional organizations began to argue that long-term prosperity and stability required the rejection of nineteenth-century values that emphasized decentralization and local community autonomy. A quote from the 1910 proceedings of the Minnesota Academy of Social Sciences is representative of this changing mood:

> The people of this country face momentous changes. . . . There seems to be a growing consciousness that the state has not done its duty . . . for the protection of the general welfare. And the people are determined that the laissez-faire policy must be given up and that a strong state is needed to cope with impending developments.[22]

Couched in terms of a "modern crime problem," progressive arguments for police reform stressed that the "decentralized nature" of existing police organizations presented a "serious handicap to effective and economical" law enforcement. The idea of a state police was advanced as the best remedy for this defect, as it would provide centralized and coordinated statewide police forces.[23] Rhetoric aside, the primary factors leading to the development of the state police were the increase in immigration from eastern and southern Europe and the desire to curb the growing labor movement.

The thesis of this book is that, rather than being a unique occurrence, the creation of the state police followed a recurring pattern in the history of social control. As those at the top of the social class hierarchy perceive a threat to their position of dominance, new and improved methods of preserving the status quo will be established. Whether it be the Royal Irish Constabulary, the Royal Canadian Mounted Police, or the Colorado Rangers, the idea of centralization was used to bolster or replace social control mechanisms that had become inadequate in the face of greater challenges from below. As with immigration restriction, prohibition, scientific management, commission forms of city government, eugenics, the juvenile court, and education reform, centralized state police forces were part of a massive effort on the part of the dominant segments of society to preserve their values and ideals of social order.

## NOTES

1. Jerome Hall, *Theft, Law, and Society* (Indianapolis, IN: Bobbs Merrill, 1956); William J. Chambliss, "A Sociological Analysis of the Law of Vagrancy," *Social Problems* 12 (Summer 1964): 67–77.

2. Ernest K. Alix, *Ransom Kidnapping in America, 1874–1974: The Creation of a Capital Crime* (Carbondale, IL: Southern Illinois University Press, 1978); Howard S. Becker, *Outsiders: Studies in the Sociology of Deviance* (New York: Free Press, 1963); Joseph R. Gusfield, *Symbolic Crusade: Status Politics and the American Temperance Movement* (Urbana: University of Illinois Press, 1963); Alfred R. Lindesmith, *The Addict and the Law* (Bloomington: Indiana University Press, 1965); Pamela A. Roby, "Politics and Criminal Law: Revision of the New York State Penal Law on Prostitution," *Social Problems* 17 (Summer 1969): 83–109.

3. Steven Vago, *Law in Society* (Englewood Cliffs, NJ: Prentice-Hall, 1988), p. 121.

4. William J. Chambliss, "The State and Criminal Law," in *Whose Law? What Order?: A Conflict Approach to Criminology*, edited by William J. Chambliss and Milton Mankoff (New York: John Wiley and Sons, 1976), p. 67.

5. Hall, *Theft, Law, and Society*; Chambliss, "A Sociological Analysis"; Douglas Hay et al., *Albion's Fatal Tree: Crime and Society in Eighteenth Century England* (New York: Pantheon Books, 1975); E. P. Thompson, *Whigs and Hunters: The Origin of the Black Act* (New York: Random House, 1975).

6. Gusfield, *Symbolic Crusade*.

7. Becker, *Outsiders*; Lindesmith, *The Addict*; Troy Duster, *The Legislation of Morality: Law, Drugs, and Moral Judgment* (New York: Free Press, 1970).

8. Alix, *Ransom Kidnapping*; Roby, "Politics and Criminal Law"; Ronald L. Akers, "The Professional Association and the Legal Regulation of Practice," *Law and Society Review* 3 (May 1968): 463–482; Edwin M. Lemert, "Legislating Change in the Juvenile Court," *Wisconsin Law Review* 1967 (Spring 1967): 421–448.

9. James Hayes, "History and Development of State Police and State Highway Patrols and Methods of Handling the Minor Vehicle Violator" (M.A. thesis, Harvard University, 1935); Walter E. Kaloupek, "The History and Administration of the Iowa Highway Safety Patrol," *Iowa Journal of History and Politics* 36 (October 1938): 339–386; Oscar G. Olander, *Michigan State Police: A Twenty Year History* (Michigan Police Journal Press, 1942); Leo J. Coakley, *Jersey Troopers: A Fifty Year History of the New Jersey State Police* (New Brunswick, NJ: Rutgers University Press, 1971); Gerda Ray, "Contested Legitimacy: Creating the State Police in New York, 1890–1930" (Ph.D. diss., University of California at Berkeley, 1990); Stanley L. Swart, "The Development of State-Level Police Activity in Ohio, 1802–1928" (Ph.D. diss., Northwestern University, 1974).

10. Beginning in 1929 and continuing throughout the 1930s, various amendments were enacted that gradually transformed the highway patrol into a large state police force with increased powers of arrest and wider jurisdiction.

11. U.S. Department of Commerce, *Fourteenth Census of the United States, 1920*, vol. 3 (Washington, DC: Government Printing Office, 1923), pp. 18, 50.

12. Ibid., pp. 75, 106, 112.

13. Ibid., pp. 310–311.

14. Ibid., pp. 920, 1270.

15. Allen E. Levett, "Centralization of City Police in the Nineteenth Century United States" (Ph.D. diss., University of Michigan, 1975), p. 19.

16. Ibid.

17. Ibid., p. 24

18. Joel Summerhays, "American Police Reform: An Alternative Perspective" (Ph.D. diss., University of California at Berkeley, 1979), p. 204.

19. Edwin Schur, *The Politics of Deviance: Stigma Contests and the Uses of Power* (Englewood Cliffs, NJ: Prentice-Hall, 1980), p. 70.

20. The point must be emphasized that there are formulations within the Marxist tradition which are less "instrumental" in their view of the relation of the ruling class to the state; they stress structural elements such as fractions within the ruling class, the autonomy of the state, and stabilization of the total system of capitalist relations. But the work of this Marxist tradition has been highly abstract, with little or no empirical analysis of concrete societal features such as the police. See, for example, Louis Althusser, *For Marx* (New York: Pantheon Books, 1969); Claus Offe, "Political Authority and Class Structures: An Analysis of Late Capitalist Societies," *International Journal of Sociology* 2 (Spring 1972): 73–108; Nicos Poulantzas, *Political Power and Social Classes* (London: NLB/Sheed, 1973).

21. Levett, "Centralization of City Police," pp. 74–75.

22. F. C. Miller, "The State Police," *Papers and Proceedings of the Third Annual Meeting of the Minnesota Academy of Social Sciences*, ed. William A. Schaper, vol. 3, no. 3 (Index Press, 1910), p. 98.

23. New Jersey State Chamber of Commerce. Bureau of State Research "State Police Problem in America," *State Research*, supplement to *New Jersey* 4, no. 4 (January 1917): 2.

# Suggestions for Further Research on the State Police

The data and conclusions about the development of the state police presented in this book were intended to fill the void that exists with regard to current understanding and knowledge about the development of this form of police in the United States. Much remains to be done. My research has convinced me that the state police, along with small-town and rural police forces, offer police scholars a wealth of issues and data sources for future study. The following discussion will briefly identify four areas of study that seem to be the most logical next areas of inquiry for expanding our knowledge about not only state police but the police in general.

The first area for study is the legislative process creating state-controlled police agencies in other states. Besides the studies of Illinois and Colorado presented in this volume, only New York and Ohio have been studied with regard to development of a state police (see the studies by Ray for New York and Swart for Ohio, listed under those state headings below). States such as Michigan, Pennsylvania, and New Jersey should be examined in detail to provide a more complete picture of the various interest groups promoting centralized paramilitary state police forces and those who opposed such efforts. Also, study of the legislative process leading to the development of state police in such states as Montana, California, or North Dakota would provide a comparison with the industrial states. Finally, additional comparative legislative analysis may uncover regional differences (North versus South, Northeast versus Midwest) with regard to the pattern of state police development.

A second area for research should focus on the state police movement, both locally and nationally, and the various organizations that were formed to promote state police reform. The existence of such groups as the State Police Auxiliary Committee in Illinois and the New York State Police Committee suggests the strong possibility that regional and national organizations may have acted in a cooperative if not coordinated effort to advance the state police idea nationwide. Questions for research would focus on membership, operation, and financial support for such groups in order to clarify the role they played in state police development. Related questions should focus on the study of the creation and operations of such organizations as the Northwestern Traffic Institute and the American Institute of Criminal Law and Criminology in Chicago and the National Institute of Public Administration in Washington, D.C., with regard to their role in promoting police reform such as the state police.

A third area of study should focus on social-biographical research of the various prominent individuals who actively worked for passage of state police laws. Individually, studies of writers such as Katherine Mayo and Frederick Van de Water would prove insightful as to the personal reasons for their involvement in the state police movement and provide a window into a segment that was actively seeking major reform of society's police operations. Bruce Smith deserves particular attention as he was one of the foremost proponents of efficient and centralized policing. Biographical analysis of Smith would illuminate many issues, people, and agencies involved in working for police reform. Study of the prominent superintendents such as John C. Groome of Pennsylvania, George Olander of New York, and Oscar Olander of Michigan would provide insights into the backgrounds of the men who shaped the early state police forces. Finally, we also need to know what kind of men became state police officers: What were their backgrounds, training, and attitudes toward their job?

Fourth, although much remains to be done concerning the origins and development of the state police, questions of actual enforcement activity are of equal if not greater importance. To understand fully the role of the state police in the overall police system, it is necessary to discern what it was these agencies did once they were established. Did state police provide improved crime control in rural areas? Were they used extensively against labor to break strikes? Did cooperation among the different levels of police improve, or was there open hostility on the part of local officials? Was the problem of differential enforcement of certain laws eliminated? Whose interests were actually served by the operation of the state police? These and other issues concerning the actual operation of the state police need to be studied in order to assess the overall impact state police had on social order.

To aid those interested in pursuing research into the origins or operations of the early state police forces in the United States, I have included a bibliography of all sources on the state police uncovered during my research for this book.

## BIBLIOGRAPHIES AND DIGESTS

Corcoran, Margaret M. "State Police in the United States: A Bibliography." *Journal of Criminal Law and Criminology* 14 (1924): 544–555.

Indiana. Bureau of Legislative Information. "Summary of Statutory Provisions of the Various States in Regard to State Police." Indianapolis, 1913.

Lambert, June. "Digest of the Laws of the Various States Relating to State Police." Albany, NY: New York State Library, Legislative Reference Section, 1929.

Library of Congress. Division of Bibliography. "List of References on State Police and Similar Law Enforcing Organizations." Washington, DC, 1923.

Rhode Island State Library. Legislative Reference Bureau. "Digest of Legislation in the Several States Relating to State Police and State Departments of Public Safety." Providence, 1923.

# GENERAL WORKS—BOOKS

Miller, George E., and David M. Baldwin. *State Traffic Law Enforcement*. Chicago: National Safety Council, 1944.

Monroe, David G. *State and Provincial Police*. Evanston, IL: State and Provincial Section, International Association of Chiefs of Police and the Northwestern University Traffic Institute, 1941.

Smith, Bruce. *The State Police*. New York: Macmillan, 1925.

Vollmer, August, and Alfred Parker. *Crime and the State Police*. Berkeley: University of California Press, 1935.

# GENERAL WORKS—ARITICLES AND BOOK CHAPTERS

Adams, Lynn G. "The State Police." *Annals of the American Academy of Political and Social Science* 146 (November 1929): 34–40.

Allen, W. H. "Local Versus State Constabulary." *Annals of the American Academy of Political and Social Science* 17 (1901): 100–101.

Barrows, David P. "State Police." *California Monthly* (February 1932): 26.

Borkenstein, Robert. "State Police." In *Encyclopedia of Crime and Justice*, vol. 3, edited by Sanford H. Kadish. New York: Free Press, 1983.

Breckinridge, John B. "State Police." *Kentucky Law Journal* 52 (1963): 125–133.

Burke, C. "Experiences of the State Police." *American Magazine* 98 (1924): 26–28.

Buwalda, Irma W. "State Police." *The Tax Digest* 13 (May 1935): 149–151.

Cawcroft, Ernest. "The Sheriff and a State Constabulary." In *County Government*, by the New York Constitutional Convention Commission, 61–68. Albany, NY: J. B. Lyon, 1915.

Champion, Alfred H. "Modern Crime Control: Will State Police Prove the Remedy." *The Tax Digest* 12 (1934): 364–365, 386–393.

Chernin, Milton. "State Police." Legislative Problems no. 14. Berkeley: University of California, Bureau of Public Administration, 1934.

Conover, Milton. "State Police." *American Political Science Review* 15 (February 1921): 82–93.

———. "State Police Developments, 1921–1924." *American Political Science Review* 18 (November 1924): 773–781.

Cooper, Weldon. "The State Police Movement in the South." *Journal of Politics* 1 (November 1939): 414–433.

Day, Frank. "State Police and Highway Patrols." In *The Book of the States*, 461–466. Chicago: Council on State Governments, 1964.

Federal Bureau of Investigation. "State-Wide Law Enforcement Agencies." *Law Enforcement Bulletin* 7, no. 7 (1938): 28–42.

French, J. W. "Trooper on the Highway." *Journal of Industry and Finance* (April 1931): 8–10.

Fuld, Leonard F. "Police Problems: State Constabulary." In *Police Administration*, 416–425. New York: Putnam, 1909.

Hall, E. G. "State Constabulary: Military Police." In *Minnesota State Federation of Labor Official Year Book*, 48–55. Minnesota State Federation of Labor, 1922.

Hallam, Oscar. "State Organization for the Apprehension of Criminals." Report of the Commission on Criminal Apprehension of Minnesota. St. Paul, MN: Commission on Criminal Apprehension, December 31, 1930.

Harwood, Jonathan H. "State Police Forces." *Traffic Quarterly* 3, no. 1 (January 1949): 5–13.

Hatton, Augustus R. "The Control of Police." In *Cincinnati Conference for Good City Government and the Fifteenth Annual Meeting of the National Municipal League,* edited by Clinton R. Woodruff, 157–171. National Municipal League, 1909.

Hays, Gurd M. "State Constabulary Best Insurance When the Guard Leaves." *International Socialist Review* 18 (1917): 88–89.

Henderson, C. R. "Rural Police." *Annals of the American Academy of Political and Social Science* 40 (1912): 228–233.

Hickey, Edward J. "Trends in Rural Police Protection." *Annals of the American Academy of Political and Social Science* 291 (January 1954): 22–30.

Howie, Wendall D. "Troopers Given Hearty Endorsement." *The State Trooper* 6 (1924): 11–12, 29.

Hurley, Robert T. "Should State and City Police Cooperate?" [1929] In *Proceedings of the Annual Conventions of the International Association of Chiefs of Police, 1926–1930,* vol. 5, 100–102. New York: Arno Press, 1971.

Leathers, Harland F. "A Centralized State Police System." *Duke Bar Association Journal* 4 (1936): 86–92.

Leonard, Donald S. "Relationships and Cooperation Between State and Municipal Police." [1930] In *Proceedings of the Annual Conventions of the International Association of Chiefs of Police, 1926–1930,* vol. 5, pp. 111–118. New York: Arno Press, 1971.

Mathews, J. M. "Enforcement of State Law." In *Principles of American State Administration,* 410–462. New York: Appleton, 1917.

Miller, F. C. "The State Police." *Papers and Proceedings of the Third Annual Meeting of the Minnesota Academy of Social Sciences,* edited by William A. Schaper, vol. 3, no. 3, 96–126. Index Press, 1910.

New Jersey State Chamber of Commerce. Bureau of State Research. "State Police Problem in America." *State Research.* Supplement to *New Jersey* 4, no. 4 (January 1917): 1–210.

Olander, Oscar G. "Municipal or State Police?" *Police "13–13"* 4 (1929): 10–11.

——. "Should State and City Police Be Under One Control?" *The Police Journal* (New York) 17 (January 1930): 24–25, 31.

Palmer, Milton R. "The State Police as an Asset." *American Industries* 23 (August 1922): 19–23.

——. "Making the Highways Unsafe for Highwaymen." *Illinois Journal of Commerce* 4 (September 1922): 13.

——. "Rhode Island Demands Police." *The State Trooper* 6 (1925): 5.

Peterson, Virgil W. "Local and State Law Enforcement Today." *Current History* 53 (1967): 8–14, 49–50.

——. "Developments of Local and State Law Enforcement." *Current History* 60 (1971): 327–334.

Puttkammer, E. W. "The Organization of a State Police." *Journal of Criminal Law and Criminology* 26 (January–February 1936): 727–740.

Rapport, Victor A. "A Unified State–Wide Police Force." *Journal of Criminal Law and Criminology* 30 (January–February 1940): 706–711.

Ray, P. O. "Metropolitan and State Police." *Journal of Criminal Law and Criminology* 10 (November 1919): 351–355.

——. "Metropolitan and State Police." *Journal of Criminal Law and Criminology* 11 (November 1920): 453–467.

Roosevelt, Theodore. "The Need for a State Police." *The Trooper: State Police Magazine of Illinois* 1 (1924), 6.

Shartel, Stratton. "What Is State Police: What Will It Do; What Will It Cost?" *Bank News* 1 (February 1929): 5–7.

Smith, Bruce. "The State Police." In *Readings in American Government*, edited by Finla G. Crawford, 625–632. New York: Knopf, 1927.

——. "The State Police." In *Rural Crime Control*. New York: Columbia University, Institute of Public Administration, 1933.

——. "The State Police: An Experiment in Rural Protection." *Police Journal* (London) 3 (January 1930): 20–29.

——. "Factors Influencing the Future Development of State Police." *Journal of Criminal Law and Criminology* 23 (1932): 713–718.

——. "State Police: Some Possible Lines of Future Development." *State Government* 7 (1934): 51–54.

——. "History of State Police Organizations." *Our Sheriff and Police Journal* 30 (1935): 9–25.

——. "State and Federal Police." In *Police Systems in the United States*. Rev. ed. New York: Harper and Brothers, 1949.

"Social Service and a State Constabulary." *Social Service Review* 5, no. 2 (March 1917): 14–17.

Stone, Donald C. "A State Police Act." In *The Book of the States, 1939–40*, 132–134. Chicago: Council of City Governments, 1939.

U.S. Commission of Industrial Relations. "Pennsylvania State Police." In *Final Report and Testimony*, U.S. Senate, 64th Cong. 1st sess., 1923. Vol. 29, serial no. 6939, 10929–11025.

Whitten, Robert H. "Police." In *Public Administration in Massachusetts*, 80–99. Columbia University Studies in History, Economics and Public Law, 8, no. 4. New York, 1898.

Woltman, Frederick, and William L. Nunn. "Cossacks." *The American Mercury* 15 (December 1929): 399–406.

## GENERAL WORKS—UNPUBLISHED MANUSCRIPTS

Anderson, Leslie L. "State Police Systems in the United States." M.A. thesis, University of Minnesota, 1923.

Chamber of Commerce of the United States. "State Police and the State Highway Patrols." Washington, 1931.

Gladston, Edward A., and Thomas W. Cooper. "State Highway Patrols: Their Functions and Financing." Paper presented at the 45th annual meeting of the Highway Research Board. Northwestern University Traffic Institute Library, Chicago, 1966.

Gourley, G. Douglas. "State Police Systems." Chap. 4, vol. 1 in *Effective Police Organization and Management*. A consultant paper submitted to the Office of Law Enforcement Assistance, United States Department of Justice. Northwestern University Traffic Institute Library, Chicago, 1967.

Hayes, James. "History and Development of State Police and State Highway Patrols and Methods of Handling the Minor Vehicle Violator." M.A. thesis, Harvard University, 1935.

Smith, Thomas S. "Democratic Control and Professionalism in Police Work: The State Police Experience." Ph.D. diss., University of Chicago, 1968.

Vanderwood, Paul J. "The Rurales: Mexico's Rural Police Force, 1861–1914." Ph.D. diss., University of Texas at Austin, 1970.

Woo, Tao Fu. "State Police and State Highway Patrols." M.S. thesis, University of Colorado, 1949.

## STATE-SPECIFIC MATERIALS

### Alaska

"Alaska May Get Force of Federal Troopers." *The State Trooper* 1 (1920): 35.

### Arizona

Miller, Joseph. *The Arizona Rangers*. New York: Hastings House, 1972.

Winsor, Mulford. "The Arizona Rangers." *Our Sheriff and Police Journal* 31 (1936): 49–61.

### California

Cato, E. Raymond. "The Highway Patrol in California." *Our Sheriff and Police Journal* 30 (1935): 7, 28.

Gammage, Allen Z. "The California Highway Patrol: A Study in Administration." Ph.D. diss., University of Texas, 1959.

Graves, Richard. "Will California Have a State Police?" *Western City* 11 (1935): 23, 26.

Kenney, John P. *The California Police*. Springfield, IL: Charles C. Thomas, 1964.

### Colorado

"Colorado Joins the Ranks." *The State Trooper* 2, (1920): 18.

Vorse, A. O. "Colorado State Police Are Organized." *The State Trooper* 2 (1921): 9–10.

Warren, Frederick S. "Colorado Legislative Committee Urges State Police Organization." *The State Trooper* 12 (December 1930): 13–14.

———. "Colorado's New State Highway Courtesy Patrol Is Now in Effective Operation." *The State Trooper* 17 (December 1935): 5–6.

### Connecticut

Rapport, Victor A. "The Growth and Changing Functions of the Connecticut Department of State Police." *Journal of Criminal Law and Criminology* 30 (September–October 1939): 359–369.

### Georgia

Watkins, Ben T. "The Georgia Highway Patrol Bill." *Southern Lawyer* 1 (January 1937): 14–16.

# Illinois

Barth, Frank F. "Why Illinois Should Have a State Police Force." *Illinois Journal of Commerce* 4 (August 1922): 7, 30, 32.

——. "New Illinois State Police Bill Is Very Heartily Endorsed." *Illinois Journal of Commerce* 5 (February 1923): 11–12.

——. "State Police-Labor-Politics." *The Trooper: State Police Magazine of Illinois* 1 (January 1924): 24.

"The Cure for Herrin." *The State Trooper* 8 (December 1926): 16.

DeLong, Earl H., and Fred E. Inbau. "A Law Enforcement Program for the State of Illinois." *Journal of Criminal Law and Criminology* 26 (1936): 727–740.

Dunlap, Al. "Increasing Crime Demands State Police for Illinois." *Illinois Journal of Commerce* 6 (1924): 13, 28.

"Illinois Deserves a Real State Police Department." *The Illinois Policeman* 3 (1937): 16–17, 20.

"Illinois State Police." Scrapbook of newspaper clippings, articles, and legislative notes. Chicago Historical Society.

Leach, Paul R. "Illinois Needs State Police Force." *The State Trooper* 2 (September 1920): 7–8, 37.

——. "Strong Opposition to Creation of a State Police in Illinois." *The State Trooper* 1 (June 1920): 19, 21, 23.

——. "West Frankfort Riots Point the Moral: Illinois Disturbances Show Present Need for an Efficient Police Force." *The State Trooper* 2 (October 1920): 9–10.

——. "State Police Up in Illinois Again." *The State Trooper* 2 (January 1921): 13–14.

——. "Issue Is Joined in Illinois." *The State Trooper* 2 (March 1921): 13–14.

O'Brien, Daniel L. "Half-Century Mark for the Illinois State Police." *The Police Chief* 39 (1972): 62.

"Police Bill Needs Amending." *Illinois Journal of Commerce* 7 (1925): 10.

"The Proof of the Pudding: Illinois Eats Mud in Bank Robberies and Other Crimes." *Illinois Journal of Commerce* 6 (1924): 12.

Staley, Eugene. "State Constabulary or Military Police." In *History of the Illinois State Federation of Labor*. Chicago: University of Chicago Press, 1930.

State Police Benevolent Group. *Illinois State Police: A Division of the Department of Law Enforcement, 1922–1972*. Springfield, IL: State Police Benevolent Group, 1972.

Stephens, George E. "Labor Rules the Legislature." *Illinois Journal of Commerce* 7 (1925): 7, 22.

"Trouble in Illinois." *The State Trooper* 5 (1924): 16.

"The Wet Drive." *The State Trooper* 6 (1925): 16.

# Indiana

"Indiana Bankers Are for Troopers." *The State Trooper* 6 (1925): 6.

"Indiana Discovers the Need of a Strong State Police." *The State Trooper* 2 (1921): 18.

# Iowa

"Iowa Sees the Dawn." *The State Trooper* 8 (1927): 16.

"Iowa Solons Get Driver's License and State Public Safety Measure." *The State Trooper* 12 (1931): 13–14.

"Iowans Look Forward to Having a State Police in Near Future." *The State Trooper* 12 (1931): 11–12.

Kaloupek, Walter E. "The History and Administration of the Iowa Highway Safety Patrol." *Iowa Journal of History and Politics* 36 (October 1938): 339–386.

McKeown, William H. "Iowa Considers the Establishment of a State Police Organization." *The State Trooper* 12 (1930): 9–10.

——— . "Iowans Believe State Police Force Needed to Protect Rural Districts." *The State Trooper* 12 (1931): 9–10.

## Kansas

Kansas Legislative Council. "State Police: Analysis of Existing Laws and of the Experience of Other States with Special Application to Kansas." Research report. Topeka, 1934.

"Kansas Police Bill Contains Newest Ideas." *The State Trooper* 2 (1921): 12.

## Kentucky

Kentucky Department of Law. "State Police." *Kentucky Law Journal* 52 (1963–1964): 125.

## Maine

"Maine Gets in Line." *The State Trooper* 6 (1925): 16.

## Maryland

Winebrenner, David C. *The First Chapter of the History of the Maryland State Police Force.* Baltimore, MD: Commissioner of Motor Vehicles, 1921.

## Massachusetts

Jones, Marshall E. St.E. "A History of the Massachusetts State Police Force as a Changing Social Organization." Ph.D. diss., Harvard University, 1936.

Massachusetts State Police. *The Thin Blue Line: Massachusetts Department of Public Safety.* Publication no. 987. Boston, 1968.

Powers, William F. *The One-Hundred Year Vigil: The Story of the Nation's First State-wide Enforcement Agency.* Massachusetts: Department of Public Safety, Boston, 1965.

## Michigan

"Editor Talks Plainly about State Police." *The State Trooper* 2 (1920): 27.

"Farm Bureau Secretary Praises the Constabulary." *The State Trooper* 2 (1920): 43.

"The Farmer and the State Police." *The Michigan State Police Journal* 1 (January 1920): 19.

"For the Enemies It Has Made." *The Michigan State Police Journal* 1 (March 1920): 21, 23.

Olander, Oscar G. "Michigan State Police." *Journal of Criminal Law and Criminology* 23 (1932): 718–722.
——— . *Michigan State Police: A Twenty Year History*. Lansing: Michigan Police Journal Press, 1942.
Palmer, Milton R. "Michigan Wants the State Police." *The State Trooper* 2 (1921): 5–6.
"Resolutions Adopted by State Labor Federation Endorse Various Movements." *The Michigan State Police Journal* 1 (November 1919): 39, 41.
Scully, Charles B. "Motor Car Bandits and the Rural Dweller of Today." *The Michigan State Police Journal* 1 (1919): 13–14.
"State Farm Bureau Favors Continuing the State Police." *The State Trooper* 2 (1920): 18.
"State Police Deserve Commendation." *The State Trooper* 2 (1920): 9–10.
Vaughan, Coleman C. "How the Michigan State Police Came to be Organized." *The Michigan State Police Journal* 1 (1919): 9.

## Minnesota

Jones, J. J. "Minnesota State Highway Patrol Unique in Character." *The Police Journal* 17 (October 1930): 13, 25.
"Minnesota Wants the State Police." *The State Trooper* 12 (1930): 20.

## Missouri

Heinberg, J. G., and A. C. Breckenridge. *Law Enforcement in Missouri—A Decade of Centralization and Central Control of Apprehension and Prosecution (1931–1941)*. University of Missouri Studies, vol. 17, no. 1. Columbia, 1942.
Watson, Richard A. *Law Enforcement in Missouri: State Highway Patrol*. Columbia, MO: University of Missouri, Bureau of Government Research, 1960.

## New Jersey

Coakley, Leo J. *Jersey Troopers: A Fifty Year History of the New Jersey State Police*. New Brunswick, NJ: Rutgers University Press, 1971.
"Labor Is Satisfied." *The State Trooper* 9 (1928): 16.
McDonough, J. J. "The New Jersey State Police." *The Police Journal* (New York) 13 (March 1926): 5–16.

## New Mexico

Hornung, Chuck. *The Thin Gray Line: The New Mexico Mounted Police*. Fort Worth, TX: Western Heritage Press, 1971.

## New York

"Arguments for a State Police." *Outlook* 106 (1914): 145–146.
Dawson, Edgar. "New York State Police." *American Political Science Review* 11 (August 1917): 539–541.

Dutton, George P. "Crime Cut One-Third by New York State Police." *Illinois Journal of Commerce* 4 (1922): 11, 24, 26.

Fletcher, George. "How the New York State Police Keep the Peace." *National Police Journal* 15 (1920): 31–33.

Greely, Helen H. "Shall New York State Have a State Constabulary?" In *Proceedings of the Second Conference for Better County Government in New York State*, 49–59. Syracuse, New York, 1916.

"I Want the State Troopers." *Outlook* 117 (1917): 451.

King, J. S. "The 'Cop' in the Country: Fine Work Done by the New York State Police." *Illinois Journal of Commerce* 6 (1923): 11, 18.

Kirwan, William E. *The New York State Police: History and Development of Collective Negotiations*. New York: New York State Police, 1969.

Mayo, Katherine. "New York State Troopers." *Outlook* 118 (April 1918): 622–623.

New York Committee for State Police. *First Annual Report*. Albany, 1917.

——— . *Second Annual Report*. Albany, 1918.

——— . "The State Speaks." *Third Annual Report*. Albany, 1919.

——— . "The Governors Speak." *Fourth Annual Report*. Albany, 1920.

New York. Division of State Police, *The New York State Police: The First Fifty Years, 1917–1967*. Albany, 1967.

"New York State's New Rural Police." *The Rural New Yorker* 76 (1917): 1365.

Ray, Gerda. "Contested Legitimacy: Creating the State Police in New York, 1890–1930." Ph.D. diss., University of California at Berkeley, 1990.

Shelton, Pamela T. *History of the New York State Police, 1917–1987*. Albany, NY: Trooper Foundation of the State of New York, 1987.

"The 'State Constabulary' Bill." *The Rural New Yorker* 76 (1917): 289.

Stockbridge, F. P. "New York State Troopers." *World's Work* 35 (1918): 264–272.

Van de Water, Frederick F. *Grey Riders: The Story of the New York State Troopers*. New York: G. P. Putnam's Sons, 1922.

## North Carolina

Sherril, Basil L. "Twenty-Five Years of Service." *Popular Government* 20 (May 1954): 3–6.

"State Police Needed." *The State Trooper* 11 (1929): 16.

## North Dakota

Lawler, Thomas J. "The History and Administration of the North Dakota Highway Patrol." M.A. thesis, University of North Dakota, 1961.

## Ohio

Burnside, L. B. "Ohio General Assembly to Consider a Bill for Rural Motorized Police Body." *The State Trooper* 6 (1925): 12.

——— . "Sentiment for State Police Grows in Ohio and Legislature Faces Strong Pressure." *The State Trooper* 7 (1926): 12.

——— . "Ohio Situation Unusual." *The State Trooper* 8 (1926): 13–14.

——— . "Ohio Still Seeks to Establish Adequate State Highway Police." *The State Trooper* 8 (1927): 8.

——— . "State Police for Ohio Sought." *The State Trooper* 10 (1929): 13.

Swart, Stanley L. "The Development of State-Level Police Activity in Ohio, 1802–1928." Ph.D. diss., Northwestern University, 1974.

## Oklahoma

Stephens, Alva R. "History of the Oklahoma Highway Patrol." M.A. thesis, University of Oklahoma, 1957.

## Oregon

Barton, Frank. "General Butler Begins His Work on Organizing Oregon State Police." *The State Trooper* 12 (1931): 7–8.

"Oregon's State Police Are Proving Their Worth." *Northwest Police Journal* (February 1932): 11–13.

## Pennsylvania

Conti, Philip. *The Pennsylvania State Police: A History of Service to the Commonwealth, 1905 to the Present.* Harrisburg, PA: Stackpole Books, 1977.

Faber, Elmer. *Behind the Law: True Stories Compiled from the Archives of the Pennsylvania State Police.* Greensboro, PA: Charles M. Henry, 1933.

Garrett, P. W. "The State Police Problems in America." *State Research*, supplement to *New Jersey* 4 no. 4 (January 1917): 7–38.

Guyer, John P. *Pennsylvania's Cossacks and the State's Police.* Reading, PA: John P. Guyer, 1924.

Holmes, Lawrence G. "An Analysis of State Police." *Trade Winds* (May 1925): 16–20.

Jaekel, Blair. "Pennsylvania's Mounted Police." *World's Work* 23 (1912): 641–652.

Mayo, Katherine. *Justice to All: The Story of the Pennsylvania State Police.* New York: G. P. Putnam's Sons, 1917.

——— . "Cherry Valley." *Atlantic Monthly* 121 (February 1918): 175–181.

——— . "Soldiers of Law and Order: Some Adventures of the Pennsylvania State Police." *Outlook* 118 (March 20–Apri 13, 1918): 447–448, 486, 537–542.

——— . "Murder of Sam Howell." *Outlook* 118 (April 1918): 584–586.

——— . "No Story at All." *Atlantic Monthly* 121 (April 1918): 507–515.

——— . "Guardians of the Countryside." *Country Life in America* 35 (December 1918): 61–63.

——— . *The Standard-Bearers: True Stories of Heroes of Law and Order.* Boston: Houghton Mifflin, 1918.

. "Demobilization and State Police." *North American Review* 209 (June 1919): 786–794.

——— . "Under the Yellow Flag." *North American Review* 210 (July 1919): 86–99.

——— . "Hand-Picked Job: An Incident in the Work of the State Police." *North American Review* 210 (August–September 1919): 253–264, 367–378.

——— . "Great Day for the Country." *Outlook* 129 (December 1921): 558–560.

——— . *Mounted Justice: True Stories of the Pennsylvania State Police.* Boston: Houghton Mifflin, 1922.

——— . "State Troopers, Operator." *Outlook* 133 (February 1923): 398–400.

"Pennsylvania State Constabulary." *Nation* 81 (1905): 49–50.

Pennsylvania State Federation of Labor. *The American Cossack*. Harrisburg: Pennsylvania State Federation of Labor, 1915.

"Pennsylvania's Constabulary." *Nation* 90 (1910): 281–282.

Perry, C. E. "Origin of the Pennsylvania State Police." *The Police Journal* (New York) 14 (October 1926): 6.

"Policing a State." *Nation* 96 (1913): 382–383.

Purdy, E. Wilson. *Pennsylvania State Police*. Harrisburg: Pennsylvania State Police, 1963.

Reinsch, P. S. "The Pennsylvania Constabulary." In *Readings on American State Government*, 217–221. Boston: Ginn, 1911.

"State Police of Pennsylvania, A Model of Efficiency." *American City* 24 (1921): 371–372.

U.S. Commission on Industrial Relations. "Pennsylvania State Police." *Final Report and Testimony*, U.S. Senate, 64th Cong., 1st sess., 1923. Vol. 29, serial no. 6939, 10929–11025.

"What the Steel Strikers Think of the Police." *Literary Digest* 63 (November 1919): 46–52.

"What Those Cossacks Think of the Steel Strikers." *Literary Digest* 63 (December 1919): 50–56.

## Rhode Island

Clark, Frank. "Battle Lines Are Forming." *The State Trooper* 7 (1925): 13.

"Organizations Favor Rhode Island Force for Splendid Work Against Law-Breakers." *The State Trooper* 7 (1925): 8.

Palmer, Milton R. "Rhode Island Demands Police." *The State Trooper* 6 (1925): 5.

Powers, William F. *In the Service of the State: The Rhode Island State Police, 1925–1975*. Providence: Rhode Island Bicentennial Commission Foundation, 1975.

Sherwood, Grace M. "State Police Organization Has Enviable Record." *Providence Magazine* 40 (March 1929): 110, 112, 114.

## Tennessee

"State Police a Cure for Lynchings." *World's Work* 35 (1918): 585–586.

"Tennessee Plans Highway Patrol." *The State Trooper* 11 (1930): 20.

## Texas

Baenziger, Ann P. "The Texas State Police During Reconstruction: A Reexamination." *Southwestern Historical Quarterly* 72 (1967): 470–491.

Fidler, Paul E. "The Texas Highway Patrol." *Texas Municipalities* 22 (April 1935): 91–95.

Field, William T. "The Texas State Police, 1870–1873." *Texas Military History* 5 (Fall 1965): 136–138.

Nunn, William C. "A Study of the State Police During the E. J. Davis Administration." M.A. thesis, University of Texas, 1931.

Ogdan, G. W. "Watch on the Rio Grande." *Everybody's Magazine* 25 (1911): 353–365.

Paine, Albert B. *Captain Bill McDonald, Texas Ranger: A Story of Frontier Reform*. New York: J. J. Little & Uves, 1909.

Rathbun, C. M. "Keeping the Peace Along the Mexican Border." *Harper's Weekly* 50 (1906): 1632–1643.

Samora, Julian, Joe Bernal, and Albert Pena. *Gunpowder Justice: A Reassessment of the Texas Rangers*. South Bend, IN: University of Notre Dame Press, 1979.

Sullivan, W. J. L. *Twelve Years in the Saddle for Law and Order on the Frontiers of Texas*. Austin, TX: Van Boekmann-Jones, 1909.

Ward, James R. "The Texas Rangers, 1919–1935: A Study in Law Enforcement." Ph.D. diss., Texas Christian University, 1972.

Webb, Walter P. *The Texas Rangers: A Century of Frontier Defense*. Boston: Houghton Mifflin, 1935.

## Utah

Gray, Robert M. "A History of the Utah State Bureau of Criminal Identification and Investigation." *Utah Historical Quarterly* 24 (April 1956): 171–179.

## Virginia

McCoy, Harold G. "Virginia Inaugurates Highway Patrol." *The State Trooper* 6 (1924): 17.

## West Virginia

Crow, Lester E. "West Virginia Welcomes State Troopers." *The State Trooper* 1 (1920): 4–5, 21.

Quenzel, C. H. "A Fight to Establish the State Police." *Journal of Criminal Law and Criminology* 34 (May–June 1943): 61–67.

## Wisconsin

"State Police, Patterned after Michigan Force, Still Sought for Wisconsin." *The State Trooper* 10 (1929): 17.

Wisconsin. Motor Vehicle Department, Enforcement Division. *25 Years of Service*. Madison, 1965.

"Wisconsin Press Wants Troopers." *The State Trooper* 10 (1929): 14.

"Wisconsin Seeking State Police, Has Praise for Michigan Department." *The State Trooper* 12 (1930): 28.

"Wisconsin Studies Policing." *The State Trooper* 12 (1931): 25.

# Bibliography

## BOOKS AND ARTICLES

Akers, Ronald L. "The Professional Association and the Legal Regulation of Practice." *Law and Society Review* 3 (May 1968): 463–482.

Alix, Ernest K. *Ransom Kidnapping in America, 1874–1974: The Creation of a Capital Crime.* Carbondale, IL: Southern Illinois University Press, 1978.

Allswang, John M. *A House for All Peoples: Ethnic Politics in Chicago, 1890–1936.* Lexington: University Press of Kentucky, 1971.

———. *Bosses, Machines, and Urban Voters: An American Symbiosis.* Port Washington, NY: Kennikat Press, 1977.

Alpert, Geoffrey P., and Roger G. Dunham. *Policing Urban America.* Prospect Heights, IL: Waveland Press, 1988.

Althusser, Louis. *For Marx.* New York: Pantheon Books, 1969.

———. *Lenin and Philosophy and Other Essays.* New York: Monthly Review Press, 1971.

Baenziger, Ann P. "The Texas State Police During Reconstruction: A Reexamination." *Southwestern Historical Quarterly* 72 (1967): 470–491.

Baker, Ray S. "The Reign of Lawlessness: Anarchy and Despotism in Colorado." *McClure's Magazine* 23 (May 1904): 43–57.

———. "Organized Capital Challenges Organized Labor: The New Employer's Association Movement." *McClure's Magazine* 23 (July 1904): 279–292.

Banton, Michael. *The Policeman in the Community.* London: Tavistock, 1964.

Bartollas, Clemens. *American Criminal Justice: An Introduction.* New York: Macmillan, 1988.

Bayley, David H. *Patterns of Policing: A Comparative International Analysis.* New Brunswick, NJ: Rutgers University Press, 1985.

Becker, Howard S. *Outsiders: Studies in the Sociology of Deviance.* New York: Free Press, 1963.

Berman, Jay S. *Police Administration and Progressive Reform: Theodore Roosevelt as Police Commissioner of New York*. Westport, CT: Greenwood Press, 1987.

Bittner, Egon. *The Functions of the Police in Modern Society*. Chevy Chase, MD: National Institute of Mental Health, 1970.

Bordua, David J. *The Police: Six Sociological Essays*. New York: John Wiley and Sons, 1967.

Breathnach, Seamus. *The Irish Police: From Earliest Times to Present Day*. Dublin: Anvil Books, 1974.

Broeker, Galen. *Rural Disorder and Police Reform in Ireland, 1812–36*. London: Routledge and Kegan Paul, 1970.

Brown, Lorne, and Caroline Brown. *An Unauthorized History of the Royal Canadian Mounted Police*. Toronto: James Lewis & Samuel, 1973.

Buenker, John D. "Urban Immigrant Lawmakers and Progressive Reform in Illinois." In *Essays in Illinois History in Honor of Glenn Huron Seymour*, edited by Donald F. Tingley. Carbondale, IL: Southern Illinois University Press, 1968.

———. "The Illinois Legislature and Prohibition, 1907– 1919." *Journal of the Illinois Historical Society* 62 (Winter 1969): 363–384.

———. *Urban Liberalism and Progressive Reform*. New York: W. W. Norton, 1973.

Bunyan, Tony. *The History and Practice of the Political Police in Britain*. London: Julian Friedman, 1976.

Burke, C. "Experiences of the State Police." *American Magazine* 98 (1924): 26–28.

Carte, Gene E., and Elaine H. Carte. *Police Reform in the United States: The Era of August Vollmer, 1905–1932*. Berkeley: University of California Press, 1975.

Center for Research on Criminal Justice. *The Iron Fist and the Velvet Glove: An Analysis of the United State Police*. Berkeley: Center for Research on Criminal Justice, 1988.

Chambliss, William J. "A Sociological Analysis of the Law of Vagrancy." *Social Problems* 12 (Summer 1964): 67–77.

Chambliss, William J., and Milton Mankoff. *Whose Law? What Order?: A Conflict Approach to Criminology*. New York: John Wiley and Sons, 1976.

Chamelin, Neil C., Vernon B. Fox, and Paul M. Whisenand. *Introduction to Criminal Justice*. Englewood Cliffs, NJ: Prentice-Hall, 1975.

Coakley, Leo J. *Jersey Troopers: A Fifty Year History of the New Jersey State Police*. New Brunswick, NJ: Rutgers University Press, 1971.

Cole, George F. *The American System of Criminal Justice*. 5th ed. Pacific Grove, CA: Brooks-Cole, 1989.

Conklin, John E. *Criminology*, 2nd ed. New York: Macmillan, 1986.

Conley, John. "Criminal Justice History as a Field of Research: A Review of the Literature, 1960–1975." *Journal of Criminal Justice* 5 (Spring 1977): 13–28.

Conover, Milton. "State Police." *American Political Science Review* 15 (February 1921): 82–93.

———. "State Police Developments, 1921–1924." *American Political Science Review* 18 (November 1924): 773–781.

Conti, Philip. *The Pennsylvania State Police: A History of Service to the Commonwealth, 1905 to the Present*. Harrisburg, PA: Stackpole Books, 1977.

Critchley, T. A. *A History of Police in England and Wales, 1900–1966*. London: Constable, 1967.

Dawson, Edgar. "New York State Police." *American Political Science Review* 11 (August 1917): 539–541.

Dubofsky, Melvyn. "The Origins of Western Working Class Radicalism, 1890–1905." *Labor History* 7 (Spring 1966): 131–154.

Dunham, Roger G., and Geoffrey P. Alpert. *Critical Issues in Policing: Contemporary Readings*. Prospect Heights, IL: Waveland Press, 1989.

Duster, Troy. *The Legislation of Morality: Law, Drugs, and Moral Judgment*. New York: Free Press, 1970.

Felkenes, George T. *The Criminal Justice System: Its Functions and Personnel*. Englewood Cliffs, NJ: Prentice-Hall, 1973.

Fidler, Paul E. "The Texas Highway Patrol." *Texas Municipalities* 22 (April 1935): 91–95.

Fogelson, Robert. *Big-City Police*. Cambridge, MA: Harvard University Press, 1977.

Fuld, Leonard F. *Police Administration*. New York: Putnam, 1909.

Gibbons, Don C. *Society, Crime, and Criminal Behavior*. 5th ed. Englewood Cliffs, NJ: Prentice-Hall, 1987.

Goldstein, Herman. *Problem-Oriented Policing*. New York: McGraw-Hill, 1990.

Gottfried, Alex. *Boss Cermak of Chicago: A Study of Political Leadership*. Seattle: University of Washington Press, 1962.

Graves, Robert M. "A History of the Utah State Bureau of Criminal Identification and Investigation." *Utah Historical Quarterly* 24 (April, 1956): 171–179.

Gray, Robert M. "A History of the Utah State Bureau of Criminal Identification and Investigation." *Utah Historical Quarterly* 24 (April 1956): 171–179.

Grob, Gerald N., and George A. Billias. *Interpretations of American History*. Vol. 2, *Since 1865*. 2nd ed. New York: Free Press, 1972.

Gusfield, Joseph R. *Symbolic Crusade: Status Politics and the American Temperance Movement*. Urbana: University of Illinois Press, 1963.

Guyer, John P. *Pennsylvania's Cossacks and the State's Police*. Reading, PA: John P. Guyer, 1924.

Haber, Samuel. *Efficiency and Uplift: Scientific Management in the Progressive Era, 1890–1920*. Chicago: University of Chicago Press, 1964.

Hall, Jerome. *Theft, Law, and Society*. Indianapolis, IN: Bobbs Merrill, 1956.

Harring, Sidney L. "The Development of the Police Institution in the United States." *Crime and Social Justice* 5 (Spring–Summer 1976): 54–59.

———. *Policing a Class Society*. New Brunswick, NJ: Rutgers University Press, 1983.

Harring, Sidney L., and Lorraine M. McMullin. "The Buffalo Police, 1872–1900: Labor Unrest, Political Power and the Creation of the Police Institution." *Crime and Social Justice* 4 (Fall–Winter 1975): 5–14.

Hay, Douglas, et al. *Albion's Fatal Tree: Crime and Society in Eighteenth Century England*. New York: Pantheon Books, 1975.

Hays, Samuel P. *The Response to Industrialism, 1885–1914*. Chicago: University of Chicago Press, 1957.

———. "The Politics of Reform in Municipal Government in the Progressive Era." *Pacific Northwest Quarterly* 55 (October 1964): 157–169.

Hickey, Edward J. "Trends in Rural Police Protection." *Annals of the American Academy of Political and Social Science* 291 (January 1954): 22–30.

Higham, John. *Strangers in the Land: Patterns of American Nativism, 1860–1925*. New Brunswick, NJ: Rutgers University Press, 1955.

Hofstadter, Richard, and Michael Wallace. *American Violence: A Documentary History*. New York: Random House/Vintage Books, 1970.

Holmes, Lawrence G. "An Analysis of State Police." *Trade Winds* (May 1925): 16–20;

Holten, N. Gary, and Melvin E. Jones. *The System of Criminal Justice*. 2nd ed. Boston: Little, Brown, 1982.

Hornung, Chuck. *The Thin Gray Line: The New Mexico Mounted Police*. Fort Worth, TX: Western Heritage Press, 1971.

Horrall, S. W. "Sir John MacDonald and the Mounted Police Force for the Northwest Territories." *Canadian Historical Review* 53 (June 1972): 179–200.

Illinois. *Blue Book of the State of Illinois: 1923–1924.* Springfield, 1923.

Inciardi, James A. *Criminal Justice.* Orlando, FL: Academic Press, 1984.

Jaekel, Blair. "Pennsylvania's Mounted Police." *World's Work* 23 (1912): 641–652

Johnson, David R. *American Law Enforcement: A History.* St. Louis, MO: Forum Press, 1981.

Kaloupek, Walter E. "The History and Administration of the Iowa Highway Safety Patrol." *Iowa Journal of History and Politics* 36 (October 1938): 339–386.

Keiser, John H. "John H. Walker: Labor Leader from Illinois." In *Essays in Illinois History in Honor of Glenn Huron Seymour,* edited by Donald F. Tingley. Carbondale, IL: Southern Illinois University Press, 1968.

Kelly, Alfred H. *A History of the Illinois Manufacturers' Association.* Chicago: University of Chicago Libraries, 1940.

Kirwan, William E. *The New York State Police: History and Development of Collective Negotiations.* New York: New York State Police, 1969.

Kolko, Gabriel. *The Triumph of Conservatism: A Reinterpretation of American History, 1900–1916.* New York: Free Press of Glencoe, 1963.

——— . *Main Currents in Modern American History.* New York: Harper and Row, 1976.

Kratcoski, Peter C., and Donald B. Walker. *Criminal Justice in America: Process and Issues.* 2nd ed. New York: Random House, 1984.

Lane, Roger. *Policing the City: Boston, 1822–1885.* Cambridge, MA: Harvard University Press, 1967.

Lemert, Edwin M. "Legislating Change in the Juvenile Court." *Wisconsin Law Review* 1967 (Spring 1967): 421–448.

Liebman, Robert, and Michael Polen. "Perspectives on Policing in Nineteenth-Century America." *Social Science History* 2 (Spring 1978): 346–360.

Lindesmith, Alfred R. *The Addict and the Law.* Bloomington: Indiana University Press, 1965.

Link, Arthur S. "What Happened to the Progressive Movement in the 1920s?" *American Historical Review* 64 (July 1959): 833–851.

Link, Arthur S., and William B. Catton. *American Epoch: A History of the United States since the 1890s.* New York: Alfred A. Knopf, 1963.

Link, Arthur S., and Richard L. McCormick. *Progressivism.* Arlington Heights, IL: Harlan Davidson, 1983.

Lundman, Richard J., ed. *Police Behavior: A Sociological Perspective.* New York: Oxford University Press, 1980.

Manning, Peter K. *Police Work: The Social Organization of Police.* Cambridge, MA: MIT Press, 1977.

Mannle, Henry W., and J. David Hirschel. *Fundamentals of Criminology.* Englewood Cliffs, NJ: Prentice-Hall, 1988.

Mayo, Katherine. *Justice to All: The Story of the Pennsylvania State Police.* New York: G. P. Putnam's Sons, 1917.

——— . "Cherry Valley." *Atlantic Monthly* 121 (February 1918): 175–181.

——— . "Soldiers of Law and Order: Some Adventures of the Pennsylvania State Police." *Outlook* 118 (March 20–April 3, 1918): 447–448, 486, 537–542.

——— . "New York State Troopers." *Outlook* 118 (April 1918): 622–623.

——— . "Guardians of the Countryside." *Country Life in America* 35 (December 1918): 61–63.

——. *The Standard-Bearers: True Stories of Heroes of Law and Order*. Boston: Houghton Mifflin, 1918.

——. "Demobilization and State Police." *North American Review* 209 (June 1919): 786–794.

——. "Hand-Picked Job: An Incident in the Work of the State Police." *North American Review* 210 (August–September 1919): 253–264, 367–378.

——. *Mounted Justice: True Stories of the Pennsylvania State Police*. Boston: Houghton Mifflin, 1922.

——. "State Troopers, Operator." *Outlook* 133 (February 1923): 398–400.

Merriam, Charles E. *Chicago: A More Intimate View of Urban Politics*. New York: Macmillan, 1929.

Miller, F. C. "The State Police." In *Papers and Proceedings of the Third Annual Meeting of the Minnesota Academy of Social Sciences*, edited by William A. Schaper. Vol. 3, no. 3, 96–126. Index Press, 1910.

Miller, Joseph. *The Arizona Rangers*. New York: Hastings House, 1972.

Mills, J. Warner. "The Economic Struggle in Colorado: Dominant Trusts and Corporations." *The Arena* 35 (February 1906): 150–158.

——. "The Economic Struggle in Colorado: Eight-Hour Agitation Strikes and Fights." *The Arena* 36 (October 1906): 375–390.

Monkkonen, Eric H. *Police in Urban America, 1860–1920*. Cambridge: Cambridge University Press, 1981.

Murphy, Paul L. "Sources and Nature of Intolerance in the 1920s." *Journal of American History* 51 (July 1964): 60–76.

Murray, Robert K. *Red Scare: A Study of National Hysteria, 1919–1920*. New York: McGraw-Hill, 1955.

New Jersey State Chamber of Commerce. Bureau of State Research "State Police Problem in America." *State Research*. Supplement to *New Jersey* 4, no. 4 (January 1917): 1–210.

New York. Division of State Police. *The New York State Police: The First Fifty Years, 1917–1967*. Albany, 1967.

Niederhoffer, Arthur. *Behind the Shield: The Police in Urban Society*. Garden City, NJ: Doubleday, 1967.

Noble, David W. *The Progressive Mind, 1890–1917*. Chicago: Rand McNally, 1970.

Offe, Claus. "Political Authority and Class Structures: An Analysis of Late Capitalist Societies." *International Journal of Sociology* 2 (Spring 1972): 73–108.

Olander, Oscar G. "Michigan State Police." *Journal of Criminal Law and Criminology* 23 (1932): 718–722.

——. *Michigan State Police: A Twenty Year History*. Lansing: Michigan Police Journal Press, 1942.

Palmer, Milton R. "The State Police as an Asset." *American Industries* 23 (August 1922): 19–23.

Palmer, Stanley H. "The Irish Police Experiment: The Beginnings of Modern Police in the British Isles, 1785–1795." *Social Science Quarterly* 56 (December 1975): 410–424.

——. *Police and Protest in England and Ireland, 1780–1850*. Cambridge: Cambridge University Press, 1988.

Parks, Evelyn. "From Constabulary to Police Society." *Catalyst* 5 (Summer 1970): 76–97.

Pennsylvania State Federation of Labor. *The American Cossack*. Harrisburg: Pennsylvania State Federation of Labor, 1915.

Perry, C. E. "Origin of the Pennsylvania State Police." *The Police Journal* (New York) 14 (October 1926): 6.

Peterson, Richard. "Conflict and Consensus: Labor Relations in Western Mining." *Journal of the West* 12 (January 1973): 1–17.

Peterson, Virgil W. "Local and State Law Enforcement Today." *Current History* 53 (1967): 8–14, 49–50.

——— . "Developments of Local and State Law Enforcement." *Current History* 60 (1971): 327–334.

Poulantzas, Nicos. *Political Power and Social Classes.* London: NLB/Sheed, 1973.

——— . *Classes in Contemporary Capitalism.* London: NLB, 1975.

Powers, William F. *The One-Hundred Year Vigil: The Story of the Nation's First Statewide Enforcement Agency.* Boston, MA: Department of Public Safety, 1965.

——— . *In the Service of the State: The Rhode Island State Police, 1925–1975.* Providence: The Rhode Island Bicentennial Commission Foundation, 1975.

Prassel, Frank R. *The Western Peace Officer: A Legacy of Law and Order.* Norman: University of Oklahoma Press, 1972.

Purdy, E. Wilson. *Pennsylvania State Police.* Harrisburg: Pennsylvania State Police, 1963.

Pursley, Robert D. *Introduction to Criminal Justice.* New York: Macmillan, 1987.

Puttkammer, E. W. "The Organization of the State Police." *Journal of Criminal Law and Criminology* 26 (January–February 1936): 727–740.

Radzinowicz, Leon A. *History of the English Criminal Law and Its Administration from 1750.* Vol. 3. New York: Macmillan, 1968.

Rapport, Victor A. "The Growth and Changing Functions of the Connecticut Department of State Police." *Journal of Criminal Law and Criminology* 30 (September–October 1939): 359–369.

——— . "A Unified State-Wide Police Force." *Journal of Criminal Law and Criminology* 30 (September–October 1940): 706–711.

Ray, P. O. "Metropolitan and State Police." *Journal of Criminal Law and Criminology* 10 (November 1919): 351–355.

——— . "Metropolitan and State Police." *Journal of Criminal Law and Criminology* 11 (November 1920): 453–467.

Reid, Sue T. *Criminal Justice.* 2nd ed. New York: Macmillan, 1990.

Reiner, Robert. *The Politics of the Police.* New York: St. Martin's Press, 1985.

Reinsch, P. S. "The Pennsylvania Constabulary." In *Readings on American State Government,* edited by P. S. Reinsch. Boston: Ginn, 1911.

Reiss, Albert J. *The Police and the Public.* New Haven, CT: Yale University Press, 1971.

Reith, Charles. *The Police Idea: Its History and Evolution in England in the Eighteenth Century and After.* London: Oxford University Press, 1938.

——— . *British Police and the Democratic Ideal.* London: Oxford University Press, 1943.

——— . *A Short History of the British Police.* London: Oxford University Press, 1948.

——— . *The Blind Eye of History: A Study of the Origins of the Present Police Era.* London: Faber and Faber, 1952.

——— . *A New Study of Police History.* London: Oliver and Boyd, 1956.

Reppetto, Thomas A. *The Blue Parade.* New York: Free Press, 1978.

Richardson, James F. *The New York Police: Colonial Times to 1901.* New York: Oxford University Press, 1970.

——— . *Urban Police in the United States.* Port Washington, NY: Kennikat Press, 1974.

Robinson, Cyril D. "The Deradicalization of the Policeman: A Historical Analysis." *Crime and Delinquency* 24 (April 1978): 129–151.

Roby, Pamela A. "Politics and Criminal Law: Revision of the New York State Penal Law on Prostitution." *Social Problems* 17 (Summer 1969): 83–109.

Samora, Julian, Joe Bernal, and Albert Pena. *Gunpowder Justice: A Reassessment of the Texas Rangers*. South Bend, IN: University of Notre Dame Press, 1979.

Schur, Edwin. *The Politics of Deviance: Stigma Contests and the Uses of Power*. Englewood Cliffs, NJ: Prentice-Hall, 1980.

Sherril, Basil L. "Twenty-Five Years of Service." *Popular Government* 20 (May 1954): 3–6.

Siegel, Larry J. *Criminology*. 3rd ed. St. Paul, MN: West Publishing, 1989.

Silver, Allen. "The Demand for Order in Civil Society." In *The Police*, edited by David Bordua. New York: Basic Books, 1968.

Sims, Victor H. *Small Town and Rural Police*. Springfield, IL: Charles C. Thomas, 1988.

Skolnick, Jerome H. *Justice Without Trial: Law Enforcement in Democratic Society*. New York: John Wiley and Sons, 1966.

Skolnick, Jerome H., and David H. Bayley. *The New Blue Line: Police Innovation in Six American Cities*. New York: Free Press, 1986.

Smith, Bruce. *The State Police*. New York: Macmillan, 1925.

——. "The State Police." In *Readings in American Government*, edited by Finla G. Crawford. New York: Knopf, 1927.

——. "The State Police: An Experiment in Rural Protection." *Police Journal* (London) 3 (January 1930): 20–29.

——. "Factors Influencing the Future Development of State Police." *Journal of Criminal Law and Criminology* 23 (1932): 713–718.

——. "The State Police." In *Rural Crime Control*. New York: Columbia University, Institute of Public Administration, 1933.

——. "State Police: Some Possible Lines of Future Development." *State Government* 7 (1934): 51–54.

——. "History of State Police Organizations." *Our Sheriff and Police Journal* 30 (1935): 9–25.

——. "State and Federal Police." In *Police Systems in the United States*. Rev. ed. New York: Harper and Brothers, 1949.

Staley, Eugene. *History of the Illinois State Federation of Labor*. Chicago: University of Chicago Press, 1930.

Stockbridge, F. P. "New York State Troopers." *World's Work* 35 (1918): 264–272.

Storch, Robert D. "The Plague of the Blue Locusts: Police Reform and Popular Resistance in Northern England, 1840–57." *International Revue of Social History* 20, part 1 (1975): 61–90.

Suggs, George G. *Colorado's War on Militant Unionism: James H. Peabody and the Western Federation of Miners*. Detroit, MI: Wayne State University Press, 1972.

Tarr, Joel A. *A Study in Boss Politics: William Lorimer of Chicago*. Urbana: University of Illinois Press, 1971.

Thompson, E. P. *Whigs and Hunters: The Origin of the Black Act*. New York: Random House, 1975.

Tobias, J. J. "The Policing of Ireland." *The Criminologist* 5 (November 1970): 99–104.

Torres, Donald A. *Handbook of State Police, Highway Patrols, and Investigative Agencies*. Westport, CT: Greenwood Press, 1987.

Travis, Lawrence F. *Introduction to Criminal Justice*. Cincinnati, OH: Anderson Publishing, 1990.

U.S. Department of Commerce. *Fourteenth Census of the United States, 1920*, Vol. 3. Washington, DC: Government Printing Office, 1923.

U.S. Department of Justice. *Sourcebook of Criminal Justice Statistics, 1987*. Washington, DC: Government Printing Office, 1987.

U.S. Department of Justice, Bureau of Justice Statistics. *Sourcebook of Criminal Justice Statisitcs, 1992*. Edited by Kathleen Maguire, Ann L. Pastore, and Timothy J. Flanagan. Washington, DC: Government Printing Office, 1993.

Vago, Steven. *Law and Society*. Cliffs, NJ: Prentice-Hall, 1988.

Van de Water, Frederick F. *Grey Riders: The Story of the New York State Troopers*. New York: G. P. Putnam's Sons, 1922.

Vollmer, August, and Alfred Parker. *Crime and the State Police*. Berkeley: University of California Press, 1935.

Waldron, Ronald J. *The Criminal Justice System: An Introduction*. 4th ed. New York: Harper and Row, 1989.

Walker, Samuel. "The Urban Police in American History: A Review of the Literature." *Journal of Police Science and Administration* 4 (September 1976.): 252–260.

——. *A Critical History of Police Reform*. Lexington, MA: D. C. Heath, 1977.

——. *Popular Justice: A History of American Criminal Justice*. New York: Oxford University Press, 1980.

——. *The Police in America: An Introduction*. New York: McGraw-Hill, 1983.

Webb, Walter P. *The Texas Rangers: A Century of Frontier Defense*. Boston: Houghton Mifflin, 1935.

Weinstein, James. *The Corporate Ideal in the Liberal State, 1900–1918*. Boston: Beacon, 1968.

Wells, Merle W. "The Western Federation of Miners." *Journal of the West* 12 (January 1973): 18–35.

Weston, Paul B., and Kenneth M. Wells. *Law Enforcement and Criminal Justice: An Introduction*. Pacific Palisades, CA: Goodyear, 1972.

Wiebe, Robert H. *The Search for Order, 1877–1920*. New York: Hill and Wang, 1967.

Williams, Wayne C. *Sweet of Colorado*. New York: Fleming H. Revell, 1943.

Wilson, James Q. *Varieties of Police Behavior*. Cambridge, MA: Harvard University Press, 1969.

Woltman, Frederick, and William L. Nunn. "Cossacks." *The American Mercury* 15 (December 1929): 399–406.

Yablonski, Lewis. *Criminology: Crime & Criminality*. 4th ed. New York: Harper and Row, 1990.

Zorbaugh, Harvey W. *The Gold Coast and the Slum*. Chicago: University of Chicago Press, 1929.

## UNPUBLISHED MANUSCRIPTS

Bacon, Seldon. "The Early Development of the American Municipal Police: A Study of the Evolution of Formal Controls in a Changing Society." Ph.D. diss., Yale University, 1939.

Hayes, James. "History and Development of State Police and State Highway Patrols and Methods of Handling the Minor Vehicle Violator." M.A. thesis, Harvard University, 1935.

Johnson, David R. "Crime Fighting Reform in Chicago: An Analysis of Its Leadership, 1919–1927." M.A. thesis, University of Chicago, 1966.

——. "The Search for an Urban Discipline: Police Reform as a Response to Crime in American Cities, 1800–1875." Ph.D. diss., University of Chicago, 1972.

Ketcham, George A. "Municipal Police Reform: A Comparative Study of Law Enforcement in Cincinnati, Chicago, New Orleans, New York, and St. Louis, 1884–1877." Ph.D. diss., University of Missouri, 1976.

Levett, Allen E. "Centralization of City Police in the Nineteenth Century United States." Ph.D. diss., University of Michigan, 1975.

Ray, Gerda. "Contested Legitimacy: Creating the State Police in New York, 1890–1930." Ph.D. diss., University of California at Berkeley, 1990.

Summerhays, Joel. "American Police Reform: An Alternative Perspective." Ph.D. diss., University of California at Berkeley, 1979.

Swart, Stanley L. "The Development of State-Level Police Activity in Ohio, 1802–1928." Ph.D. diss., Northwestern University, 1974.


## GOVERNMENT AND LEGISLATIVE DOCUMENTS

Alabama State Legislature. *Session Laws*. 1919, no. 551; 1931, no. 331; 1935, no. 331.

Alaska State Legislature. *Session Laws*. 1941, chap. 65, sec. 1; 1947, chap. 49; 1953, chap. 144; 1959, chap. 64, sec. 18.

Arizona State Legislature. *Session Laws*. 1903, no. 64; 1909, chap. 4.

Arkansas State Legislature. *Session Laws*. 1929, no. 299.

California State Legislature. *Session Laws*. 1929, chap. 308.

Colorado State Archives, Denver, Colorado. *Journal of the House*. 1917.

Colorado State Legislature. *Session Laws*. 1917, chap. 12; 1935, chap. 125.

——. *Journal of the House*. 1917.

——. *Journal of the House*. Special sess., 1917.

——. *Journal of the Senate*. Special sess., 1917.

——. *Journal of the House*. Special sess., 1919.

——. *Journal of the Senate*. Special sess., 1919.

——. *Journal of the House*. 1921.

——. *Journal of the Senate*. 1921.

——. *Journal of the House*. 1923.

——. *Journal of the House*. 1927.

——. *Journal of the Senate*. 1927.

Connecticut State Legislature. *Session Laws*. 1903, chap. 141.

Delaware State Legislature. *Session Laws*. 1891, chap. 47; 1898, chap. 64; 1921, chaps. 195, 196.

Florida State Legislature. *Session Laws*. 1939, chap. 19551, no. 556.

Georgia State Legislature. *Session Laws*. 1917, no. 224; 1937, no. 20.

Idaho State Legislature. *Session Laws*. 1919, chap. 103; 1921, chap. 67; 1923, chaps. 12, 152; 1939, chap. 60.

Illinois General Assembly. *Journal of the House*. 50th sess., 1917.

——. *Journal of the Senate*. 50th sess., 1917.

——. *Journal of the House*. 51st sess., 1919.

——. *Journal of the Senate*. 51st sess., 1919.

——. *Journal of the House*. 52nd sess., 1921.

——. *Journal of the Senate*. 52nd sess., 1921.

——. *Session Laws*. 1921, chap. 211.

——. *Journal of the House*. 53rd sess., 1923.

——. *Journal of the Senate*. 53rd sess., 1923.

——. *Session Laws*. 1923, p. 562.

———. *Journal of the House*. 54th sess., 1925.
———. *Journal of the Senate*. 54th sess., 1925.
———. *Journal of the Senate*. 55th sess., 1927.
———. *Journal of the Senate*. 56th sess., 1929.
Iowa State Legislature. *Session Laws*. 1915, chap. 203; 1935, chap. 48.
Kansas State Legislature. *Session Laws*. 1933, chap. 109; 1937, chap. 330.
Kentucky State Legislature. *Session Laws*. 1932, chap. 106, sec. 18.
Louisiana State Legislature. *Session Laws*. 1928, no. 296; 1932, no. 21, sec. 11; 1936, no. 94; 1942, chap. 110.
Maine State Legislature. *Session Laws*. 1917, chap. 284; 1935, chap. 303.
Maryland State Legislature. *Session Laws*. 1916, chap. 687.
Massachusetts State Legislature. *Session Laws*. 1865, chap. 249; 1871, chap. 394; 1874, chap. 405; 1875, chap. 15; 1879, chap. 305; 1919, chap. 350.
Michigan State Legislature. *Session Laws*. 1917, no. 53; 1919, no. 26.
Minnesota State Legislature. *Session Laws*. 1929, chap. 355.
Mississippi State Legislature. *Session Laws*. 1938, chap. 143.
Missouri State Legislature. *Session Laws*. 1931, pp. 230–36.
Montana State Legislature. *Session Laws*. 1935, chap. 135.
Nebraska State Legislature. *Session Laws*. 1919, chap. 173; 1927, chap. 157; 1937, chaps. 141, 176.
Nevada State Legislature. *Session Laws*. 1908, chap. 4.
New Hampshire State Legislature. *Session Laws*. 1937, chap. 134.
New Jersey State Legislature. *Session Laws*. 1919, chap. 102.
New Mexico State Legislature. *Session Laws*. 1905, chap. 9; 1919, chap. 94; 1921, chap. 12; 1933, chap. 119.
New York State Legislature. *Session Laws*. 1917, chap. 161.
North Carolina State Legislature. *Session Laws*. 1929, chap. 218.
North Dakota State Legislature. *Session Laws*. 1935, chap. 148.
Ohio State Legislature. *Session Laws*. 1933, pp. 93–96.
Oklahoma State Legislature. *Session Laws*. 1937, chap. 50.
Oregon State Legislature. *Session Laws*. 1921, chap. 371; 1931, chap. 139.
Pennsylvania State Legislature. *Session Laws*. 1905, no. 227.
Rhode Island State Legislature. *Session Laws*. 1917, chap. 1469; 1925, chap. 588.
South Carolina State Legislature. *Session Laws*. 1868, no. 11; 1878, no. 601; 1892, no. 28; 1894, no. 518; 1896, no. 61; 1903, no. 12; 1907, no. 226; 1930, no. 603; 1935, no. 232.
South Dakota State Legislature. *Session Laws*. 1917, chap. 355; 1935, chap. 97.
Tennessee State Legislature. *Session Laws*. 1915, no. 74; 1919, chap. 96; 1929, chap. 25.
Texas State Legislature. *Session Laws*. 1870, chap. 13; 1871, chap. 67; 1873, chap. 31; 1901, chap. 34; 1919, chap. 144; 1935, chap. 181.
Utah State Legislature. *Session Laws*. 1923, chap. 65; 1941, chap. 14.
Vermont State Legislature. *Session Laws*. 1925, no. 70.
Virginia State Legislature. *Session Laws*. 1924, chap. 99; 1932, chap. 342.
Washington State Legislature. *Session Laws*. 1921, chap. 108.
West Virginia State Legislature. *Session Laws*. 1919, chap. 12.
Wisconsin State Legislature. *Session Laws*. 1939, chap. 10.
Wyoming State Legislature. *Session Laws*. 1921, chap. 18; 1935, chap. 51.

## NEWSPAPERS AND MAGAZINES

*Champaign Daily-News* (Illinois), 1917–1923.
*Chicago Daily News*, 1929.
*Chicago Evening Post*, 1925.
*Chicago Tribune*, 1916–1931.
*Denver Post*, 1917–1927.
*Illinois Journal of Commerce* (Chicago), 1921–1927.
*Illinois State Federation of Labor Weekly Newsletter*, 1917–1929.
*Illinois State Journal* (Springfield), 1916–1931.
*Illinois State Register* (Springfield), 1923–1929.
*Legislative Review* (Springfield), Illinois Chamber of Commerce, 1925.
*The New Majority* (Illinois), 1919.
*New York Times*, 1903–1937.
*The Peoria Journal* (Illinois), 1921–1925.
*The Peoria Star* (Illinois), 1921.
*Rocky Mountain News* (Colorado), 1917–1927.
*Springfield Register* (Illinois), 1921.
*State Police Book* (official publication of the Information Bureau of the American Municipalities, Chicago, Illinois), 1919–192?.
*The State Trooper* (published monthly by The State Trooper Publishing Company, Detroit, Michigan), 1918–1931.
*Twin-City Review* (Illinois), 1921.
*Urbana Courier* (Illinois), 1920.

## MANUSCRIPT AND ARCHIVAL SOURCES

Chicago. Chicago Historical Society. John Fitzpatrick Papers.
———. Chicago Historical Society. Illinois Manufacturers' Association, Minutes, Directors' Meetings, 1919–1923.
———. Chicago Historical Society. "Illinois State Police." Scrapbook, qF37KA/I6.
———. Chicago Historical Society. *Lakeside Directory of Chicago, 1900–1925.*
———. Chicago Historical Society. Victor O. Olander Papers.
———. Chicago Historical Society. *Polk's Directory of Chicago, 1923.*
———. Chicago Historical Society. "Reports, Letters, Clippings of Chicago Crime Associations and Committees" Scrapbook, qF38K/S41.
———. Chicago Historical Society. *Who's Who in Chicago: The Book of Chicagoans, 1926.*
Denver. Colorado Historical Society. Colorado Fuel and Iron Co., Records, 1884–1949.
———. Colorado State Archives. Julius C. Gunter Papers.
———. Colorado State Archives. Oliver H. Shoup Papers.
———. Colorado State Archives. William E. Sweet Papers.
Urbana-Champaign. Illinois Historical Survey, University of Illinois. Champaign, Illinois. John Hunter Walker Papers.
———. University of Illinois Archives. Henry M. Dunlap Papers.

# Index

## ABOUT THE AUTHOR

H. KENNETH BECHTEL is Associate Professor in the Department of Sociology at Wake Forest University. He is coeditor of a work on Blacks in American Science, and has contributed in many ways to the literature of sociology.

ISBN 0-313-26380-9

EAN

9 780313 263804

HARDCOVER BAR CODE